HOW THE BATTLESHIP *MAINE* WAS DESTROYED

The U.S.S. Maine. Port side view.

HOW THE BATTLESHIP *MAINE* WAS DESTROYED

H. G. Rickover

WITH A NEW FOREWORD BY

FRANCIS DUNCAN, DANA M. WEGNER,

IB S. HANSEN, AND ROBERT S. PRICE

NAVAL INSTITUTE PRESS

Annapolis, Maryland

Library of Congress Cataloging-in-Publication Data

Rickover, Hyman George.
How the battleship Maine was destroyed / H.G. Rickover ; with a
new foreword by Francis Duncan . . . [et al.].
p.   cm.
Originally published: Washington : Naval History Division, Dept.
of the Navy, 1976.
Includes bibliographical references (p.   ) and index.
ISBN 1-55750-717-1
1. Maine (Battleship)   I. Title.
E721.6.R5   1994
973.8'95—dc20   94-7345

Printed in the United States of America on acid-
free paper ∞

3 5 7 9 8 6 4 2
First printing

Contents

Illustrations

Photographs identified by a number preceded by NRL are available from the Naval Historical Center, Washington, D.C. The designations LC and NA refer to the collections of the Library of Congress and the U.S. National Archives.

PHOTOGRAPHS

CHARTS

DRAWINGS AND FIGURES

Foreword to the 1995 Edition

On September 1, 1974, the *Washington Star-News* published an article by John M. Taylor titled "Returning to the Riddle of the Explosion that Sunk the Maine." The *Maine* was the battleship that exploded in Havana harbor on the night of February 15, 1898; the riddle was whether a Spanish or Cuban mine planted outside the ship, or some cause within the ship had initiated the explosion. Swept by a tide of patriotic outrage asserting that treachery had caused the loss of 266 American lives, Congress on April 25 declared war on Spain. When the fighting ended on August 12, the Americans had triumphed in Cuba, the Philippines, and Puerto Rico. The United States had become an imperial power.

Admiral H. G. Rickover, head of the naval nuclear propulsion program, a joint effort of the Navy and the Atomic Energy Commission, read the Taylor article with quickening interest. It stated that the Navy had made little use of its technically trained officers during its investigation of the tragedy. For example, George W. Melville, the Navy's Chief Engineer, was among those who strongly doubted that a mine was the agent of destruction, but he was never asked for his views. The Admiral could not believe that the Navy did not make use of all available information to determine the cause of so great a disaster.

He read the article on Sunday; early Monday morning he was in our office, brandishing the newspaper. At that time our assignment was to prepare a study of the naval nuclear propulsion program, which the Naval Institute Press published in 1990 under the title *Rickover and the Nuclear Navy: The Discipline of Technology*. Because we were naval historians, he wanted to know what we knew about the investigation of the *Maine*. Replying that we did not know any details, he asked us to see what we could find out. Our own curiosity aroused, we agreed to do so.

We turned to books on the war and biographies, only to find that the several accounts disagreed with one another. The Admiral was intrigued. If the Spanish-American War marked a decisive point in American history, why was there so little detailed knowledge about the event that precipitated the conflict—the destruction of the *Maine?*

He was no novice to history. He had written *Eminent Americans:*

Namesakes of the Polaris Submarine Fleet, published in 1972 by the Government Printing Office. It was a collection of biographical essays based on his study of published works. But going further into the question of the *Maine* meant delving into the raw material of history—government records, contemporary newspapers and periodicals, documents stored in archives, collections of personal papers, artifacts in museums, and perhaps even interviews with descendants of people involved in the catastrophe. Because of his official duties, he could not undertake research into such source materials. He asked if we would do so.

To our surprise, we found that he had some personal links to the war. As a young ensign, less than a year out of the Naval Academy, he was in the destroyer *La Vallette* in maneuvers off Panama when the fleet sank the *Iowa* on March 23, 1923, at target practice. The day before, he and other officers had gone on board, wanting to see a ship that had helped change the course of American history. On July 3, 1898, the old battleship had fired the first shot in the Battle of Santiago de Cuba, which annihilated the Spanish squadron under Admiral Cervera y Topete. Another connection was made in the late 1930s, when Lieutenant Commander Rickover was in the Philippines, assigned to the Cavite Navy Yard just south of Manila. Many buildings in the yard, including the *commandancia,* headquarters of the Sixteenth Naval District, had been built during the days of Spanish rule. Discovering that Emilio Aguinaldo, who had fought the Spanish and Americans for Philippine independence, lived nearby, Rickover called on him. Aside from an exchange of courtesies, not much was said, but Rickover had met a man who had won his place in history.

Rickover found research in primary sources fascinating. He would talk to us in the office when his working day was over, and at sea during the few idle moments that occurred when he was conducting the initial trials of nuclear submarines and surface ships. He wanted to know what we were finding out, and he wanted to exchange ideas. What problems did we face? How could he help?

It was his idea to contact the Spanish naval attaché to see what the archives in Madrid had to offer, a request that led to the appearance of hitherto unknown material. When we suggested it might be useful to find out what other navies had experienced with ship explosions, he promptly arranged for us to see the British and French naval attachés. In this and other instances he was able to open doors for us that otherwise might have been closed. In one archival foray we ran across some ciphered messages. It turned out they had already been deciphered, a fact we found out only after he had mobilized part of the intelligence community, members of which wondered why the sudden interest from high authorities in events that had occurred more than seven decades earlier. We could see the focus of his interest was changing. No longer was it how the Navy had conducted its inquiry—it was what had happened in Havana harbor on the night of February 15, 1898.

As historians, we had gone about as far as we could go. In our research, however, we had uncovered the way for another discipline to take over. In 1910 President Taft had assigned the Army Corps of Engineers the task of raising the *Maine* from the slime and mud in which she had rested for thirteen years. The next year the engineers built a cofferdam around the wreck, slowly pumping out the water, and making an annotated photographic record of the wreckage. We thought it might be feasible for professional engineers to interpret the evidence revealed in the photographs and the ship's plans.

For this purpose the Admiral obtained the services of Ib S. Hansen, then Assistant for Design Applications in the Structures Department at the David W. Taylor Naval Research and Development Center at Carderock, Maryland, and Robert S. Price, a research physicist at the Naval Surface Weapons Center at White Oak, Maryland. Both men had extensive experience in analyzing the effects of explosions on ship hulls. At the behest of the Admiral, the National Archives and Records Administration furnished copies of the plans of the *Maine* and the photographs taken by the Army. Rickover made available to Hansen and Price a room where they could spread out their work, told us to give them any support they needed, and left them alone.

While Hansen and Price began their analysis, we started to draft the historical section of the book. Frequently, we sent manuscript into his office. From his penciled comments it was evident that he had read and pondered every word, at times striking paragraphs and substituting his own, to make sure the text said exactly what he wanted it to say.

When the Hansen-Price analysis determined that an internally initiated explosion had destroyed the *Maine,* the Admiral wanted to make sure that nontechnical readers could understand their conclusion. He thought a series of isometric drawings would help. The first would show the ship at anchor, and those following would show what had happened.

He turned to the Navy for an illustrator. The Admiral knew exactly what he wanted: the ship at various stages of disintegration—and nothing else. Unfortunately, the Navy illustrators fell into two schools: one would show the *Maine* at anchor and with a fish swimming around her;

the other with the ship at anchor and with a gull flying over her. One after another the illustrators emerged, pale and wan, from a stormy interview with the Admiral. Eventually he had to go to a commercial source.

How the Battleship Maine Was Destroyed, copyrighted by the Admiral and published by the Government Printing Office, appeared in 1976. Newspapers across the country called attention to its appearance, and reviews in scholarly journals were generally favorable. All recognized that the Hansen-Price analysis was the heart of the book. Because of it the *American Historical Review* found, "The explosion which destroyed the *Maine* is mysterious no longer," and the *Journal of American History* concluded, "The *Maine* was indeed sunk by an internal explosion." The reviewer for *Technology and Culture,* referring to the 1911 photographs, made a very pertinent observation: "The camera, in effect, answered questions we are only today smart enough to ask." The Naval Institute *Proceedings* thought the Admiral's book deserved a "Well Done." The *Chicago Tribune* quoted an official Cuban source as saying that Washington had indirectly admitted that "the *Maine* explosion was a monstrous self-provocation to declare war on Spain and take over Cuba, Puerto Rico, the Philippines, and Hawaii." In 1976 Admiral Rickover granted the Spanish Navy the right to translate and publish a limited number of copies.

Not everyone agreed then or agrees now that the riddle of the *Maine* has been answered once and for all. Some critics believe that the Admiral has not made his case and that the Hansen-Price analysis is inconclusive. However, no consideration of the controversy is possible without taking his book into account.

The Admiral resented reviews that were condescending or implied that, because historians had long doubted that a mine had caused the loss of the ship, he had contributed little to solving the controversy. The photographs had been available since 1911: why had historians never used them?

He was not trying to prove that the Navy was to blame for the catastrophe, and he had nothing to gain by trying to do so. He consulted qualified authorities and experts in several fields—more than we have mentioned here—and it would have been exceedingly unwise on his part to try to force the views of such individuals into a predetermined conclusion. They were willing to help him because they, too, wanted to know what had happened. His purpose, as well as that of those whose help he obtained, was to make a contribution to American history. To that end he was willing to use his influence to gain access to various sources of information and to several fields of technical knowledge.

Admiral Rickover was convinced that the destruction of the *Maine* had important lessons to teach. Of these, the most important was the role of technology in making national decisions. Technical problems must be examined by technically qualified people who cast their analysis in terms other citizens can understand. Otherwise, fateful decisions will be made on the basis of emotions. The centenary of the loss of the *Maine* reminds us that even small wars bring in their wake long-lasting, deep, and troubling entanglements.

Francis Duncan
Dana M. Wegner

Almost twenty years ago we were individually summoned and told that an admiral wanted some expert help in examining the effects of explosions on a ship. Much to our surprise we learned that the admiral was Rickover, and with even more amazement that the ship was the *Maine*. About all we knew about the *Maine* was the cry "Remember the *Maine*." In fact, we had used this expression more than once in the promotion of our daily work, the development of technology to increase the resistance of Navy ships to weapons explosions, without really knowing much about what was behind the expression. A request from Admiral Rickover was tantamount to an order, even if it was couched in terms of volunteering, and the summons definitely had two sides to it, both flattering in having been asked, and frightening in having to walk into the lion's den. For there is no denying it, the Admiral's reputation in the technical community was one of a severe uncompromising taskmaster. As it turned out, the volunteer task became a most fascinating and engrossing one, and the lion turned into a most agreeable gladiator. He gave us a totally free hand, spared no effort in providing support by directing the collection of all conceivable evidence, and implored us to find the truth, whatever it was. And with the help of the historians Dr. Francis Duncan and Dana Wegner, who dug out all the available source material, we believe the truth about the cause of the *Maine* disaster has been uncovered. Having no prior notion of what happened, nor any knowledge of what the source material contained, we recall that the first thing that struck us when we started to examine it was that the conclusions of both the 1898 and the 1911 inquiries were not accompanied by any solid technical explanations of their derivation. Considering the consequences, that was startling, to say the least. It became our task to reexamine the evidence, and try to derive a conclusion based on technical considerations alone. In doing this we were better positioned than the official boards of 1898 and 1911 since we essentially had the same evidence, were absolutely under no pressure to justify any specific finding, and had available to us all the technical progress in the field of explosion effects predictions since then. The fact that the boards appear not to have availed themselves of the expertise existing at the time does not help their case. Our case and its justifications are explained in the original appendix A. Most of the reviews appearing after the publication of the book have been favorable, but a few have presented arguments contradicting some of our technical ones. In general, these contradictions have not been based on reexaminations of the source material but on interpretations of the words used, or on their own unverified postulates concerning physical events. Part of the reply to this is in the form of a confession. We did not fully explain and show everything we knew about the pertinent effects of explosions on ships, for much of the proof for this was classified information. Fortunately, the World War II ship-damage data has been made available to the public since the book was published, and some of this is utilized in the addendum to appendix A included in this edition (immediately following appendix A). The addendum is intended to provide further clarification of some key points. One of the ship-damage cases used in the addendum is that of the USS *California,* which was damaged and sunk at Pearl Harbor. It was raised and repaired in 1942 for further use during the war. Interestingly, the officer in charge of restoring the electrical systems was one Commander Hyman G. Rickover.

Ib S. Hansen
Robert S. Price

Foreword to the 1976 Edition

The sinking of the U.S.S. *Maine* in Havana Harbor, Cuba, early in 1898, was one of the more notable events in American history. It was of special significance because of its relationship to the ensuing Spanish-American War, the acquisition by the United States of overseas territory, and the emergence of the nation as a world power. In 1898, the Navy had little familiarity with explosive effects on the steel ships introduced only recently into the Fleet. Naval officers advanced various theories. Some believed that the cause had been an underwater explosion external to the ship. Others believed that a more likely source was an explosion within the hull, either accidental or as the result of a surreptitiously placed explosive device. The matter has been the subject of recurring debate ever since.

In this work, Admiral H. G. Rickover makes a unique contribution by studying the loss of the *Maine* in the light of modern technical knowledge. That knowledge has been derived from theoretical and experimental investigations of explosives, explosive effects, and the dynamic response of hull structures, as well as from the Navy's extensive wartime experience and testing programs of recent years.

With characteristic thoroughness, Admiral Rickover also undertook extensive research in archival materials to explore events associated with the loss of the *Maine* and to place it in historical perspective. The result is this volume which presents significant new insights in an important event of American history.

I should like to acknowledge the valued advice of two distinguished members of the Secretary of the Navy's Advisory Committee on Navy History, Dr. Richard W. Leopold and Dr. Caryl P. Haskins, who generously reviewed this manuscript prior to the decision to undertake its publication.

EDWIN B. HOOPER
Vice Admiral, USN (Ret.)
Director of Naval History

Preface

In recent years, students of American history have given increasing attention to the Spanish-American War. There is good reason for this interest, for from this brief conflict the United States emerged with possession of the Philippines and became a major power in the Far East. At that time the European nations—Great Britain, France, Russia, and Germany—were competing among themselves for spheres of influence. Asia was awakening: Japan was becoming a major power and China was standing on the brink of a revolution which was to last for decades and which was to transform profoundly the Far East. Because of the acquisition of the Philippines, the United States could not avoid involvement in these events. The role of the United States in the Far East is one of the deepest concerns of all thoughtful Americans.

My own interest in the Spanish-American War goes back many years, for I recognized it as a turning point in American history. In 1974, the *Washington Star-News* published an article by John M. Taylor, "Returning to the Riddle of the Explosion that Sunk the Maine," which aroused my curiosity. Mr. Taylor observed that no one had yet determined whether the *Maine* had been destroyed by a mine or an accidental explosion. That I knew. But Taylor also remarked that Charles D. Sigsbee, commanding officer of the *Maine* and therefore an interested party, was allowed to attend sessions of the Navy's court of inquiry and even to question witnesses. Furthermore, Taylor pointed out that Rear Admiral George W. Melville, Chief of the Bureau of Steam Engineering, had said that the cause of the disaster was a magazine explosion. However, he was not asked to testify, although he occupied an official position which required professional competence. These points raised in my mind questions as to how the Navy had investigated the event which had played a major part in bringing about the war with Spain.

Most historians had considered the despatch of the *Maine* to Havana from the aspect of diplomacy, and the report of the court of inquiry as a major factor in the origins of the war. How the court was selected and how it carried out its assignment had never been given serious consideration. Examination of these issues unexpectedly led to related subjects and these have dictated the organization of the book.

Chapter 1 describes the *Maine* and its commanding officer.

Chapter 2 summarizes the historical background of American-Cuban relations and the possibility of war as considered by some naval officers.

Chapter 3 relates the development of President McKinley's policy toward Cuba; the size and organization of the Navy which would have to carry out that policy; and the selection of the *Maine* as the ship to be held in readiness to go to Havana.

Chapter 4 deals with President McKinley's decision to send the *Maine* to Havana; the arrival at the Cuban capital; and the ship's destruction.

Chapter 5 covers the selection of the court of inquiry; the regulations under which it operated; and the warlike atmosphere in Washington.

Chapter 6 follows the investigation of the court of inquiry; the drawing up of its report; its receipt in Washington; and the outbreak of war.

Chapter 7 recounts the investigation made by the Navy in 1911 when the ship was raised; and summarizes the engineering analysis completed in 1975 which reexamines the loss of the *Maine*. This analysis is a technical appraisal of the evidence; it reaches a new conclusion on the cause of the disaster.

Chapter 8 assesses the impact of the *Maine* upon American history.

Three appendices follow: the text of the 1975 engineering analysis; a survey of international law in 1898 as it related to the *Maine;* and a brief summary, useful as a comparison, of the way the French conducted their investigation of the loss of a battleship by an accidental magazine explosion.

In my belief, a study of the destruction of the *Maine* throws important new light upon the men and institutions which fought the war with Spain and left us a legacy that still influences our nation.

Acknowledgments

This monograph would not have been possible without the contributions of several people. When questions about the naval court of inquiry which investigated the loss of the *Maine* crossed my mind, I talked the matter over with Dr. Francis Duncan, Associate Historian, Energy Research and Development Administration. He and I had frequently discussed naval history. He was at once interested and volunteered to investigate the historical sources, provided he could limit his assistance to whatever he could do outside of his regular assignments. His help was invaluable. His research assistant, Mr. Dana M. Wegner, learned of the project and became interested. Mr. Wegner's special field is the Union Navy during the Civil War. He agreed to work in his spare time with Dr. Duncan. Mr. Wegner not only did research in historical materials, but he made most of the plans and drawings.

Because of the controversy over the sinking of the *Maine*—whether a mine or an accident had destroyed the vessel—I decided to ask for information from foreign naval archives. Captain Adolfo Gregorio, Spanish Naval Attaché, obtained several documents from the naval archives of his government; these show clearly that the Spanish authorities in Madrid and in Havana had not expected a visit from the *Maine*. Rear Admiral L. R. Bell Davies, RN, Commander of the British Naval Staff in Washington, obtained information on the experience of the Royal Navy with shipboard explosions during the general period of the *Maine* disaster. Rear Admiral Emile J. Chaline, the French Naval Attaché, obtained similar information from the French archives. The information that these three officers provided was very helpful.

For certain background on American naval experience and procedures, I turned to Vice Admiral Edwin B. Hooper. USN (Ret.), Director of Naval History, and Dr. Dean C. Allard, head of the operational archives branch of the Naval History Division. Vice Admiral Julien J. LeBourgeois, USN, President of the Naval War College, obtained for me the college's plans in the event of a war with Spain. Because of my interest in the international law aspects of the disaster, Admiral LeBourgeois asked Professor William T.

Mallison of the George Washington University Law School, then holding the Charles H. Stockton Chair of International Law, and Mrs. Sally V. Mallison to investigate certain questions. Rear Admiral B. R. Inman, USN, Director of Naval Intelligence, had the Spanish and French documents translated. Rear Admiral Jon L. Boyes, USN, Director, Naval Telecommunications, and Lieutenant General Lewis Allen, Jr., USA, Director, National Security Agency/Central Security Services, and Richard A. von Doenhoff, National Archives and Records Service, were able to locate deciphered versions of messages that had been sent in cipher from the American naval attaché in Madrid just before the outbreak of the war in 1898.

Certain individuals graciously made available to me papers in their possession: Mr. Philip L. Alger, Mrs. R. E. Sampson, Mr. W. T. Cluverius, and Rear Admiral R. M. Watt, Jr., USN (Ret.).

As the research continued, it became apparent that it might be possible to analyze the wreckage of the *Maine* to see whether an internal or external explosion had led to the loss of the ship. Fortunately, the naval board of inspection in 1911, which examined the wreck before it was raised and towed to sea and sunk, had created a volume of photographs, drawings, overlays, and reports. At my request, Dr. James B. Rhoads, Archivist of the United States, lent me the material. Finding qualified individuals who could interpret the information was exceedingly important, for their findings might make it possible to determine how the *Maine* had been lost. Mr. Ib S. Hansen, David W. Taylor Naval Ship Research and Development Center, and Mr. Robert S. Price, Naval Surface Weapons Center, were interested in the challenge and volunteered to examine the evidence.

Mr. Hansen and Mr. Price studied the testimony and findings of the court of inquiry of 1898, the conclusions of the board of inspection of 1911, and the technical data gathered for the board's consideration. Mr. Dana M. Wegner provided the historical technical information which Mr. Hansen and Mr. Price needed. Dr. Philip K. Lundeberg, Curator of the Division of Naval History, Smithsonian Institution, gave the benefit of his knowledge of mines and mining techniques of the Spanish-American War period. The Hansen-Price analysis throws new and significant light upon the destruction of the *Maine*.

I want to express my appreciation to several individuals for their assistance. Vice Admiral Edwin B. Hooper and Dr. Dean C. Allard offered comments on details and general interpretation which greatly improved the manuscript. Dr. Richard W. Leopold, an authority on

American diplomatic history, carefully reviewed the manuscript and gave me scholarly and perceptive comments which were invaluable. Evan M. Duncan, a student of French naval history, offered helpful suggestions on evaluating the investigation of the explosion on board the French battleship *Jena*. Members of my own staff who took the time to read parts of the manuscript and gave useful suggestions were: Preston G. Athey, Philip R. Clark, Mark Forssell, Catherine V. Golnik, Robert L. Kingsbury, Kenneth A. MacGowan, James W. Vaughan, and Barbara J. Whitlark.

I gratefully acknowledge these contributions.

January 1976   H. G. Rickover
Washington, D.C.

HOW THE BATTLESHIP *MAINE* WAS DESTROYED

CHAPTER 1

The Explosion

At 9:40 p.m., Tuesday, February 15, 1898, the American battleship *Maine* exploded in the harbor of Havana, Cuba. Out of a complement of 354 officers and men, 266 lost their lives. The tragedy was one of a series of events that led the United States into the Spanish-American War and a new age.

The *Maine* had been at Havana and moored at the same buoy since January 25. Her purpose had been to defend American interests during the civil war which Cuba was fighting against Spain. With its two tall stacks and two military masts, each with fighting tops, the *Maine* easily dominated the scene. The ship had an overall length of 319 feet, an extreme beam of 57 feet, a normal displacement of 6,682 tons, and a design speed of 17 knots. Like all capital ships of its day, the battleship carried a variety of guns. The main battery consisted of four 10-inch guns, divided equally between two turrets, and six 6-inch guns. As a secondary battery, the *Maine* had seven 6-pounders. The several calibers resulted in part from the inability to determine ranges accurately over 3,000 yards. The larger guns, which had a slow rate of fire, were to attack the armor of the opposing ship, while the smaller guns were to fire rapidly and sweep the enemy decks. Four torpedo tubes, two on each side, above the waterline but below the weather deck, completed the armament. Armor protected certain areas of the ship; 8-inch plates shielded the 10-inch guns in their turrets, and an armor belt with a maximum thickness of 12 inches extended along 180 feet of the waterline on each side. The New York Navy Yard laid the keel on October 17, 1888, and six years and eleven months later—on September 17, 1895—the Navy placed the battleship in commission. So far as active service was concerned, the *Maine* was still a new ship.[1]

1

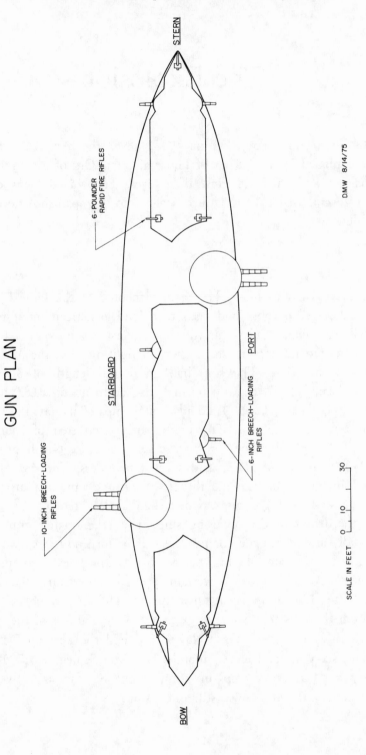

GUN PLAN

BOW

STERN

STARBOARD

PORT

IO-INCH BREECH-LOADING RIFLES

6-INCH BREECH-LOADING RIFLES

6-POUNDER RAPID FIRE RIFLES

SCALE IN FEET

0   IO   30

DMW 8/14/75

The lengthy time of construction revealed the status of American naval technology. During the Civil War, the United States had built the largest and most advanced navy in the world, but the service had dwindled into insignificance in the two decades following Appomattox. The decline was more than a matter of numbers of ships. In marine engineering, naval architecture, and the manufacture of armor and ordnance, the United States was far behind. When Congress on August 3, 1886, authorized construction of the *Maine* as one of "Two sea-going double-bottomed armored vessels of about 6,000 tons," the Navy and American industry had little technical experience. The government placed its first large order for domestically manufactured armor plate and gun forgings on June 1, 1887, with the Bethlehem Iron Company for the *Maine,* the *Texas* (the second vessel Congress authorized in 1886), and for the completion of five monitors. As Bethlehem built its armor plant, relying on European technology, new processes for improving armor appeared and the government changed its specifications. As a result, the completion of the ship was delayed. Building the engines also proved difficult, for they were among the first vertical, inverted, three-cylinder, triple-expansion engines built for the Navy. The attempt to use steel castings was disappointing. By 1898, the *Maine* was already surpassed and the Navy had designated the ship as a second-class battleship.[2]

To modern eyes, the *Maine* would have an unusual appearance. The ship was painted in peacetime colors: white hull and white boats, straw-colored superstructure, masts, and stacks, and black guns and searchlights. More significantly, the ship had an unusual deck arrangement which had been dictated by the location of the 10-inch turrets. Instead of being on the center-line, as is the case with modern ships, the forward turret was on the starboard side and the after turret on the port side, diagonally opposite. The superstructure of the *Maine* was divided into three sections: the forward one with the searchlight and foremast; the center one with the stacks, pilothouse and most of the boats; and the after one with its searchlight and the mainmast. The breaks between the three were to allow the turrets on each side to rotate and fire across the deck. Most of the officers were berthed aft and most of the men were housed forward. Since the explosion had taken place near the bow, casualties among the crew had been heavy. Only two officers had lost their lives.[3]

When the explosion occurred, Captain Charles D. Sigsbee, commanding officer of the *Maine,* was at his desk writing letters. He was fifty-three years old. Born in Albany, New York, he attended the Naval Academy from 1859 to 1863, graduating in time to see active service in the Civil War. His career was similar to that of most naval officers of his generation. He experienced not only the monotonous duty of blockading, but he also took part in the battle of Mobile Bay and the attacks on Fort Fisher in North Carolina. After the war he served at home and abroad, gradually reaching positions of higher rank and greater responsibility. It is impossible to say whether Sigsbee, like some officers, had suffered from the boredom of naval life in peacetime and service in a Navy which was becoming antiquated. He might not have been discontented; he prided himself on his shiphandling and he spent years in hydrographic work. In 1880, he published *Deep-Sea Sounding and Dredging* and gained an international reputation. He had some interest in technical matters. He had invented an electrically operated device to handle some of the deep-sea data, and he had worked on developing a rheostat.[4]

He had one blemish on his record. In 1886, a board inspected the *Kearsarge,* the Civil War veteran he commanded. The board reported that the ship was dirty and that the commanding officer had failed to comply with ordnance instructions and to drill the marines sufficiently. Sigsbee was able to explain these deficiencies; he pointed out that they stemmed from the age of the ship and recent bad weather.[5]

Sigsbee was the second commanding officer of the *Maine,* taking over on April 10, 1897, only a few weeks after he had been promoted to captain. The ship already had a troubled career. It had caught fire while under construction; it had run aground in February, 1896; five men were washed overboard off Cape Hatteras on February 6, 1897 (only two were recovered); and two men were injured two days later when a piece of ammunition exploded. Early in his command, Sigsbee had taken the *Maine* into New York Harbor through the treacherous Hell Gate without a pilot. While proceeding down the East River, he found himself in a dangerous situation. To avoid ramming a crowded excursion steamer, he plowed into Pier 46. There is evidence that at least one high-ranking officer thought Sigsbee had used poor judgment in operating in crowded and restricted waters without a pilot. On the other hand, his split-second decision to hit the pier instead of the steamer prevented a heavy loss of life and won him a letter of commendation.[6]

Because of the tension in Havana, Sigsbee—from the ship's arrival—had ordered certain precautions. No visitors were allowed to roam the ship unescorted, and no small boats were permitted to approach without challenge. At night the ship had a greater degree of readiness than that usually called for: marines carried small arms ammunition in their belts, boxes of 1-pounder and 6-pounder ammunition were stowed near the guns and sentries were posted about the decks. To Sigsbee, the disaster meant one thing: as he wrote in 1912, "I surmised from the first that the explosion initiated from outside the vessel." He believed that his ship was under attack; his first order on reaching the deck after the explosion was to post sentries to repel boarders.[7]

The *Maine* was one of the causes of the first war of the United States with a foreign power since the conflict with Mexico half a century earlier. Congress declared war on April 25. Between the declaration and the signing of an armistice, 110 days elapsed. Within that brief time, the Americans were strikingly triumphant. In the Caribbean, Cuba assumed independence under the close scrutiny of Washington, while Puerto Rico became an American possession. In the Pacific, the United States annexed the Hawaiian Islands— a byproduct of the war since they were, technically at least, an independent republic. From Spain, the Americans acquired the island of Guam and the Philippine archipelago. The territorial changes in the Caribbean were the logical outgrowth of a long trend toward American domination. It was the acquisitions in the Far East which were astonishing. The American flag flying over Manila signaled the sudden emergence of the United States as a new power. For so short a struggle, the consequences were long-lasting.

The war was also important in American military history, for in certain respects the conflict foreshadowed those which were to follow. President William McKinley did not hesitate to exercise his powers as Commander-in-Chief. He installed a war room on the second floor of the White House. In addition to walls covered with large-scale maps, the room contained 25 telegraph instruments and 15 telephones. These gave McKinley direct and private access to his key officials and departments. As the Army found itself unable to cope with the shifting burdens he placed on it, McKinley intervened. He might, perhaps, have done the same with the Navy had its successes been less striking or had the war gone on longer. The Army achieved one important victory out of the war—reform and the creation of a general staff.[8]

The Navy fared differently. John D. Long, Secretary of the Navy, wrote, "May it not be said that not one error has been made?" Long was too skillful and experienced a politician to have meant these words literally, but he was voicing an important opinion. To him the Navy had been tested and its administration proved sound. Others disagreed. Alfred Thayer Mahan, the famous naval strategist and historian, wrote caustically in an article, "We cannot expect ever again to have an enemy so entirely inapt as Spain showed herself to be . . . ." Mahan, never popular in the Navy, was now a retired officer. How much he represented naval opinion is therefore difficult to assess. But a similar view was held by another prominent officer reaching the crest of a distinguished career. Captain Henry C. Taylor had been president of the Naval War College and had commanded a battleship during the war. Even before the conflict he was convinced that the Navy needed a professional staff; a group of officers who would be responsible for seeing that the Navy was prepared for war. Nothing that occurred changed his mind. Men such as Mahan and Taylor believed that the easiness of victory could breed a complacency which ignored the need for reform.[9]

Changes in territory and in military organization are fairly easy to describe; weighing the larger significance of the war is much more difficult. The close of the nineteenth century was bringing an end to an era of American history. The frontier had disappeared, business and industry were growing larger and more complex, labor was becoming organized more strongly, and cities were expanding rapidly. These developments would have continued regardless of the war with Spain. Nonetheless, the conflict did make a difference. The nation achieved a greater sense of unity—a spirit which McKinley wisely fostered as he insisted that former Confederates be placed in high ranks of the Army. There was a greater confidence and an end to isolation. Imperialism and navalism, as difficult as these terms are to define, took on a new and troubling prominence. Theodore Roosevelt's adage of "speak softly, and carry a big stick; you will go far" and William Howard Taft with "dollar diplomacy" struck a new tone in foreign affairs.

Perhaps as much as Concord, Fort Sumter, and Pearl Harbor, the loss of the *Maine* symbolized the passage of one era and the beginning of another.

CHAPTER 2

Cuba

From the earliest days of the Republic, American political leaders had been interested in Cuba; they could not be otherwise. The island was large, wealthy in natural resources, close to the United States, and dominated the entrances into the Gulf of Mexico. The American policy was to prevent British or French acquisition—even if that meant supporting Spanish possession—but in the belief that at some time the island must fall to the United States. Presidents Polk, Pierce, and Buchanan urged purchase of Cuba. For several reasons, among them Spanish pride and the complexities of the slavery issue in the United States, these efforts were frustrated. The Civil War removed the factor of slavery, but the nation's interest turned toward internal development and, for a while, the Cuban question was dormant.

The lull was only temporary. In 1868 the Cubans, tired of corruption and misrule, rebelled against Spain. In 1873 the Spanish seized the *Virginius,* a commercial vessel flying the American flag and sailing the high seas off Jamaica. The ship had been engaged in running arms to the Cubans at various times and its right to fly the American flag was doubtful. The Spanish executed the captain and 52 members of the crew and passengers. President Grant mobilized the Navy. However, the country was in no mood for war; the panic of 1873 had just begun and the Navy and Army were weak. Diplomacy settled the crisis and peace gradually returned to the island after Madrid promised reforms in 1878. Still, the rebellion had shown that disorders in Cuba could embroil the United States.

Tired of broken promises, the Cubans in early 1895 rebelled again. This time the risk of entanglement was more serious for the United States. American business had made sizeable investments on the island, particularly in sugar, and these were endangered. More important, however, was a new spirit, difficult to summarize and assess, which existed in the United States. Memories of the Civil War had receded and leaders of that struggle had left positions of power. A new feeling of confidence was reflected in the interest which greeted Mahan's writing on naval

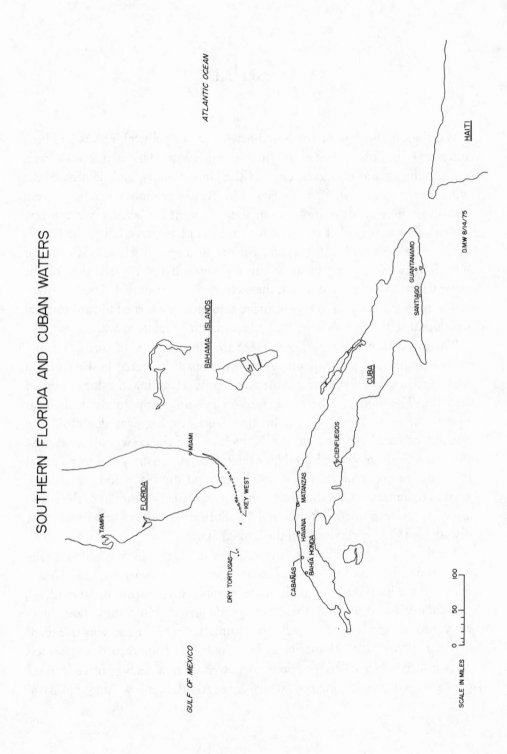

history and strategy, the construction of the New Navy, and a vigor in diplomacy which manifested itself in the Venezuelan crisis of 1895 in which the United States threatened war with Britain. Not all individuals were animated by these same beliefs; many disagreed with Mahan, fought against building battleships, and sought restraint in dealing with England. Nonetheless, the United States in 1895 was different from what it had been in 1873. Moreover, the Cuban insurrection raised a storm of moral outrage as the modern press brought into millions of homes incident after incident of the horrors of war.[1]

The horrors were real enough, even if exaggerated by the yellow press. They stemmed from the nature of the conflict; the Spanish held the principal cities and seaports, while the insurgents, avoiding fixed battle, moved through the countryside burning and wrecking in an effort to destroy the island's value to Spain. To deprive the rebels of their mobility, the Spanish divided the countryside by blockhouses, trenches, and barbed wire fences. To cut off the rebels from food and supplies, the Spanish, in 1896, adopted the *reconcentrado* policy—herding the rural population into concentration camps. Here conditions were appalling; starvation and disease took their greatest toll from the aged, women, and children.

President Grover Cleveland proclaimed neutrality on June 12, 1895. American citizens—and anyone else under United States jurisdiction—were forbidden to engage in activities directed against the established government of a friendly power. It was illegal to serve in Cuban forces, persuade others to do so, or to outfit or arm vessels for Cuban service. The Department of the Treasury, through its collectors of customs, and the Navy, with its ships, attempted to enforce the law. Enrique Dupuy de Lôme, the Spanish minister in Washington, gathered information from whatever sources he could—including spies and detectives—to ferret out prospective breaches of neutrality and turned his evidence over to the American government for action. Obviously, Cleveland's policy, although grounded in law, aided Spain and not Cuba. On the other hand, he vigorously defended the rights of American citizens in Cuba against Spanish intrusion. To prevent the possibility of an incident which might unleash a train of events he could not control, Cleveland stopped the

Navy from making its customary courtesy calls to Cuban ports. He kept the North Atlantic Squadron, the Navy's most important combat force, out of the Gulf of Mexico and the Caribbean where it usually went for maneuvers during the winter months.[2]

Congress strongly criticized Cleveland for his policy of neutrality. In 1896, the Senate proposed a resolution granting belligerent rights to the Cubans. The House of Representatives not only welcomed the move but went even further by urging American intervention. In conference the House yielded to the Senate but Cleveland ignored the congressional action. He could do so because it was a concurrent resolution, not binding on him or the nation. To Cleveland, Congress was encroaching upon the power of the presidency. More practically, he saw no organization among the insurgents capable of assuming the authority and obligations of a government.[3]

Consul General Fitzhugh Lee represented the United States in Havana. It was not an easy job to defend American lives, property, and interests during a civil war, or to determine which of the claimants for his protection were truly American citizens. Lee was no mere cipher. A nephew of Robert E. Lee, he had risen to be a Confederate cavalry general during the Civil War. Later he served as governor of Virginia and wrote a biography of his famous uncle. He was given the position in Cuba by Cleveland in 1896. He did not speak Spanish or know much about Cuba. Blunt and outspoken, he believed Spain, even if she wished, could never mend her ways. Nor did he have faith in the ability of the insurrectionists to establish a government. He did, however, see a chance for personal gain if he could persuade wealthy Americans to join him and invest in a Havana streetcar system. He was not easy to control, for he did not hesitate to interpret along his own lines the policy laid down by the State Department. He believed that the United States must ultimately intervene and he wanted naval vessels ready to be sent to him. Cleveland was cautious. By the end of his term, he had come to the conclusion that Lee should be replaced. The actual decision and timing he left to his successor.[4]

Geography dictated that the Navy would play a major role in the event of a Cuban crisis. It was, therefore, only common sense for some officers to think about what should be done if civil war in Cuba led to hostilities with Spain. Individual contributions to the various plans are hard to determine, but there were two places where planning for possible naval operations took place. One was the Naval War College on Coaster's Harbor Island, Newport, Rhode Island. The other was the Navy Department in Washington.

Established in 1884 to instruct officers in strategy and tactics, the college led a precarious existence, for naval officers could see little practical use for it. Mahan's lectures on sea power, for all their scholarly brilliance, made few converts among his fellow officers. Commander Henry C. Taylor brought a new perspective to the college when he became president in November, 1893. He believed that the Navy suffered from poor organization and administration, as well as a lack of professionalism among its officers. Placing less stress upon lectures on naval history, he emphasized war games and planning. The usual procedure was for a handful of students to arrive during the summer. They were divided into committees and set to work upon a major strategic problem. At the end of the term, the group discussed their solutions and, in the fall, the staff drew up a plan. The college had studied the Venezuelan crisis in 1895. Now Taylor assigned Cuba as a major exercise.[5]

By November, 1896, the college worked out an elaborate document which listed three possible basic strategies. The United States could attack Spain in Europe, the Philippines, or Cuba and Puerto Rico. The plan discarded the first two courses. A campaign against Spain would require a major effort on the other side of the Atlantic and the outcome would be doubtful. A vigorous attack on the Philippines was almost certain of success, but would not bring the enemy to terms. The Caribbean was the proper theater of operations. Occupying Cuba and Puerto Rico might not cause Spain to seek peace, but the islands were near at hand. There was another reason for focusing upon the West Indies; one which went beyond the scope of planning for a campaign and implied a postwar interest—"The strategic relation of Cuba to the Gulf of Mexico is so close and intimate that the value of that island to the United States in a military and naval way is incalculable."

In the event of war, the college saw that the proximity of Cuba gave the United States a great advantage. Because the Spanish Navy in the West Indies was weak, it should be possible for the Americans to complete important military moves before Spain could bring reinforcements to bear. It might take as long as 30 days before Spain could bring a considerable force across the Atlantic. But, in 25 days from the outbreak of war, the United States could land 30,000 men in Cuba, 50,000 during the following 20 days, and as many thereafter as needed. Even after the Spanish arrived, the two fleets would be equal. The Americans should welcome an engagement, but not go out of their way to seek one. The chief military objective was Havana, not the Spanish fleet. As the political, military, and commercial center of the island, the Cuban capital was well-defended. Perhaps a naval demonstration might stir up disaffected troops and elements of the civil population so that Spanish authorities would have to surrender the city, but American planners could not count on it. In all probability, the Army would have to invest Havana. The college proposed several feints for landings, with the real force going ashore at Cabañas and Bahía Honda.[6]

In a separate paper—probably in his own handwriting—Taylor drew up a summary. The Navy in Asia and the Pacific would demonstrate against the Philippines. Ships on the European Station would observe Spanish movements and fall back on the United States where they would join the main fleet in its campaign against Cuba. Only after the Americans had been successful in the West Indies would steps be taken against Spain itself. Taylor doubted whether a move against the Spanish homeland was worth the effort. It might even backfire if it caused the Spanish to unite in patriotism. He had no patience with arguments that the Army or Navy alone could take Cuba—"For the Cuban campaign all the military resources of the U.S. afloat & ashore must be developed and put in use instantly." If there was to be an error, it should be on the side of overpreparation. The November plan, Taylor's synopsis, and later corrections, went to the Secretary of the Navy and a few high-ranking officers.[7]

The plan was curiously unrealistic. It assumed that the United States would be prepared to move at the declaration of war, that the Army and the Navy had been mobilized, that shore facilities and shipping existed to embark, transport, and supply a force of 30,000 men in the first 25 days of the campaign and additional forces as necessary. There was no recognition that the total authorized strength of the Army in 1897 was only 25,000 officers and men. Spain was assumed to be waiting motionless in the Caribbean. No thought was given to the possibility that the preparations in the United States might stimulate a response by Spain. Finally, the plan proposed that the Americans land an army and keep it supplied before the Spanish Navy had been defeated.[8]

In Washington, Secretary of the Navy Hilary A. Herbert was aware of the work of the college. In August, 1896, he established a board to consider the college's plan and whether, in the event of hostilities, the Navy might itself successfully fight a war with Spain and leave only a limited part for the Army. To study these questions, Herbert selected five high-ranking officers—among them Taylor—who occupied important positions. On December 12, 1896, the board completed its own plan. The members began from the fundamental premise that Spanish forces could not maintain themselves in Cuba without supplies from overseas, especially food. If war came, the Navy should blockade the deepwater ports of Cuba and Puerto Rico, bombard the military depots at Havana and San Juan, and open supply lines to the insurgents, while the Army should be prepared to garrison selected ports. The Navy's European Squadron should leave the Mediterranean, the Asiatic Squadron should leave the Far East, and both should combine in the Atlantic with ships from the United States. Together this force was to capture the Canary Islands for a base from which to operate in Spanish waters. The board, with Taylor in dissent, disapproved the plan prepared by the War College. Herbert accepted the board's position.[9]

Six months later—on June 30, 1897—a new board issued a plan which narrowed the differences between the two earlier efforts. Cuba resumed its position as the main objective. Because of its strong defenses, Havana could not be taken from the sea: therefore the Navy would seize nearby ports so that the Army could land and mount an offensive against the Cuban capital. The most the Spanish Navy could do was to send a few cruisers which might occasionally disrupt the blockade. To counter this possibility, the Navy should send a squadron of fast ships to Spanish waters. The board believed that the Philippines, virtually ignored in the plan of December 12, 1896, should be an active area of operations. The Asiatic Squadron should steam to Manila and cooperate with the Philippine insurgents. Possibly the city would fall to a joint attack. If this was the case, the United States would have a controlling voice as to the future of the islands.[10]

Cuba was only one of several problems the nation faced. Most citizens were far more worried about the aftermath of the panic of 1893. Falling farm prices, massive unemployment, labor unrest, the use of federal troops to quell rioting in Chicago; all were issues transforming politics and investing it with an emotion and a passion that had not been felt for decades. The Democrats, as the party in power, were on the defensive. Their task was not made easier by Cleveland's conservatism and financial orthodoxy. As the summer of 1896 and the time of the conventions drew near, the Democratic ranks were shattered while the Republicans were confident.

The Republicans were expansionists. Their platform called for American control of Hawaii, construction and ownership of a trans-isthmian canal across Nicaragua, and purchase of the Danish West Indies. As for Cuba:

> We watch with deep and abiding interest the heroic battle of the Cuban patriots against cruelty and oppression, and best hopes go out for the full success of their determined contest for liberty. The government of Spain, having lost control of Cuba, and being unable to protect the property or lives of resident American citizens, or to comply with its Treaty obligations, we believe that the government of the United States should actively use its influence and good offices to restore peace and give independence to the island.

The Democrats were far more restrained. They simply declared that the Monroe Doctrine had to be maintained and that, "We extend our sympathy to the people of Cuba in their struggle for liberty and independence." [11]

The presidential campaign was tumultuous. William Jennings Bryan, the Democratic candidate, jarred the Republicans from their complacency, but in the end the Republican candidate, William McKinley, was elected.

On December 7, 1896, Cleveland sent his last State of the Union Message to Congress. A good portion of it was devoted to Cuba. He found it difficult to see any progress toward peace, for the opposing forces were too evenly balanced. Spain held Havana, the seaports, and the major cities, but the insurgents controlled the countryside. In some areas, the Spanish maintained a semblance of civil government, but the rest of the island was under military occupation or in a state of anarchy. Both forces were committing excesses: the United States could not help being concerned, not simply on the grounds of sentiment and philanthropy, but because Cuba was so near.

The President saw no easy solution. Some Americans had proposed granting belligerent rights to the insurgents, but he believed that this course would injure the interests of the United States. Others had recommended recognizing Cuban independence, but Cleveland saw no organization that could be called a government. The possibility of buying the island had been explored, but Spain was unwilling to sell. Intervention would mean war, but the United States was a peaceful nation which believed that right, not might, should rule its conduct. The best hope seemed to be some measure of autonomy, but mutual distrust created an almost insuperable obstacle. Nonetheless, the United States offered its friendly services to guarantee a settlement. Time was running out. In measured phrases Cleveland wrote:

> It would be added that it cannot be reasonably assumed that the hitherto expectant attitude of the United States will be indefinitely maintained. . . .

When the inability of Spain to deal successfully with the insurrection has become manifest and it is demonstrated that her sovereignty is extinct in Cuba for all purposes of its rightful existence, and when a hopeless struggle for its reestablishment has degenerated into a state which means nothing more than the useless sacrifice of human life and the utter devastation of the very subject-matter of the conflict, a situation will be presented in which our obligations to the sovereignty of Spain will be superseded by higher obligation, which we can hardly hesitate to recognize and discharge.[12]

The tenor of the message was striking. Cleveland was near the end of his term in office, yet the words he used warned Spain that American patience was limited and that Madrid had to find a solution soon. Privately, Cleveland had little doubt about the future. A few days before the end of his administration, he met with McKinley. The retiring President was almost certain that a war with Spain was inevitable.[13]

CHAPTER 3

Increasing Pressure

McKinley was enigmatic. A man of great personal charm, he talked easily with individuals and groups and he listened eagerly, seeking avidly for information. He held his own counsel and kept his thoughts to himself, often preferring to work through persons he trusted rather than through organizations. His views on Cuba were unknown. His campaign speeches gave no clue, for he had dealt with domestic issues and ignored Cuba completely. His inaugural address was not much more enlightening. On foreign relations, he declared that his goal was to cultivate peace with all nations. "It will be our aim to pursue a firm and dignified foreign policy, which shall be just, impartial, ever watchful of our national honor and always insisting upon enforcement of the lawful rights of American citizens everywhere." He could not rule out force, but: "War should never be entered upon until every agency of peace has failed; peace is preferable to war in almost every contingency. Arbitration is the true method of settlement of international as well as local or individual differences." [1]

Platitudes were one thing; reality another. McKinley could not ignore the insistent clamor of the yellow press, the restlessness of Congress, nor the possibility that American lives in Cuba were in danger. His first Cabinet meeting discussed a request from Lee for the Navy to station a vessel in Havana. As Secretary of the Navy John D. Long recalled the discussion, the Cabinet believed the measure was too strong. If McKinley held this view, he did not hold it long. [2]

By the summer of 1897, McKinley knew what he wanted to do. He carefully edited the instructions to General Stewart L. Woodford, his new minister to Madrid. Woodford was to assure Spain of the friendly attitude of the United States, but the war in Cuba must end. He was to point out that, so far, Spanish efforts to quell the rebellion had led only to devastation and, in the present condition, some incident could occur which would release forces beyond control. Therefore it was in the interest of both countries that the war end, but Spain had to take the initiative and take it soon. Spain should offer proposals to the Cubans which would bring peace; the United States would do what it could to help. But, Woodford was to warn, if Spain could not end the war the United States would step in.[3]

In any active role the United States might take, the Navy was certain to play a leading part. The Navy in late 1897 was small. Its strength lay in its four first-class battleships, the *Indiana, Massachusetts, Oregon,* and *Iowa;* two second-class battleships, the *Texas* and the *Maine;* and two armored cruisers, the *Brooklyn* and the *New York.* There were also sixteen other cruisers, fifteen gunboats, six double-turreted monitors, a ram, a dynamite gunboat, and five torpedo boats. The Navy was expanding rapidly; five first-class battleships, sixteen torpedo boats, and one submarine were under construction. There were about 1,200 officers in active service (a number which included engineers) and about 11,750 enlisted men. In so small a Navy, the senior officers knew each other well and nearly all were veterans of the Civil War.[4]

Responsibility for the Navy's readiness fell upon the Secretary of the Navy. He was a member of the Cabinet and reported directly to the President. It was possible to divide the Navy into two parts; one was military or operational, the other was the organization which existed to support the Navy afloat. In both areas, the Secretary had important responsibilities. In operational matters, he directed ship and squadron movements and selected officers for major commands. As one officer wrote to him in 1898, "The gift of the command lies entirely with yourself. There is absolutely no other rule. If you think it proper to give a junior captain a good ship you can do so." On the support side of the Navy, the Secretary got into technical matters when lower levels could not settle conflicting views. A political figure chosen by the President, the Secretary could not make all the decisions; he had to rely on his officers for advice.[5]

Most of the administrative and technical functions which supported the operational Navy were divided among eight bureaus: Navigation, Ordnance, Equipment, Construction and Repair, Steam Engineering, Medicine and Surgery, Supplies and Accounts, and Yards and Docks. The bureau chiefs reported directly to the Secretary. So too, did the

Judge Advocate General, the Department's chief legal officer. Of these men, the Chief of the Bureau of Navigation was the most powerful. He was charged with promulgating and enforcing the orders of the Secretary to the fleet. In addition, he was influential in personnel matters. Because his recommendations on detailing junior officers were almost always accepted, his choice of assignments could make or break a career. In so far as the Navy had a chief military officer, it was the Chief of the Bureau of Navigation. It was significant that his office was near to that of the Secretary.

Four bureaus—Construction and Repair, Ordnance, Equipment, and Steam Engineering—were particularly important in the building of the *Maine*. Construction and Repair was in charge of all design, construction, and repair of naval ships. Ordnance had the responsibility for all that related to weapons and ammunition; it recommended the armament to be carried by all armed vessels and the armor specifications, but placing the armor plates and guns on board the ship fell to Construction and Repair. Steam Engineering controlled the design, building, and repair of steam propulsion plants, as well as the steam machinery used in turning gun turrets. The Bureau of Equipment supplied a variety of material—such as sails and awnings, ground tackle, cordage, and mess outfits.[6]

Relations between the bureaus were often strained. The background of the bureau chiefs was one reason. Most often the Chiefs of the Bureaus of Ordnance and Equipment were line officers—men who were eligible for command at sea but to whom the technical aspects of the Navy were secondary. In contrast, staff officers who devoted their professional careers to their specialties headed the other two bureaus; the "Chief Constructor" was in charge of Construction and Repair and the "Engineer-in-Chief" of Steam Engineering. Relations were particularly bad between the line officers and engineers. Engineers at sea were under the cognizance of the Engineer-in-Chief and occasionally were discriminated against by some line officers. But the changing technology which tended to upset the lines of organizational jurisdiction was the fundamental cause of strained relations among the bureaus.[7]

McKinley had chosen John D. Long to be Secretary of the Navy. He was a politician, a former governor of Massachusetts who had run an honest and competent administration, and a congressman who had served in Washington when McKinley had been a representative from Ohio. The two men were still close; Long and his family were frequent dinner guests at the White House. Long deliberately made no effort to acquire a detailed knowledge of any branch of his Department. He wrote in his journal:

> I make [it] a point not to trouble myself overmuch to acquire a thorough knowledge of the details pertaining to any branch of the service. Such knowledge would undoubtedly be a very valuable equipment, but the range is so enormous I could make little progress, and that at great expense of health and time, in mastering it. My plan is to leave all such matters to the bureau chiefs, or other officers at naval stations or on board ship, limiting myself to the general direction of affairs. What is the need of my making a dropsical tub of any lobe of my brain, when I have right at hand a man possessed with more knowledge than I could acquire, and have him constantly on tap? At best there is enough for me to do, and to occupy my attention. Some of it is spent on important things, and a very large part on small things, especially personal matters—personal frictions, personal delinquencies, personal appeals, and personal claims.

Long was a capable official, only mildly interested in reform. To an extent he was self-deprecating. When a principle was involved—when he believed that his civilian authority was being challenged by naval officers—he could be adamant. But he was passive and stubborn rather than active and aggressive.[8]

The Assistant Secretary, Theodore Roosevelt, had enough enthusiasm and energy for several people. McKinley had chosen the young New Yorker—he was only 39 in October, 1897—partly to please Senator Henry Cabot Lodge, an important Republican leader. Roosevelt was a valuable and hardworking official; he handled material and contract matters and naval intelligence; he was chairman of the board of officers which was working out ways to end decades of strife by merging the engineer corps into the line officers. Roosevelt was fascinated by all activities of the Navy, from operational affairs such as target practice to technical matters such as ship design.[9]

He recognized the danger from the practice of locating coal bunkers adjacent to magazines. The idea behind the arrangement was that coal-filled bunkers would give additional protection from enemy projectiles. However, there was a risk that spontaneous combustion of the bituminous coal could overheat the magazines. Since 1895 there had been three coal bunker fires in the *Olympia,* four in the *Wilmington* and at least one in the *Petrel,* the *Lancaster,* and the *Indiana.* There had been several bunker fires recently in the *Brooklyn,* and it was well known that those on board the *Cincinnati* and *New York* almost caused the magazines to explode. The *Oregon,* too, had been endangered. Because many of the Navy's ships—including the *Maine*—had bunkers and magazines with a common bulkhead between them, Roosevelt recommended in November 1897 that Long appoint a board to make a thorough investigation of various types of coal and the causes of spontaneous combustion. He did more; he had the American naval attachés get information on the procedures foreign navies followed to prevent spontaneous ignition of coal.[10]

On Friday, September 17, 1897, Roosevelt dined with McKinley. The two men talked about naval affairs and Spain, and continued their conversation during a drive the following Monday. Roosevelt left with the President a paper describing the condition of the fleet. He believed the North Atlantic Squadron of seven "ironclads" under Rear Admiral Montgomery Sicard was in "splendid trim."

> The fleet on the Atlantic Coast is therefore available for almost any emergency that seems likely to arise. We should, however, have as much warning as possible if any emergency is at all probable. It is impossible to keep all of these ships ready all the time. . . .

As for the Asiatic Squadron, which consisted of the cruisers *Olympia, Boston,* and gunboats *Yorktown* and *Machias*:

> This squadron would probably be quite competent to take the Philippines, or at least create a heavy diversion there, but they could do nothing themselves as against Japanese cruisers.

As a whole, Roosevelt was confident:

> I think the Navy is equal to any strain that can be placed upon it; but of course, and especially if to be used against two opponents, it would be of the greatest consequence to receive warning as much in advance as possible, and to be allowed to take the initiative instead of waiting and letting the enemy develop his plans.[11]

Roosevelt summarized his talk with McKinley for Lodge. The Assistant Secretary had stated that, in the event of war, American initiative was needed if trouble was to be avoided with both Spain and Japan. If the United States had its main fleet ready at Key West before war was declared, if four fast cruisers harassed the coast of Spain as quickly as possible, if an expeditionary force landed in Cuba, the war would probably be over in six weeks. In the meantime, the Asiatic Squadron could blockade Manila or even take the city. But the key to everything was initiative.[12]

In late summer of 1897, an anarchist murdered the conservative Spanish premier Antonio Cánovas del Castillo. Momentarily the prospects for peace brightened, for Práxedes Mateo Sagasta, the liberal leader who formed a new government on October 6, 1897, opposed the Cuban war. Sagasta recalled General Valeriano Weyler y Nicolau—"Butcher" Weyler, as he was known in the American press—and replaced him with General Ramón Blanco y Erenas who was instructed to fight the Cubans in a Christian and humane manner. Furthermore, in November Sagasta took the first steps to establish an autonomous government in Cuba. It was, of course, far too much to say that the change of policy had been the result of American pressure but still, a liberal government might be easier to deal with. Lee remained pessimistic. He did not believe the insurgents would accept autonomy. Nor would the Spanish elements who had commercial and business interests; these people, he thought, would prefer annexation to the United States rather than genuine autonomy or independence.[13]

Although the accession of a new government in Madrid eased tensions, there was no guarantee that Spanish efforts to placate Cuba would be successful. The McKinley administration began to take measures to prepare for possible emergency in Havana. On October 8, 1897, Long ordered the *Maine* detached from the North Atlantic Squadron, which was operating off Chesapeake Bay, and sent to Port Royal, South Carolina. The ship arrived at her new station on October 12. Rear Admiral Arent S. Crowninshield, Chief of the Bureau of Navigation, wrote Sigsbee on October 21 that the *Maine* was at Port Royal because it was near enough to Cuba so that the ship would be available, and yet far enough away so that it would not be conspicuous. Crowninshield advised Sigsbee to keep the *Maine* filled with coal. To Sigsbee, the stay at Port Royal was dull and the possibility of a more active duty was attractive.[14]

At London there was another straw in the wind. The British shipbuilding industry was constructing vessels for several foreign navies, among them the Japanese, Brazilian, Chilean, and Spanish. Spain had six destroyers on order, but there were rumors that Madrid might have trouble paying for them. Lieutenant John C. Colwell, the American naval attaché, understood that Spain was negotiating for more naval vessels of an undisclosed number and class. He heard, too, that the Spanish were interested in the Brazilian cruisers being built. Although Colwell did not say so, perhaps the Brazilians and their builders were trying to stimulate the United States to buy, for there was gossip that the South American country was in financial difficulty.

At any rate, "I am authoritatively informed that the United States can purchase the Brazilian vessels named at their contract prices, and though they might not be taken possession of or removed from their builders' yards, they could in that way be kept out of Spanish hands." [15]

For the *Maine* the pace of events began to quicken. In response to a routine circular, the ship's division officers—those responsible for such areas as ordnance, engineering, and navigation—drew up a list of repairs and alterations, all of which appear to have been minor. On October 28, Sigsbee forwarded the list to Sicard and, on November 15, the *Maine* left for Norfolk. From November 21 to 23, the ship took on coal at nearby Newport News. On December 3, two things happened. Roosevelt informed the Chiefs of the Bureaus of Construction and Repair, Steam Engineering, Ordnance, and Equipment, that all of the work on the *Maine* had to be completed by December 10, since the ship was scheduled to leave the yard the next day. Also on December 3, Long sent secret and confidential plans to the *Maine* and *Detroit*. (The plans have not been found, but from other evidence it appears that if the *Maine* and the *Detroit* at Key West received a code message from Lee consisting of the letter "A," the battleship was to go to Havana and the cruiser to Matanzas, a port about 50 miles from the Cuban capital.) On December 6, the *Maine* was drydocked. An inspection revealed that the antifouling paint was in bad condition, the bottom was encrusted with barnacles, and a heavy growth of seaweed marked the waterline. The *Maine,* with a clean hull, was refloated on December 10 and five days later arrived at Key West.[16]

The *Maine* at Key West was the precursor of a much larger force, for the North Atlantic Squadron was to resume its winter exercises in the Gulf of Mexico. On January 3, 1898, Roosevelt wrote to Rear Admiral Sicard asking for the plan of maneuvers. He told Sicard that the squadron would consist of the *New York,* the *Indiana, Massachusetts, Iowa, Maine, Texas,* the monitor *Terror,* and one other cruiser. Roosevelt promised that, except for an emergency, Sicard could count on these ships until April 1.[17]

On December 6, 1897, McKinley sent his first State of the Union Message to Congress. In foreign affairs, the only serious problem he saw was the

NRL(M)39251

On board the Maine. *View of port side of main deck looking forward. The upper gun is a 6-pounder; the lower is a 6-inch gun. The foremast was eventually placed at Annapolis. Photograph taken at Bar Harbor, Maine, August, 1897.*

struggle between Spain and Cuba. Although both sides were waging a bitter and uncivilized war, he believed the Spanish policy of *reconcentrado* was proving in practice to be one of extermination. As a neighboring nation, the United States could only wait a reasonable time for peace and order to be restored. He reviewed the possibilities. The United States could recognize the insurgents as belligerents; Cuba as an independent state; or intervene, either as a neutral to enforce rational compromise or in favor of one side or the other. One thing he ruled out: "I speak not of forcible annexation, for that cannot be thought of. That, by our code of morality, would be criminal aggression. . . ." But:

> If it shall hereafter appear to be a duty imposed by our obligations to ourselves, to civilization and humanity to intervene with force, it shall be without fault on our part and only because the necessity for such action will be so clear as to command the support and approval of the civilized world.[18]

CHAPTER 4

The *Maine* to Havana

The war in Cuba had transformed Key West from a quiet town with a small naval station into a center of activity. Since it was only 90 nautical miles from Havana, the port was well situated for the Navy to carry out the policy of neutrality. The small unprotected cruisers *Montgomery* and *Detroit,* and the torpedo boats *Cushing, Dupont,* and *Ericsson* were engaged in searching out filibustering expeditions—as attempts to supply aid to the Cuban insurgents were called. Key West was also important because it was linked by telegraph to Washington and by undersea cable to Havana. The main disadvantage of the port was an extensive coral reef which limited the anchorage available for large vessels. Consequently, the North Atlantic Squadron during its maneuvers was to operate out of the Dry Tortugas, a small cluster of low-lying islands about 60 miles to the west.[1]

At Key West, Sigsbee waited for a message from Lee. Almost daily he sent a cable to the consul general. Because of Spanish censorship, the contents were innocuous and even trifling, but they served the purpose of making sure that no one had interrupted the cable traffic and that he and Lee could contact each other. For an exchange of information on serious matters they depended on secret letters smuggled in and out of Havana. Knowing that he would have to respond quickly if he received a summons from Lee, Sigsbee hoarded the coal taken on board at Newport News. It was bituminous coal, susceptible to spontaneous combustion, but it had better burning qualities than the anthracite coal he received from the naval station at Key West.[2]

Lee was convinced that Spain could not end the rebellion by granting autonomy. He believed that Spanish authority in Havana was precarious and that a presidential or congressional action in Washington, such as recognizing the rights of belligerency, could set off a serious disturbance. Therefore, he wrote the State Department on December 22, 1897, that a naval vessel or two should be sent to Havana before any such measure was taken. The Spanish population in the city was divided. Some of them, mostly businessmen and their employees, detested autonomy for it threatened their interests.

This group had organized and armed itself and, in Lee's view, threatened the control of General Blanco over the city. Consequently, Lee thought that Blanco himself might feel relief if American naval vessels were in the harbor. At all events, Lee believed the presence of naval ships would help him meet his responsibility for protecting American lives and property.[3]

In Washington, too, there were doubts about autonomy. Alvey A. Adee, a career diplomat and Second Assistant Secretary of State, analyzed the provisions and found them wanting. Spain was not offering Cuba an organic and fundamental charter but simply legislative acts; what the *Cortes* had granted, the *Cortes* could take away. It was uncertain whether Spain could enforce sufficient peace to give autonomy a chance. Spanish finances were bad and the stability of the Spanish government in Madrid was open to question. Consequently, Adee believed that McKinley was correct in not pledging to support autonomy and was wise to continue to wait and see if it would be successful.[4]

If Lee and Adee were correct, a serious threat lay over Havana. Possibly autonomy might work but it might also fail with results that could be disastrous. There was not only the suffering on the island for McKinley to consider, there were also the practical domestic politics of congressional emotions and the position of the United States in foreign affairs. Several American diplomats were reporting German activities in Central America. McKinley had already warned Spain that American patience was almost exhausted. On January 11, 1898, the administration took its first step to prepare the Navy for the uncertain future. Long ordered Rear Admiral Thomas Selfridge, Commander-in-Chief of the European Squadron, to retain those men whose enlistments were about to expire. A year later, Long recalled the despatch as ". . . probably the first important order given in contemplation of war."[5]

On January 12, a riot broke out in Havana. It was not, as Lee had feared, a reaction against a Washington move. The mob was made up of elements of the Spanish civil population demonstrating against some Havana newspapers which favored autonomy. The presence of Spanish army officers in the mob was ominous. Lee alerted Sigsbee but decided that the situation was not serious enough to call for the *Maine,* for the next day the city was quiet. In Washington, Adee read the event differently. Extremely influential because of his long service and background, Adee saw in Lee's despatches evidence that autonomy was failing, and that it lacked support among the Spanish civilians and army officers.

Adee believed that the civilians, organized as "volunteers" might over-
throw the weak autonomous government and the authority of Blanco.
Adee thought that if Havana were plunged into chaos, the rest of the
island would quickly follow. On January 12, when news of the rioting
arrived, he advised William R. Day, the Assistant Secretary of State, that
the naval squadron in the Gulf of Mexico should be prepared for any
emergency.[6]

Day was an important figure in the administration and an example
of McKinley's practice of working through individuals who were personally linked to him. McKinley had selected John Sherman as Secretary
of State. Because the elderly Sherman was in poor health, McKinley asked
Day to serve as Assistant Secretary of State. The two men had been close
friends and political associates for years; Day had been one of that group
which had rescued McKinley from financial difficulties. Day accepted the
assignment reluctantly, for he was a lawyer, not a diplomat. Shrewd and
discreet, he relied heavily upon Adee. Yet Day also sought advice from
outside the Department. In November 1897 he consulted John Bassett
Moore, professor of international law at Columbia. Day was concerned
about Congress and wondered if the legislative branch had the authority
to force American intervention. Moore assured him that the matter was
one for the President to decide. Moore added that intervention would
mean war.[7]

After the riot of January 12, the administration considered the possibility
of intervention in the near future. An unsigned memorandum in the State
Department files, marked as submitted to McKinley on January 14, argued
that Spain must leave the island, Cuba must indemnify the Spanish for their
losses, and the United States should recognize Cuban independence. But the
President would have to act. "Has not the time come for some kind of
intervention on the part of the United States, friendly or forceful. Is not 'the
near future' which calls for 'intervention with force' if necessary, upon us."
That same day the Cabinet discussed the issue, but the mood according to
Long was not warlike. In the Secretary's view, "My own notion is that Spain
is not only doing the best it can, but is doing very well in its present treatment of the island." As he saw it, Spain had granted autonomy and put an
end to the barbarities of the earlier administration. "Our government certainly has nothing to complain of, every American interest has been protected
as far as possible." Still, he admitted that the stability was fragile and danger

to American life and property was ever present. Perhaps ships would have to be sent to Havana.[8]

Theodore Roosevelt was certain that the riot meant that war was near. He was exhilarated at the prospect. When it came, he told Long, he would resign his position and go at once to the front. On January 14, Roosevelt prepared for Long a lengthy summary of the Navy's strength in the Caribbean, Atlantic, and Pacific, along with ideas on what each force should do. In two respects—ammunition and numbers of men—the Navy was deficient. Above all, Roosevelt warned, the United States should not drift unprepared into war.[9]

Woodford, the American minister, had a long and confidential audience in Madrid with María Cristina, the Queen Regent, on January 17. She wanted an end to the rebellion. She had done all she could. Only American assistance kept the war going. Now it was up to McKinley. He should issue a proclamation calling upon the American people to stop aiding the rebellion and he should break up the group of Cuban exiles and sympathizers known as the New York junta. For his part, Woodford explained as best he could the limitations on presidential power. He was candid on another subject: the United States doubted the ability of General Blanco to maintain order. Even more bluntly, Woodford referred to rumors of conspiracies in Madrid.[10]

On January 20, Enrique Dupuy de Lôme, the Spanish minister, called on Day. Until the riot in Havana broke out, Dupuy was guardedly optimistic, reporting to his superiors in Madrid that autonomy seemed to be removing the irritations that rasped the relations between Spain and the United States. He knew about plans to move the North Atlantic Squadron south for maneuvers; he was not aware, judging from his despatches, of the order signed by Long on January 11 to the European Station to retain those men whose enlistments had expired. Dupuy, a shrewd professional diplomat, underestimated the determination of McKinley to see an end to the struggle on the island. When he spoke to Day on January 20, Dupuy was clearly delivering the same message that the Queen Regent gave Woodford. The Spanish diplomat declared that he was pessimistic, not about the situation in Spain or Cuba, but about the attitude of the United States. Echoing the words of the Queen Regent, he said that it was only the American people who kept the insurrection alive; therefore, it was only a "courageous act of statesmanship" by the American President which could prevent a break between the two nations in the near future. Autonomy, he stated, was an unqualified success. Spain, indeed, could bring peace to the island by May 1.

The conversation turned to specific problems. Dupuy complained that Lee, by his conduct and outspoken views, was proclaiming the failure of autonomy. The Spanish minister was also disturbed by press statements that the Navy was preparing in Cuban waters for any emergency. The press was speculating that, if Spain mobilized her fleet in these waters, a clash and war were inevitable. Lee's attitude and the rumors about ships were disquieting to Madrid. Day remarked that Lee had not been authorized to make any statement on autonomy. As for ships, if Lee needed them, he should have them. Day did not see how Spain could object if the United States exercised its right to protect its citizens and property. Sending ships, countered the minister, would be an unfriendly act and taken as the first step in intervention. Landing marines in Havana, or forces anywhere in Cuba, would be seen as a cause of war. He wanted Day to make sure that these views got to the President.[11]

McKinley was in a difficult position. If Lee, Adee, and Day were correct, the situation in Havana was so explosive that no one could tell what would happen. A ship might well have a calming effect and protect American lives. On the other hand, Dupuy had just warned that Spain would regard the presence of an American naval vessel as a dangerous and unfriendly act. How to introduce a ship into Havana without precipitating a war was a difficult problem. If these were the thoughts in the minds of McKinley and Day, it might account for the question which Day asked Lee on January 22: What were the numbers and types of naval vessels of other nations in Havana? Lee replied promptly: None, but two German ships were expected soon.[12]

Day's query could have alerted Lee that the policy of prohibiting American naval vessels from visiting Havana was under reconsideration. Twice Lee had written that German naval ships were to call at Havana, and he could see no reason why the Navy could not do likewise. He even suggested pretexts: a ship could enter claiming a shortage of fuel because of chasing a filibustering expedition, or that it wanted to send despatches to Washington. But whatever the reason, he argued for a large ship; one which would impress the Spanish and dissuade anyone from making a foolish attempt against it.[13]

At 10 o'clock on the morning of January 24, Dupuy called again at the State Department. He learned, not surprisingly, that his efforts of a few days earlier had failed: McKinley would not go beyond the policy he had set forth in his December congressional message but he would give autonomy a fair chance. Day then introduced a new element. The President intended to send naval vessels on friendly visits to Cuba quite soon. Since Spain and the United States were at peace, and since autonomy was proving so successful, Spain could not possibly object. Dupuy could do little more than say that the visits should not have been stopped in the first place.

After the Spanish diplomat departed, Day hurried to the White House. He, McKinley, Long, and perhaps Nelson A. Miles, Commanding General of the Army, and Joseph McKenna, Justice of the Supreme Court, considered the matter. McKinley made his decision: the *Maine* would go to Havana. Messages went out at once. Lee and Woodford were informed that the *Maine* would leave in a day or two. The message for Sigsbee, however, ordered him to depart immediately. At the Assistant Secretary's request, Dupuy returned that afternoon to the State Department for his second interview of the day. In Day's words, "I told him the President had despatched the *Maine* to Cuba." [14]

The sequence of events was important. Lee and Woodford had been told that the *Maine* would leave in a day or so; Dupuy was informed in his first interview that the ship would depart quite soon; the message to Sigsbee ordered him to proceed to Havana; and Dupuy, in his second interview, was told that the *Maine* had already been sent. In all probability McKinley, by acting fast, was introducing a battleship into the heart of the Cuban capital before Spain could protest. The quickness of the move was hardly in conformance with customary international law, but it cut through any possible delays that might result from Spanish objections. The *Maine* would protect American interests and be available to take advantage of whatever opportunities time might bring. By his action McKinley also accomplished something else. Both parties in Congress had been turbulent and critical of his Cuban policy. Republican and Democratic leaders alike applauded his move.[15]

Why a battleship instead of a cruiser was chosen to go to Havana is a matter of conjecture. Lee believed that a large ship would make the strongest impression upon the Spanish authorities and the population of Havana. Sigsbee, too, thought that the size of the vessel making the visit was important. McKinley and his advisors might have considered the *Maine* as the logical choice: since October 1897 the ship had been set aside for an emergency in Cuba; and available since mid-December at Key West awaiting a summons from Lee. Given the American belief

that matters in Cuba were coming to a crisis, sending the *Maine* instead
of a smaller ship was a natural decision, if not a wise one.[16]

On the evening of January 24, the *Maine* was at anchor with the
North Atlantic Squadron at the Dry Tortugas. Under Rear Admiral
Montgomery Sicard, the squadron consisting of the armored cruiser
New York (flagship) and the battleships *Iowa, Indiana,* and *Massachusetts,* had left Hampton Roads, Virginia, on January 16. Off North Carolina the *Texas* joined the squadron so that Sicard had with him all the
Navy's battleships except the *Oregon,* which was on the West Coast,
and the *Maine.* After a slow passage, partly because of leaky boiler tubes
on the *Indiana,* Sicard arrived off Key West on January 23. The *Maine*
and the unprotected cruisers *Montgomery* and *Detroit* joined the squadron.
To Sigsbee, the appearance of the North Atlantic Squadron must have
brought some relief from boredom, although he liked having an independent command. At Key West the *Maine* remained at anchor, but its steam
launches were used on night patrols against filibustering expeditions. Now
his time of waiting was almost over. To his wife he wrote: "In certain
events the *Maine* is to be the chosen of the flock; it being so ordered by
the Department." [17]

Because the *Maine* was to take part in the squadron exercises, changes
had to be made in the arrangement by which Lee could contact Sigsbee.
Caution was essential, for Key West was notorious for news leaks and
more than once the Navy was embarrassed to find its confidential
orders in the newspapers. Under Long's orders, Sigsbee turned over to
Lieutenant Albert Gleaves, commanding the torpedo boat *Cushing,* details on how to reach Lee. Gleaves was to leave Key West immediately to
find Sicard (and the *Maine*) if one of three things happened: all traffic
over the Havana cable stopped; Lee did not answer cables sent to him; or
he sent certain prearranged code phrases. "Pay nothing" meant to stand
by. "Vessels might be employed elsewhere" meant come at once. If
Gleaves had reason to reach Lee by letter he could do so through the
business agent, captain, or purser of the *Olivette,* a small steamer running
between Key West and Havana. Gleaves should be careful not to compromise these men; only an officer in civilian clothes should contact them.

Gleaves was also warned that the affairs in Havana were critical and that Lee believed the Navy would have to send vessels sooner or later.[18]

About 9 o'clock on the evening of January 24, Sigsbee at the Dry Tortugas saw the running lights of a vessel which was narrow, low in the water, and coming at a good speed from the direction of Key West. Anticipating that it was a torpedo boat (it was the *Dupont*) with his orders, he went on board the *New York* after leaving word to prepare the *Maine* for getting underway. The telegraphic order from Long to Sicard stated:

> Order the Maine to proceed to Havana, Cuba, and make friendly call—Pay his respects to the authorities there—Particular attention must be paid to usual interchange of civility—Torpedo boat must not accompany Maine—The squadron must not return to Key West on this account

Two hours later the *Maine* left the anchorage.[19]

Sigsbee's parting remark to Sicard was that he would try to make no mistakes. Not knowing what his reception might be, Sigsbee spent the night hours getting ammunition to the guns. In mid-morning of January 25, the *Maine* was off the Cuban capital, flags flying, steaming at full speed and, except for outward appearances, at general quarters. At first, Sigsbee considered entering without a pilot but decided against it. When the pilot, Julian Garcia Lopez, came on board, Sigsbee asked if the *Maine* was expected and what kind of a welcome he might receive. Lopez replied that he had known nothing of the *Maine*'s arrival and that the Americans had nothing to fear so long as they behaved themselves. As Lopez later recalled the scene, he showed a chart of the harbor to Sigsbee, pointed to a mooring in the man-of-war section of the harbor, and asked if the location was satisfactory. Sigsbee was pleased. Throngs of people crowded the waterfront as the *Maine* entered the harbor. Lopez, with a skill which won Sigsbee's tribute, moored the battleship to buoy four.[20]

Long was relieved that all had gone well. Sigsbee reported that ". . . the *Maine* presents a most formidable appearance. Her surroundings and her present deep draft seem to greatly exaggerate her size." To Lee, the arrival of the battleship was the culmination of months of effort. He believed now he had been overanxious about the effect the ship might have. Sigsbee made his first official call in full uniform and attracted attention but nothing more. Lee wrote: "I . . . am so happy that we have reached and quietly crossed over the bridge which for a long time we have seen in front of us." The *Washington Evening Star* interviewed several naval officers. Rumors that Havana was protected by mines and torpedoes did not worry them. They pointed out

NRL(O)18114

The Maine enters Havana Harbor, January 25, 1898.

that all up-to-date nations, including the United States, used mines and torpedoes to protect their harbors. However, these weapons were not armed in time of peace. The *Maine* was completely safe, for the Spanish would not put mines in a harbor which was in daily use by its own as well as ships of other countries.[21]

Lee had been worried. When he heard from Day that the *Maine* was to come, he promptly advised postponing the visit six or seven days, and also asked to be notified as to date and hour of arrival. He transmitted the request of the Spanish authorities that the ship be detained until they could get instructions from Madrid, and he forwarded the Spanish argument that there could be no objection to the delay if, as the Americans alleged, the visit was friendly. At the palace the Spanish had been excited; one official suggested that it was time the Spanish fleet appeared. Lee had been abrupt—were the authorities going to help him preserve peace or were they going to precipitate a crisis?[22]

To the harbor officials, the arrival of the *Maine* had all the characteristics of a hasty act. The health authorities, always concerned with the danger of yellow fever, could not understand why Sigsbee was not prepared to offer proper documents to show he had a clean bill of health. Had they known that the ship was without proper credentials, they would have recommended placing it in quarantine.[23]

In Washington the Navy continued its preparation. On January 27, Crowninshield, Chief of the Bureau of Navigation, cabled Dewey on the cruiser *Olympia* in Yokohama, Japan, to hold men whose enlistments had ended. With this same measure the Navy had alerted all its major commands—in Europe, the Caribbean, the North Atlantic, and now the Far East—of possible trouble with Spain. On January 31, the cruiser *Montgomery* under Commander George A. Converse, left the North Atlantic Squadron to visit and report conditions at Matanzas, a harbor some miles to the east of Havana, and Santiago, almost at the opposite end of the island.[24]

Dupuy continued his efforts to convince the State Department that the autonomous government in Cuba was in charge. He informed Day that Sigsbee, although punctilious in fulfilling the exchanges of courtesies with Spanish military officials, completely neglected the autonomous government. The Spanish minister presumed that the prejudice of Lee was at the bottom of it all, but it was hard to understand why the Americans, who professed to favor autonomy, now ignored the government established under that policy. Prodded by Washington, Sigsbee repaired the omission; he had considered

HAVANA HARBOR 1898

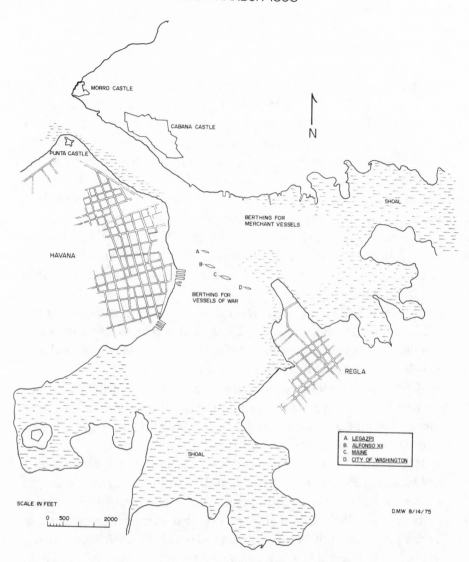

the autonomous government as if it were a legislative body in a minor colony.
Dupuy's letters on the autonomous government were among the last the
diplomat delivered to the United States government. The *New York Journal*
obtained a private letter he had written. In it Dupuy described McKinley
as a coarse politician. Even worse, the Spanish diplomat viewed autonomy

as a sham. To the American newspaper public, it was one further evidence of Spain's duplicity.[25]

Beneath a veneer of official courtesy the Spanish and Americans at Havana eyed each other warily. Both sides sought to avoid incidents. Long ordered Sigsbee not to allow the crew liberty; Madrid ordered the Havana authorities to avoid trouble when the American sailors came ashore. In a few days Sigsbee felt that the situation was sufficiently calm to permit officers to visit the city. Nonetheless, he kept ammunition readily available for all guns, sufficient steam up to move the heaviest turrets, and armed sentries posted about the decks. As was his duty, and as Roosevelt requested, Sigsbee gathered intelligence on Havana's defenses. For the crew, the novelty of being in the harbor wore off quickly; over 350 men were crowded into an armored, poorly ventilated ship, swinging at its buoy day after day. Even the bumboats shunned the *Maine*.[26]

Sigsbee, at least, had guests to entertain. These were well-established members of Havana society. From them and Lee, Sigsbee received his impressions of the political situation. Admitting that his observations were not firsthand, Sigsbee believed that Spain had no future in Cuba. The local Spanish opinion had no faith that autonomy could bring peace. Very recently (perhaps Sigsbee meant since the January 12 riot), the Spanish civilians had begun to shift toward favoring annexation to the United States. He thought the educated Cubans would probably accept American annexation.[27]

How long was the *Maine* to stay? The Navy planned to send the battleship to New Orleans by February 17 for the Mardi Gras. Furthermore, the longer the ship remained in Havana, the greater the danger from yellow fever. To questions from Washington, Lee replied that there was no danger to health before April or May. More important, to withdraw the *Maine,* unless it were replaced by an equally large and powerful ship, would be to lose all that had been gained. "We are masters of the situation now and I would not disturb or alter it." Persuaded by Lee, Washington decided to leave the *Maine* in Havana.[28]

Now that the *Maine* was present, Lee changed the code. "Vessels might be employed elsewhere" was given the meaning that the *Maine* needed help. Yet he and Sigsbee were worried that the cable might be cut and there would be no way to summon assistance. Therefore, another ship should join

NRL(O)4436

Five hours before explosion. A photograph of the Maine at Havana reportedly taken on the afternoon of February 15, 1898.

the *Maine*. Perhaps at some time Washington might want to take action, but this might precipitate a crisis endangering the *Maine*. He wrote to Day on February 2, 1898: "Sigsbee seems to think [that the] fleet would get tangled up, as it were, inside the harbor, but it might be slowly cruising conveniently near!" Sigsbee was convinced that his ship exerted a calming influence. He thought, however, that a torpedo boat should begin to make a series of visits; each time staying a little longer, until the Spanish got used to the idea. He warned that the new arrival should bring its own water, for the Spanish were perfectly capable of deliberately contaminating the supply from Havana. Day, Long, and presumably the President accepted the reasoning. On February 10, Long informed Sigsbee and Sicard that the torpedo boat *Cushing* was to go to Havana on February 15, if the weather was good, ostensibly to bring stores. The torpedo boat would return to Key West almost at once.[29]

The *Cushing,* named after the Civil War hero who sank the Confederate ironclad gunboat *Albemarle* by a spar torpedo, was one of the Navy's first steel torpedo boats. Built by the famous Herreshoff Manufacturing Company at Bristol, Rhode Island, the *Cushing* had been commissioned in 1890. It was small: 140 feet overall length, 15 feet extreme beam, a normal displacement of 116 tons, and an average draft of only 4 feet 10 inches. Armed with three 6-pounders and three torpedo tubes, and designed to carry a crew of 20 men and two officers, it was capable of making 23 knots.[30]

Despite Long's use of a ciphered cable, the Havana government learned that same day from a Spanish language newspaper of the impending visit. The authorities were not certain what to do. Every American steamer that called seemed to have left some supplies for the *Maine;* now the *Cushing* was, according to the press, about to arrive with more stores. Under Spanish law, a warship carrying provisions had to declare them for customs. Furthermore, under customary international law, the authorities were within their rights to refuse the *Cushing* entry. To do so, however, raised the possibility of a diplomatic dispute. The Spanish decided not to raise any objections.[31]

The voyage of the *Cushing* began badly. The two officers who deciphered Long's despatch neglected to transcribe the sailing date of February 15. Consequently Gleaves, to the subsequent astonishment of Long, left Key West at 7:10 in the morning of February 11. About halfway to Havana, the *Cushing* ran into heavy seas. One wave swept an officer overboard. Despite skillful ship handling and prompt action, the man was picked up too late to save his life. The torpedo boat continued on to Havana and at 3:30 p.m.

moored close by the *Maine*. The body was transferred to the battleship and sent back to the United States by commercial steamer. The day after its arrival the *Cushing* returned to Key West.[32]

Because of the error in deciphering the message, the *Cushing* was not in Havana on the night of February 15 but in its usual mooring at Key West. Gleaves was below deck when his quartermaster informed him that a man wanted to see him. Gleaves came up and recognized a secret agent. He told Gleaves that another agent in Havana had cabled that the *Maine* was blown up by a magazine explosion. Gleaves was inclined to doubt the news—Key West was full of rumors. Still, he went with the agent and Lieutenant Commander William S. Cowles, the senior officer present afloat, to the telegraph office. They waited. Hours later, the click of the telegraph filled the silent room. It was an unciphered message from Havana to be relayed to the Secretary of the Navy. The operator handed the despatch to the agent, who passed it to Cowles, who read it and handed it to Gleaves.

> *Maine* blown up in Havana harbor at nine forty to-night and destroyed. Many wounded and doubtless more killed or drowned. Wounded and others aboard Spanish man-of-war and Ward Line Steamer. Send Light House Tenders from Key West for crew and the few pieces of equipment above water. No one has clothing other than that upon him. Public opinion should be suspended until further report. All officers believed to be saved . . . Many Spanish officers, including representatives of General Blanco, now with us to express sympathy.
>
> Sigsbee [33]

CHAPTER 5

Court of Inquiry

Sigsbee's cable announcing the disaster went from Key West to Washington, arriving at the Navy Department before 1 o'clock on the morning of February 16. In Crowninshield's absence (he was in Santo Domingo exploring the possibility of acquiring a coaling station), Commander Francis W. Dickens was acting as Chief of the Bureau of Navigation. Dickens sent messages to the White House and to the Hotel Portland, where Long lived. Awakened by his daughter shortly after 1 o'clock, Long sent for Dickens and, when that officer arrived, ordered the light house tender *Fern* to Havana. Long telephoned the White House. The night watchman awakened McKinley. The President was stunned.[1]

Word of the tragedy also went from Key West to the North Atlantic Squadron. At 11:30 on the night of February 15, Lieutenant Nathaniel R. Usher, commanding the torpedo boat *Ericsson*, was ordered by Lieutenant Commander William S. Cowles of the *Fern* to prepare to get underway. Usher hurried aboard the *Fern* and learned from Cowles that the *Maine* had been lost. About 12:30 the torpedo boat left for the Dry Tortugas. At 5:30 in the morning of February 16, the *Ericsson* found the *New York*. Shortly before noon, Sicard left on the armored cruiser for Key West; there he could receive despatches from Washington and Havana.[2]

Cowles departed for Havana on the morning of February 16 and arrived at the scene of the disaster about 4:00 in the afternoon. It was hard for the crew of the *Fern* to recognize the wreck as the battleship they had known. The *Maine* was resting upright on the bottom; the stern superstructure was above the water and the mainmast was upright and nearly vertical; amidships the vessel was a shambles of twisted wreckage; of the forward part of the battleship—about a third of its length—nothing remained above the water except a few jagged pieces of metal. All ships in the harbor were flying their flags at half-mast. Parts of bodies were still drifting ashore. From the moment of the explosion, Spanish and Cubans had risked their lives to pick up survivors; these were being cared for at hospitals.[3]

NRL(O)4573

View of the port side of the wreck. Searchlight and mast are toward the stern. One of the funnels is just forward of the mainmast. A Spanish guard boat patrols the wreck. Photograph taken shortly after the disaster.

NRL(O)4572

View of the wreck from the stern looking forward. Taken soon after the explosion, this photograph shows the after superstructure deck awash. Forward of the mainmast can be seen the inverted wreckage of the central superstructure and one of the funnels.

Broadly speaking, there were two possible explanations for the disaster: the ship had been destroyed by an accident or by a deliberate act. If it was an accident, then Sigsbee had to explain how it could have occurred on board the ship for which he was responsible. If it was a deliberate act of destruction perpetrated by the crew, Sigsbee was still responsible. But if the act had been carried out by the Spanish authorities on the island, by dissident Spaniards acting against their own government, or by Cuban insurgents, Spain was at fault for she was responsible for the safety of the ship in the harbor, so long as the vessel obeyed the port regulations. There was a possible dividing line separating the accident from the act. If the explosion originated *inside* the ship, then it was probably accidental and Spain was guiltless. If the explosion originated *outside* the ship, then it was probably deliberate and Spain was to blame. Given the strained relations between the United States and Spain, determining the origins of the catastrophe was a matter with serious implications. On February 16, Segismundo Moret, Minister of Colonies, cabled Blanco that ". . . it would be advisable for Your Excellency to gather every fact you can to prove the Maine catastrophe cannot be attributed to us." On February 17, Sigsbee cabled Long: "Probably the Maine destroyed by mine, perhaps by accident. I surmise that her berth was planted previous to her arrival, perhaps long ago. I can only surmise this." [4]

In Washington people were taking sides, even if as yet there were no technical facts upon which to base a conclusion. Long noticed how political views colored the reactions. Individuals who felt that the United States should stay out of Cuba were convinced the *Maine* was destroyed by an accidental explosion. They argued that the Spanish did not have a chance to destroy an alert naval vessel. Those who believed the United States should intervene were equally convinced the Spanish had sunk the ship. They were confident that all the normal precautions of naval routine made an accident impossible. Both positions, although Long did not comment on the point, raised a difficult issue for the Navy; either the *Maine* was not alert or normal precautions were not observed. With no knowledge of technology, Long wanted to suspend judgment, but he was inclined to believe that an accident was the cause. In his view, every modern warship, filled with powerful explosives, was liable to sudden destruction. [5]

The *Washington Evening Star* in a survey of naval officers found that most attributed the loss to an accident, some to a mine, and a few to a bomb smuggled aboard. According to the press, the bureau chiefs tended to absolve themselves. Philip Hichborn, Chief Constructor, was confident that the ship's design was sound; Rear Admiral Royal B. Bradford, Chief of the Bureau of Equipment, was certain that the coal his bureau furnished was of good quality; and Engineer-in-Chief George W. Melville suspected a magazine explosion. The possibility of an accident perhaps had the most adherents. Lieutenant Frank F. Fletcher, on duty at the Bureau of Ordnance, wrote in a personal letter to Gleaves: "The disaster to the *Maine* is the one topic here now. Everybody is gradually settling down to the belief that the disaster was due to the position of the magazine next to the coal bunkers in which there must have been spontaneous combustion." [6]

Long realized that an investigation might raise awkward questions. Rear Admiral Charles O'Neil, Chief of the Bureau of Ordnance, heard a disturbing rumor. Someone thought that Sigsbee had gone into Havana with warheads on the torpedoes. Since the warheads when armed with primers were sensitive to shock, something could have detonated them. By themselves, they could not have accounted for the magnitude of the damage but they could have triggered a major explosion. Of course, even if Sigsbee had armed the torpedoes, he could have removed the warheads later. Long agreed that Sicard should find out the facts. O'Neil suggested that Sicard be prudent: "It would not read well in the papers, that a vessel entering a friendly port, put the war-heads on her torpedoes, if such was the case, and therefore the matter is left to your discretion." [7]

In one instance the clash between those who believed in an accident and those who were convinced of a deliberate act of destruction took on a bitter note. Philip R. Alger was the Navy's leading ordnance expert. In an interview published in the *Washington Evening Star* on February 18, he said:

> As to the question of the cause of the Maine's explosion, we know that no torpedo such as is known to modern warfare, can of itself cause an explosion of the character of that on board the Maine. We know of no instances where the explosion of a torpedo or mine under a ship's bottom has exploded the magazine within. It has simply torn a great hole in the side or bottom, through which water entered, and in consequence of which the ship sunk. Magazine explosions, on the contrary, produce effects exactly similar to the effects of the explosion on board the Maine. When it comes to seeking the cause of the explosion of the Maine's magazine, we should naturally look not for the improbable or unusual causes, but those against which we have had to guard in the past. The most common of these is through fires in the bunkers. Many of our ships have been in danger various times from this cause and not long ago a fire in the Cincinnati's

bunkers actually set fire to fittings, wooden boxes, etc., within the magazine and had it not been discovered at the time it was, it would doubtless have resulted in a catastrophe on board that ship similar to the one on the Maine.

I shall again emphasize the fact that no torpedo exploded without a ship has ever produced, or, according to our knowledge, can it produce an explosion of a magazine within.[8]

Roosevelt was upset. The day after the explosion he met, according to the *New York Times,* with all the bureau chiefs and other high ranking officers in the city and discussed the *Maine.* Whatever opinions Roosevelt heard, his own views were hardening toward the conviction that there had been no accident. Consequently, Alger's public comments were disturbing. Roosevelt thought that the ordnance expert was taking the "Spanish side." Alger could not possibly know anything about the matter; furthermore, Roosevelt wrote O'Neil, "All the best men in the Department agree that, whether probable or not, it certainly is *possible* that the ship was blown up by a mine . . . ." He thought the truth might never be found, but he could not rid himself of the thought that the *Maine* had been the victim of an "act of dirty treachery." He was manifestly unfair. It was certainly improper to describe the expert's opinion on a technical matter as unpatriotic. Ten days had elapsed between the interview and Roosevelt's letter; an interval which suggests that Alger was not keeping quiet. Perhaps, as Alger's relatives believed, Roosevelt was trying to suppress a report the ordnance expert had written, but so far no such document has come to light.[9]

Roosevelt was worried lest such views weaken the Navy's standing before Congress. An advocate of a strong Navy, he was shocked to hear that two Republican congressional leaders—the powerful Thomas B. Reed, Speaker of the House, and Senator Eugene Hale, Chairman of the Committee on Naval Affairs—had stated that the disaster proved the United States must stop building battleships. To Roosevelt this attitude was timorous, weak, and cowardly. He wrote a long letter to Senator Henry Cabot Lodge, perhaps for use among the latter's colleagues. Roosevelt argued that battleships were delicate instruments, and that even the most advanced naval powers had accidents. These were to be expected: they were as inevitable as losses in war. Men who lived on board the ships recognized and accepted the hazard; the nation which they defended could not do less. The loss of the *Maine* was the price the United States paid to assume its role as a great naval power.[10]

The Navy had procedures for investigating accidents. Chapter XL of *Regulations for the Government of the Navy of the United States,* the latest edition of which was published in 1896, set forth rules on courts of inquiry. They were fact-finding bodies, established to deal with important cases where evidence was not clear, where crime or criminal acts were suspected, or where serious blame existed but without certainty of where the culpability should be assigned. From the findings of the court, the convening authority—the President of the United States, the Secretary of the Navy, or the commander of a fleet or squadron—would decide if further action was necessary. The court was to be composed of not more than three officers; a fourth, who served as judge advocate, summoned witnesses, recorded proceedings, and assisted in laying the conclusions before the convening authority. If the conduct or character of an officer was under investigation, the three members of the court were, if possible, not to be inferior in rank. For his own defense the officer could call witnesses and conduct cross examinations.[11]

Despite the tense relations with Spain and the magnitude of the disaster, McKinley and Long—either of whom could have convened a court of inquiry—left the matter to Rear Admiral Sicard. Sicard was in ill health; officers of the squadron doubted if he could stand the strain of war. Born in 1836 in New York City, he attended the Naval Academy from 1851 through 1855. In the Civil War he saw hard and active service. He participated in the bombardments that led to the fall of New Orleans and in the engagement with the batteries at Vicksburg, and he led a part of the naval landing force that attacked Fort Fisher, North Carolina. From 1881 to 1890 he was Chief of the Bureau of Ordnance. He became Commander-in-Chief of the North Atlantic Squadron in 1897. On February 16, 1898, Long cabled Sicard to keep the surviving officers and men available so they could be examined by a naval court of inquiry.[12]

On the same day, Sicard proposed that the court consist of Captain French E. Chadwick, Lieutenant Commander William P. Potter, and Lieutenant Edward E. Capehart, with Lieutenant (junior grade) Frank Marble as judge advocate. The list was unusual. All four were from the *New York;* Chadwick was captain, Potter was executive officer, and the other two were junior officers. Furthermore, none was senior to Sigsbee whose actions, after all, had to be weighed. Perhaps the principle guiding Sicard was that the court must be established quickly. In any event, he wrote Long that if the selection was not satisfactory, he would have to draw upon the squadron at the Dry Tortugas.[13]

Court of Inquiry, 1898. From left to right: Captain French E. Chadwick, member; Captain William T. Sampson, president; Lieutenant Commander William P. Potter, member; Ensign Wilfred V. N. Powelson, who directed the Navy's diving operation; Lieutenant Commander Adolph Marix, judge advocate; and a civilian stenographer. Photograph taken on board the Mangrove.

Someone in Washington overruled Sicard, for the final composition of the court was Captain William T. Sampson (who was senior to Sigsbee) as president, Captain French E. Chadwick, and Lieutenant Commander William P. Potter as members, with Lieutenant Commander Adolph Marix as judge advocate. A few years later, Long recalled the reasons for the selection:

> These officers had high professional standing, and the President and his cabinet believed that their findings would be accepted. Captain Sampson had served as chief of the Bureau of Ordnance and as head of the torpedo-station at Newport. He was, therefore, well qualified to determine the question whether an internal or external explosive agent had destroyed the Maine. Prior to assuming command of the New York, Captain Chadwick had occupied the office of chief of the Bureau of Equipment. He was an expert in all matters relating to coal and electricity. Lieutenant-Commander Potter was an officer of technical experience and calm judgment. Lieutenant-Commander Marix had been executive officer of the Maine, and was familiar with details of her structure and organization.[14]

Sicard issued the court's precept on February 19. It authorized the court to meet on any ship of the squadron, at Key West and in Havana. The court was to inquire diligently into all circumstances, to determine whether the ship had been lost by the negligence of any officer or member of the crew, and to report if further proceedings should be taken against any individual. In a separate letter, Sicard informed Sampson that Sigsbee, Lieutenant Commander Richard Wainwright, executive officer, Lieutenant George F. M. Holman, navigator, and Chief Engineer Charles P. Howell—all from the *Maine*—had the right to be present at the court sessions so that they could, if necessary, offer evidence and cross-examine witnesses.[15]

The Spanish had already begun their own investigation. While the *Maine* was still burning, Admiral Vicente Manterola, commanding the naval station in Havana, set up a court of inquiry under Captain Don Pedro del Peral y Caballero as judge and Lieutenant Don Francisco Javier de Salas y Gonzalez as secretary. Peral had a difficult task. He could not reach a clear conclusion without information from the Americans on their shipboard routine and contents of the ship, access to the wreck, and technical information. Among his first acts was a request for an official interpreter to help

Spanish divers inspect the wreck. Surrounding the Maine *in the background are the commercial salvage ships from the Merritt and Chapman Derrick and Wrecking Company under contract to the Navy to remove valuable pieces of equipment from the wreck. Stereograph taken in March 1898.*

question the survivors. He also wanted authority, as well as divers and equipment, to examine the wreck.[16]

Two governments working around the same wreck raised some interesting issues of international law. (See: Appendix B, "Some Aspects of International Law and the Destruction of the *Maine,* February 15, 1898.") The *Maine* while visiting Havana was to all intents and purposes American territory. The ship was in technical compliance with the Spanish royal order of August 11, 1882, which allowed foreign ships and squadrons to enter its ports in time of peace as long as the visitors obeyed police and harbor regulations. (True enough, Cuba was in the throes of a civil war, the Spanish were given scant notice of the visit and no opportunity to object, and Sigsbee had been unable to present the proper documents to show that he had a clean bill of health, but the *Maine* had been allowed to enter.) Deserted, twisted and torn, lying on the bottom, the *Maine* presented a new set of circumstances. The United States and Spain each had cause to investigate. The Americans, because the wreck was their ship; the Spanish, because the disaster had occurred in their harbor. The day after the explosion, Blanco talked with Lee about the Spanish investigation. After consulting with Sigsbee, Lee replied the following day that the captain of the *Maine* intended to make his own inquiry in accordance with the regulations of the Navy Department. On February 18, Lee relayed a Spanish request to Washington for a joint examination. He had his answer the next day: the United States would conduct its own investigation, but would give every possible assistance to the Spanish.

Investigations had already begun. On February 18, Sigsbee attempted to return to the *Maine*. The Spanish, as was their right, had placed a cordon of small boats around the wreck and the officer in charge refused to allow him to approach the hulk. Sigsbee went aboard the *Alfonso XII* where he learned that the problem was one of identification. Because Sigsbee had lost his uniforms and was in civilian clothes, the explanation was plausible. The next day the coastal survey steamer *Bache* arrived with divers from the North Atlantic Squadron. To Peral it seemed unlikely that his investigation could go much further. On February 20, he summarized his findings so that his superiors could decide the next step. Basing his conclusions chiefly upon reports of three officers from the naval artillery, engineers, and torpedo brigade, who had circled the *Maine* in a small boat, Peral believed that an internal explosion had destroyed the ship, although much more information was needed to fill in the details.[17]

In the days to come the *Maine* was to be the center of intense activity, and at times was almost hidden from view by the light house tender *Mangrove* upon which the American court of inquiry was meeting, the *Fern,* the commercial salvage tug *Right Arm,* and small boats and lighters. Occasionally three groups of divers were at work simultaneously: those from the Navy, the Spanish, and from Merritt and Chapman Derrick and Wrecking Company under contract to the Navy to salvage all equipment possible. The Americans did give certain help to the Spanish: Sigsbee invited them to witness a few early diving operations, and he gave them some plans of the *Maine*.[18]

Whether a joint investigation would have been possible is difficult to say. The Spanish were convinced that the Americans—including the Navy—had too much at stake for a fair examination. Authorities in Madrid and Havana believed that they had to prove that the ship had been destroyed by an accident. Roosevelt was convinced that public opinion in the United States would not accept a joint effort. So, at least, he argued to McKinley and others. Roosevelt was probably right, considering reports which had reached Americans over the past few years about Spanish atrocities, the inflamed condition of the press after the *Maine* had blown up, and the excited—almost turbulent—state of Congress. For most Americans, only an investigation of their own could answer the question of how over 250 of their countrymen had lost their lives in a single night in Havana. Upon Sampson, Chadwick, and Potter rested a heavy responsibility. At sunrise on February 21, the light house tender *Mangrove*, with the court of inquiry on board, arrived in Havana.[19]

CHAPTER 6

Toward War

The American court of inquiry held its first meeting on February 21, on board the *Mangrove*. The session, as well as all the others, was closed to the public. As was his right, Sigsbee requested permission to be present at such times as he wished. He did not want counsel, nor did he object to any member of the court. In carefully qualified statements, Sigsbee on this and following days set forth his position. The Spanish knew he was coming (so he understood); an official pilot berthed the *Maine* at a buoy which (he was later told) was seldom used. The *Maine* had coaled at Key West. He was certain the coal was inspected before it was brought on board (he could not remember the actual event but such was the invariable custom). He did not know how much coal was in the forward bunkers, but assumed there was little. He knew that the fire alarms worked, because they occasionally went off at temperatures below that for which they were set. To the best of his knowledge, all regulations concerning the stowage of inflammables and paint and the disposal of waste and ashes were strictly enforced, for he had given the proper orders. Although he could not be precise as to the time, he was certain that he had inspected the magazines during the last three months. Finally, he had ordered special precautions to safeguard the ship from a visitor bent on sabotage.[1]

From his testimony emerges the portrait of an individual who was unfamiliar with his ship. He might have been a good seaman and a brave man, but perhaps also the victim of the new technology which was transforming the Navy. He might not have understood the complexities of the ship he commanded. He might have suffered from the division in the Navy which separated line officers from the shipboard engineers. Many line officers looked down upon engineering. The vagueness and uncertainty in his testimony might stem from a belief that giving an order was tantamount to its execution. Whatever the reasons, he appears to have been isolated from the day-to-day routine.

The court had one fact from which to begin. There was no doubt that an

LONGITUDINAL SECTION

WATERLINE

ARMORED PROTECTIVE DECK

HARBOR BOTTOM

LOCATION OF MINE: 1911

LOCATION OF MINE: 1898

FRAME 6 8 10 12 14 16 18 20 22 24 26 28 30 32 34 36 38 40 42 50 60 70 80

A PRISON
B STORES
C CREWS QUARTERS
D MAGAZINE A-6-M
E AUXILIARY MACHINERY
F TORPEDO ROOM
G WATER TANK
H MAGAZINE A-9-M
I SICK BAY
J PASSING ROOM
K HANDLING ROOM
L MAGAZINE A-14-M

M DISPENSARY
N COAL BUNKER
O OFFICE
P WASHROOM
Q FIRE ROOM
R MAGAZINE C-4-M
S ENGINE ROOM
T TURRET MACHINERY
U ARMORY
V SHAFT ALLEY
W STEERING GEAR
X WARD ROOM

SECTION SHOWS PORT SIDE
COMPARTMENTS ONLY

PORT SIDE, OUTBOARD, COAL
BUNKERS (FRAMES 24 TO 58)
HAVE BEEN OMITTED FOR
CLARITY

RIGGING, CATWALKS, AND HAND LINES
HAVE BEEN OMITTED FOR CLARITY

SCALE IN FEET   0 10 20 30

DMW 8/19/75

explosion occurred in one or more of the forward magazines. What caused the explosion was another matter. Logically there were four possibilities: an internal accident, an internal deliberate act, an external accident, or an external deliberate act. If the origin of the explosion was external, the force from outside the ship had to be sufficient to detonate a part of the magazines.

Sigsbee and his officers disposed of the internal causes to the court's satisfaction. His officers corroborated Sigsbee on the routine of taking the temperatures of the magazines and bunkers, and on carrying out the proper procedures for disposing of ashes and wastes and stowing paints. Discipline was excellent and there was no reason to believe that anyone on board had deliberately destroyed the ship. Furthermore, divers had recovered the keys to the magazines: they were where they should have been—in Sigsbee's cabin. To the court this meant that no one was in the magazines after they had been properly secured. As for armed torpedoes—the matter which had concerned O'Neil, Chief of the Bureau of Ordnance—Sigsbee had not entered Havana with the torpedoes armed and in the tubes. The detonators were stowed aft and had played no part in the disaster.[2]

If the court accepted the testimony of Sigsbee and his officers, only an external force could have set off the magazines. For this cause the wreck itself offered the best evidence, provided the damage could be analyzed. The difficulties in examining the ship were formidable. Diving conditions were poor: visibility was bad; the water was filthy and nearly opaque; soft ooze, some feet thick, hampered walking on the harbor bottom; and pieces of twisted and torn wreckage were not only difficult to identify, but were dangerous to life lines and air hoses. Most of the Navy divers were not highly professional. Because they were often unable to describe what they had felt or seen, the court soon turned to Ensign Wilfred Van Nest Powelson. He was not a member of the *Maine*'s company, but was assigned to the *Fern*. His training as a naval architect made him of particular value. He had been a naval cadet, appointed from New York in 1889 and had studied naval architecture in Glasgow, Scotland. Deciding against a career as a naval constructor, he had been commissioned as ensign of the line in 1895. Powelson spent hours with the divers, trying to make sense out of their descriptions. To assist him the Department sent drawings of the forward part of the ship.[3]

As the days passed, the major characteristics of the damage were revealed. The explosion shattered the ship forward of the second stack. Part of the forward deck was hurled up and thrown back upon itself. Fittings which remained attached to that portion of the deck were now upside down; a

TRANSVERSE SECTION THROUGH FRAME 28
LOOKING FORWARD

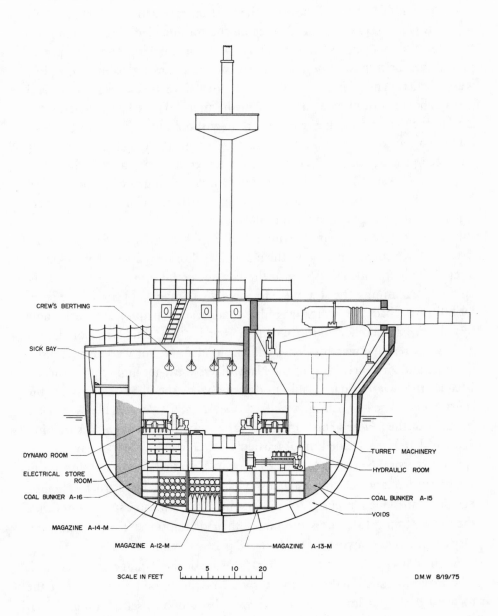

CREW'S BERTHING

SICK BAY

DYNAMO ROOM

ELECTRICAL STORE ROOM

COAL BUNKER A-16

MAGAZINE A-14-M

MAGAZINE A-12-M

TURRET MACHINERY

HYDRAULIC ROOM

COAL BUNKER A-15

VOIDS

MAGAZINE A-13-M

SCALE IN FEET   0   5   10   20

D.M.W 8/19/75

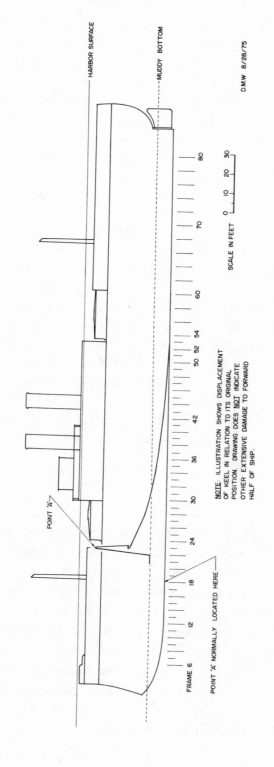

OUTBOARD PROFILE SHOWING DISPLACEMENT OF KEEL

HARBOR SURFACE

MUDDY BOTTOM

D.M.W 8/28/75

POINT "A"

POINT "A" NORMALLY LOCATED HERE

FRAME 6 12 18 24 30 36 42 50 52 54 60 70 80

SCALE IN FEET

0 10 20 30

NOTE: ILLUSTRATION SHOWS DISPLACEMENT OF KEEL IN RELATION TO ITS ORIGINAL POSITION. DRAWING DOES NOT INDICATE OTHER EXTENSIVE DAMAGE TO FORWARD HALF OF SHIP.

forward 6-pounder gun, for example, was now inverted. The forward 10-inch turret, with armor protection 8-inches thick, had vanished. On the port side the armor belt plating had been blown out. Although a large part of the bottom, particularly on the port side of the keel, had disappeared, the bow was still connected to the stern. The most baffling problem was the condition of the ship near frame 18. Frames—the ribs of a ship—were numbered from fore to aft. In the *Maine,* frames were three to four feet apart. In the vicinity of frame 18, about 59 feet from the bow, there had been a massive upheaval. One piece of bottom plating—still attached to the ship—was about four feet above the surface, even though the ship was resting on the bottom in about 36 feet of water. The keel had been driven upward so that it resembled a V, but inverted so that the acute angle was at the top. Frame 18 was just forward of the magazines which had exploded.[4]

As it heard testimony from the divers and a description of the wreckage from Powelson, the court confronted a crucial question. Could a magazine explosion alone have caused the peculiar damage to the keel? On the other hand, could a mine at frame 18 have detonated the magazines? The court turned increasingly toward the theory that a mine had set off the magazines. Sampson, on February 26, speculated about a mine; its possible explosive force and probable location, and even whether more than one mine was necessary to account for the particular characteristics of the damage. He raised these thoughts in Powelson's presence, although the ensign was not a member of the court, and even though he was directing and reporting on the activities of the divers.[5]

Almost forgotten in the excitement of the *Maine* disaster was that Spain, as a gesture of friendly reciprocity, was sending the armored cruiser *Vizcaya* to visit New York. Under Captain Antonio Eulate, the *Vizcaya* had sailed from Spain on January 29. Between Bermuda and Cape Hatteras, Eulate ran into heavy weather and finally arrived off Point Pleasant, New Jersey, on February 18. A pilot who had been on station for several days boarded the cruiser. Because a dense fog made it impossible to enter New York, the *Vizcaya* was brought to Sandy Hook and anchored at 5:55 in the afternoon. Officials from the Spanish legation and city newspapermen searched for the ship but the reporters found it first. They were welcomed aboard and Eulate learned that the *Maine* had been blown up.

The Spanish had sent one of their best ships. The *Vizcaya,* built in 1891 at Bilbao, was 340 feet in length and 65 feet in beam. The ship displaced about 6,800 tons, drew 21 feet 6 inches, and was designed for a top speed of 20 knots. A partial armor belt of 12 inches maximum thickness protected the waterline. The ship was well-armed, for in addition to two 11-inch guns—one forward and one aft—protected by barbettes, she carried ten 5.5-inch guns and six torpedo tubes above the waterline. Unlike many American naval vessels, the *Vizcaya* had a high freeboard. With her massive black hull, many reporters thought the cruiser was a handsome ship.

In the early afternoon of February 20, the *Vizcaya* finally entered the harbor. Fog and squalls made the weather miserable. American health officers boarded the ship and found that Eulate had proper credentials. Original plans called for the ship to be docked in lower Manhattan, but for greater safety the berth was shifted to the naval anchorage off Tompkinsville, Staten Island. American civic and naval authorities guarded the Spanish vessel closely. One problem in particular worried them. John P. Holland had recently completed successful surface tests of his submarine. Admiral Francis M. Bunce was enjoined to make certain the submarine did not attack the *Vizcaya.* On February 24, the cruiser left for Havana. There had been no incidents.[6]

The McKinley administration, Congress, and the nation waited for the findings of the court of inquiry. McKinley had an impatient Congress to contend with; one which, as far as Cuba was concerned, was more venturesome than he. The Republicans had a majority in both Houses (202 to 150 in the House of Representatives and 46 to 40 in the Senate), but the party was split on Cuba. McKinley could count on the support of Thomas B. Reed, Speaker of the House and a skilled parliamentarian, against intervention and war. In the Senate, McKinley had the backing of such leaders as Marcus A. Hanna, Eugene Hale, and Henry Cabot Lodge. Nonetheless, the President was in a precarious position. Senator William Allen, a Populist from Nebraska, charged that the Committee on Naval Affairs would keep to itself the facts it learned from the Department. Senator William Mason, a Republican from Illinois, proposed an independent congressional investigation to take place concurrently with that of the Department; otherwise the

Navy could be accused of trying its own case. Lodge retorted that men of the caliber of Sigsbee, Long, and Roosevelt, would not lie.[7]

Sensational newspapers were filled with schemes of how the "perfidious" Spanish had destroyed the *Maine*. At most McKinley could hope to seek a solution to Cuba short of war only as long as the court of inquiry was deliberating. In one sense the loss of the battleship gave McKinley an additional diplomatic weapon, for Madrid must realize it faced an aroused American public opinion. In an effort to relieve pressure from Congress and the newspapers, Long issued a statement of facts late in the afternoon of February 18. He had received no new evidence and still believed the *Maine* had been destroyed by an accident. Four days later he spoke again, calling for restraint. He did not expect any news from the court of inquiry for two reasons. Sampson was holding the sessions behind closed doors and the regulations provided that not even the Secretary could receive information until the court had finished its proceedings.[8]

Even as Long was speaking, the government was receiving information pointing toward a mine. Lee cabled on February 22 that divers had recovered that morning some intact copper ammunition cases from the forward 10-inch magazine. Probably, therefore, the 10-inch magazine had not exploded. Lee concluded that the evidence was beginning to prove that a "torpedo" (he meant a mine) had exploded on the port side. Reporters in Havana cabled the same theme to their newspapers. An English journalist of considerable reputation wrote Long a personal letter. Sir A. Maurice Low had come to Cuba with an open mind. He found that his colleagues—those who were responsible men, not sensationalists—were coming to the conclusion that a mine had destroyed the ship. He had bent over backwards trying to convince himself that the disaster was accidental. The naval officers were not influencing him, for they were obeying Long's injunction to keep silent on the matter. Still, he found himself drawn to the "mine theory."[9]

Weary of the turmoil and tension, Long took the afternoon off on February 25 and left Roosevelt in charge. The dynamic Assistant Secretary took hold vigorously. He ordered O'Neil to ship to New York ten 6-inch guns and twenty-two 5-inch guns for outfitting merchant ships as auxiliary cruisers. He cabled Dewey at Hong Kong to keep supplied with coal and, if war broke out, to make certain that the Spanish squadron did not leave the Far East. He was then to take the offensive in the Philippines. Long was appalled when he returned the next morning. It was not the order to Dewey that distressed him—that had been discussed earlier—it was the shipment of guns.

LC

U.S. Navy divers at work on the wreck. Helmeted diver is assisted by Navy boat crew. Stereograph taken in 1898.

They had been stored safely in the Washington Navy Yard and ready for shipment at a moment's notice. Because of Roosevelt's hasty action the guns were now at the New York Navy Yard where they were not yet needed and where they lay exposed to the weather.[10]

By this time McKinley and his key officials had a clear idea of the verdict the court would reach. Long, on the evening of February 27, discussed the *Maine* with O'Neil; just what the Secretary and the Chief of the Bureau of Ordnance said to each other the diary of neither man discloses. The next evening Long was summoned to the White House where he found McKinley and Day studying a message from Lee. The consul general was almost certain of two things: the *Maine* had been destroyed by a mine; and the Spanish government was innocent of any complicity. He elaborated on how the battleship might have been destroyed. Some individuals might have taken a barrel or a cask, loaded it with a few hundred pounds of guncotton, and surreptitiously planted it at a point where, at some time, the *Maine* would swing against it. The content of Lee's message indicated that someone on the court, or connected with it, was violating the rule that the deliberations were confidential. Clearly he had been talking with informed individuals; members of the court, divers or other men working on the wreck or officers of the *Maine*—perhaps Sigsbee, since the captain of the *Maine* was to use this explanation more than once. From his reading of Lee's message, Long thought war might still be avoided. Presumably he was basing his hope on Lee's belief that the Spanish authorities were not involved. Long sent for O'Neil to come to the White House.[11]

O'Neil was an unusual figure in the Navy. Nearly always the Chief of the Bureau of Ordnance was an Annapolis graduate—Sampson was an example—but O'Neil had risen to the position from what was the equivalent of the present rank of warrant officer. Born in Manchester, England in 1842, he entered the United States Navy in 1861. He saw a good deal of active service; his ship was one of those sunk by the Confederate ironclad *Virginia* (*Merrimack*). In 1865 he received a commission and in subsequent years specialized in ordnance, becoming Chief of the Bureau in 1897. He was to retire in 1904 under attack by the advocates of new gunnery procedures. Judging from Long's journal, he was the only individual with technical responsibilities with whom the Secretary consulted about the *Maine*. O'Neil's brief diary entries reveal no more than that he had seen photographs of the wreck and, like many people, was shocked by the magnitude of the devastation. What he thought of the makeshift mine Lee described is not known.[12]

The most significant aspect of the February 28 meeting was that McKinley, Day, Long, and O'Neil knew the trend of the court's thinking. They must have been satisfied by the prospect. If not, McKinley and Long could have insisted that qualified technical experts assist the court. Professor Philip Alger, whose abilities had won him an outstanding reputation in ordnance, was available. Professor Charles E. Munroe, president of the American Chemical Society, an authority on explosives, had promptly offered his services. Munroe was familiar with naval procedures having taken part in an earlier investigation of a paint explosion on the cruiser *Atlanta*. He received an acknowledgment but no request for assistance. At least one newspaper called attention to the absence of technically qualified members on the court.[13]

Perhaps the authorities in Washington thought that they had done all that was necessary in providing experts. On February 26, Sicard had relayed a request from the court for the services of someone who had been engaged in the construction of the *Maine* who could help identify the plates and various portions of the wreckage. Sicard suggested Frank L. Fernald, a naval constructor who had supervised the building of the *Maine*. Fernald was not sent. Perhaps he was not available, for he had retired in November, 1897. In his place the Department ordered on February 28 Naval Constructor John B. Hoover to Havana. At the moment, Hoover was assigned to Morris Heights, New York, as superintending constructor for a torpedo boat being built by the Gas Engine and Power Company. He was born in 1836 and appointed assistant naval constructor in 1875. During his career he had worked at several yards although not, so far as the records indicate, at the New York Navy Yard when the *Maine* was being built. Yet there had been some connection between him and the battleship, for he was asked to take his notes on the construction of the *Maine*. His orders were precise. He was to report to the Commander-in-Chief of the North Atlantic Squadron for such temporary duty as that officer might assign in connection with the court of inquiry, and to assist in identifying and locating the pieces of plating and framing of the forward part of the *Maine*. Hoover's part was to be quite limited and far different from the assistance that Alger, Munroe, or other technical experts might have given.[14]

On February 28, the court moved to Key West to hear the testimony of those survivors whom Sigsbee had sent from Havana as soon after the explosion as possible. After assuring that he would be called if his interests made it necessary, Sigsbee remained in Havana. Until March 2, Sampson, Chadwick, Potter, and Marix listened to the accounts of the disaster from junior officers and enlisted men. On the final day the entire court went to the army barracks where officers and enlisted men were assembled. After Sampson administered the oath to them, Marix, using the prescribed phrases in *Navy Regulations* for loss or grounding of a naval ship, asked whether any officer or man present had any fault to find with any officer or man belonging to the *Maine* on the night of its destruction. If so he was to step forward. By standing still each man acknowledged under oath that he had no complaint. Marix then asked whether there were any complaints or fault to find with any officer or man of the *Maine* while that ship was in Havana. No one stepped forward in either instance.[15]

Now that the examination of the ship's company had been completed, Long was anxious to know when Washington would get the findings. Sampson would not be hurried. Not until the divers were finished could the court draw up its conclusions and, although the divers were working as fast as possible, he could not set a final date. On the other hand some arrangements could be planned. Perhaps the *Iowa*—Sampson's command and the newest of the American battleships—could come to Havana and pick up the court when it was ready to leave. The ship need stay only part of a day; its size would show the power of the Navy and its presence would lend dignity to the court. Curiously, considering what had happened to the *Maine,* Lee's cable proposing this visit of the *Iowa* noted that there was no danger, for the harbor was safe. With the work of the court still unfinished there was no need to make that decision.[16]

McKinley could not wait for the court to finish its work before taking steps to prepare the nation. On March 6, he and Long told O'Neil to put the Bureau of Ordnance on a war footing. The next day O'Neil placed a $4,000,000 order for ammunition. (In October 1897, he had estimated the entire expense of the bureau for the year ending June 30, 1899, as about $7,434,351—which included such items as guns, ammunition, powder, and buildings.) Concurrently, the President was negotiating with Congress for appropriations. Congress left no doubt where it stood. The House on March 8 and the Senate the next day, each acting unanimously, appropriated $50,-000,000 for defense. By the middle of the month a train carrying 50 tons of ammunition was on its way to Tampa, Florida, and the North Atlantic Squadron.[17]

The Navy was alarmed by the news from Spain. On March 13, Woodford cabled that Spanish torpedo boats were preparing to cross the Atlantic. Roosevelt was worried. He had just been appointed to a naval strategy board charged with the task of planning the naval campaign. He and the board (which consisted of himself and four Navy officers) were anxious over the threat of small fast vessels capable of approaching the squadron at night, even in its anchorage, and delivering a torpedo attack. Because torpedoes would hit below the armor belt, the losses could be heavy. Consequently the board believed the Navy's job would be easier if war were declared before the torpedo boats crossed the Atlantic and before Spain had time to complete repairs on some battleships. Blockading Havana, for example, would be far more difficult if it were defended by torpedo boats. The members appealed to Long on March 16.

> For this reason, sir, we venture to state that if the report of the Court of Inquiry could be provided at once, the problem set before your Board would be very much simpler. We could then, in all probability, tell whether we should have to plan to meet the torpedo boat flotilla and the Spanish battleships now repairing in French ports or not.[18]

The board which saw that the findings of the court could lead to war, and therefore were a critical element in naval planning, were important men. Roosevelt had often given his views directly to McKinley; Rear Admiral Crowninshield was Chief of the Bureau of Navigation, Albert S. Barker and Caspar F. Goodrich were senior captains, while Commander Richardson Clover was Chief Intelligence Officer. Their views were echoed from the fleet. Sampson, a likely prospect to take command of the North Atlantic Squadron if Sicard had to be relieved for ill health, urged that Madrid be warned that the United States would destroy any torpedo boat sent over. "Self preservation demands such a course." McKinley, however, would not be rushed. Still hoping for peace, he refused to take the position that the despatch of the torpedo boats was a cause for war.[19]

The court was coming close to its end. With the examination of survivors completed, there remained the wreck with its technical question of what the damage could reveal about the origin of the disaster. On March 6, the court was back in Havana to hear the reports of Powelson and the divers. In addition the court heard Hoover. His testimony was brief. He offered measurements on the displacements of some parts of the ship from their normal position. The questions and replies were specific. The court did not ask for, nor did he offer, any general observations. The court treated Commander George A. Converse differently. He was the commanding officer of the *Montgomery,* now in Havana. Born in 1844 at Norwich, Vermont, Converse graduated from Annapolis in 1865. During his career he had considerable experience in ordnance and particularly in underwater explosions. He had been an instructor at the torpedo station at Newport, Rhode Island, served two years in the

Bureau of Ordnance and, just before his assignment to the *Montgomery,* spent four years in charge of the torpedo station. Converse, far more than Hoover, assumed the role of a technical expert.[20]

From examination of the drawings exhibited before the court, Converse, testifying on March 11, was convinced that there had been two explosions. The one which caused the bending of the bottom plates and upward thrust of the keel could have come from a large submarine mine, probably filled with gunpowder, because this slow-burning explosive would exert more force in water than more modern explosives. To have caused the damage shown in the drawing, he believed the mine was probably placed near the bottom of the harbor. The second explosion appeared to have been part of the magazines. He did not think the explosion of forward magazines *alone* could have caused distortion and displacement of the bottom plate and keel. Put another way, "Indications are that an under-water explosion produce[d] the conditions there." Marix asked Converse a specific question:

> Looking at the plan of the *Maine's* forward 10-inch and 6-inch magazines, would it be possible for them to have exploded, torn out the ship's side on both sides, and leave that part of the ship forward of frame 18 so water borne as to raise the after portion of that part of the ship, drag it aft, and bring the vertical keel into the condition that you see on the sketch?

The question was uncommonly technical, well-framed, and meticulous, almost as if the court was aware that the issue had to be raised for the record and disposed of. Possibly, although there can be no certainty, the subject had been discussed the previous day when Sigsbee and Converse met unofficially with the court. The significance of the question was that it showed the court knew of an hypothesis in which an internal explosion accounted for all aspects of the wreck, including the raised bottom plating and the upward thrust of the keel. It was a question which should also have been directed at Hoover and asked of experts in naval architecture and marine engineering. Instead it was put only to Converse, who thereby assumed the role of the only technical expert examined by the court. He replied: "It is difficult for me to realize that that effect could have been produced by an explosion of the kind supposed." Marix asked if the detonation of a mine, of the type that Converse had earlier postulated, could have exploded the forward magazines. Here Converse drew back: he could not be sure.[21]

The court held its last session in Havana on March 15. Sigsbee was confident of the outcome. He wrote to his wife, "I have no knowledge as to what the findings of this court will be but I do not fear anything which will reflect unfavorably on the Maine." Its investigation finally completed, the court returned to Key West and on March 17 moved to more spacious quarters on the battleship *Iowa*.[22]

There was no need, however, for Washington to wait for the entire document with its transcripts of the testimony; the unsigned findings could be sent up at once. Sicard cabled Long that four officers; George F. M. Holman, John J. Blandin, George Blow from the *Maine,* and Constructor Hoover would be in Washington on Saturday morning, March 19, with the findings. The Washington press was alert. The *Post* on March 18 carried a story that a special report from the *Maine* would reach the city the next day. The brief document was for the use of the President, who might or might not make it public. The *Evening Star* on March 19 reported that the group from the *Maine* had not been expected and, although they spent some time with Long, did not discuss the verdict of the court. McKinley promptly used the findings to exert further pressure on Spain. On March 20, Day cabled Woodford at Madrid that the court would show the *Maine* had been blown up by a mine. If Spain took prompt action "such as the most civilized nation would offer," the matter could be settled peacefully.[23]

The members of the court signed the findings on March 21. Sicard approved them the next day. Marix with the document wrapped and sealed, and escorted by several officers of the *Maine,* left Key West on March 22. The train arrived in Washington at 9:35 in the evening of March 24. An ensign met Marix at the station with information that Long would receive the report the next day during regular business hours. In the morning Marix went to the Department. He first saw Captain Samuel C. Lemly, the Judge Advocate General. The two men went to Long's office. Marix and the Secretary walked the short distance to the White House where, in the library, they met McKinley and Day. Later the Cabinet assembled. Marix remained nearby in case explanations were needed.[24]

It had taken only a few pages for the court to write up its conclusions. They stated that the *Maine* had arrived at Havana on January 25, 1898, and was taken to buoy number 4 by the regular government pilot. The United States consul general at Havana had notified the Spanish authorities of the impending visit the previous evening. Discipline aboard the ship was excellent and all orders and regulations in regard to the care and safety of the ship were strictly enforced. In several brief paragraphs the court described the precautions taken to assure the safety of magazines, bunkers, torpedo warheads, dry guncotton primers and detonators, and the proper stowage of varnishes, alcohol, and other combustibles. On the night of the explosion everything had been reported secure for the night at 8 o'clock. At the time of the disaster the ship was quiet and therefore least liable to accident. The court found there had been two explosions. The first had sounded like a gunshot; it lifted the forward part of the ship and forced the keel into the inverted V and some of the bottom plates upward. In the court's opinion these conditions could only have been caused by "the explosion of a mine situated under the bottom of the ship at about frame 18 and somewhat on the port side of the ship." The second explosion had folded back the protective and main decks. It was caused by the magazine. The court—as Lee's cable to Washington on February 28 had foreshadowed—was unable to find any evidence fixing the responsibility for the destruction of the *Maine* on any person or persons.[25]

After lunch the Cabinet considered the report further. At 4 o'clock the members finished. McKinley, with a single companion, walked through Lafayette Park and down some of the nearby streets. At 5 o'clock of the next afternoon, McKinley's private secretary, George B. Cortelyou, began typing the findings (the original document was largely in Marix's handwriting) in an original and ten copies. He finished at 11:00 p.m. The next day was Sunday. In the afternoon McKinley began dictating the message to Congress which would accompany the report. On Monday, March 28, the report, complete with a transcript of the testimony, was sent to Congress and released to the press. The message was short. McKinley stated he had submitted the findings to the Spanish government. He believed Spain would act honorably, guided by justice and the friendly relations which existed between the two nations. In the meantime, he counseled "deliberate consideration." [26]

McKinley had already stiffened the terms for peace. On March 26, Day sent the President's position to Woodford. In summary, McKinley wanted peace. He did not want the island. He believed Spain could not win a military victory over the insurgents. If she would revoke the *reconcentrado* order, maintain the Cubans until they could support themselves, and offer the Cubans full self-government with a reasonable indemnity, the United States would assist. Woodford promptly asked for clarification: what did full self-government mean? Day replied on March 28: it meant independence for Cuba. War was now almost inevitable.[27]

Congress, however, was in no mood for restraint. The Senate Committee on Foreign Relations began hearings on March 30. That day it heard Rear Admiral Royal B. Bradford, Chief of the Bureau of Equipment. Bradford had seen service at the Newport torpedo station in the days when it was a school. He believed he had witnessed more underwater explosions than most naval officers. He had not seen the court's full report, but from what he had read in the newspapers he had no doubt that a mine, perhaps filled with as much as 300 pounds of modern high explosives, had done the job. Probably the mine was placed before the *Maine* arrived. Captain Albert S. Barker, appearing the next day, had not seen the full report nor read the newspapers thoroughly. Still, if the court was telling the truth—and he was sure it was—a mine had been placed under the keel.

Sigsbee appeared before the committee on the last day of March. He said he had only attended some of the sessions of the court, for when he learned that the investigation was proceeding so carefully and scientifically, he did not feel his presence was necessary. He "preferred to be measured by the judgment of other people." On the cause of the explosion he was cautious. "It is, of course, merely matter of opinion. My opinion is that a mine destroyed the *Maine*. . . ."

Sigsbee dealt as best he could with the problem which was to vex him for years. How, with all of the precautions he took, could the tragedy have happened? He had two answers. A dozen men could have laid the mine, even in the face of the discipline and vigilance of his ship. Without the knowledge of any high Spanish official, these men could have made a mine out of a section of an old hogshead or even a wine cask. It could have been towed, barely awash, by a lighter and planted in its position without anyone on the *Maine* suspecting. He remarked that curiously the ship, during all of its time in Havana, had never before swung in that direction: some of his officers had told him so. But he did not rule out the possibility that the mine could have been planted before the *Maine* arrived. When the explosion occurred, the ship was in a position where her guns could have taken the Spanish shore batteries under fire. Sigsbee declared: if he had been given the task of defending the port with but a single mine, he would have chosen that very spot to place it. The mine could have been electrically controlled. Someone could have laid the wires that led to the shore-based firing position and then sent power over the lines to detonate it. Or perhaps someone had gained control of the harbor defense switchboard for a moment. Once he hinted at information he possessed which it was injudicious to disclose. He was not questioned on this point, however.[28]

On April 2 the new Spanish minister, Luis Polo de Bernabé, sent the results of the Spanish inquiry to the State Department. The Spanish recapitulated the characteristics of the ship and called attention to the royal order of 1882 which, in ordinary times of peace, allowed foreign naval ships and squadrons to enter Spanish ports with no restrictions except those of Spanish naval ordinances and police regulations. At the moment of the explosion there was no wind and the water was smooth. Since the ship was motionless, a mine would have had to be detonated by electricity rather than by contact with the hull, but neither wires nor a control station had been discovered. Further, a mine was liable to produce a column of water, but none was observed. Nor were there any dead fish which were usually found after an underwater explosion. The Spanish turned to foreign authorities to support their position that mines had sunk several vessels, but never caused magazines to explode. The report noted that every naval officer knew the dangers from spontaneous combustion of coal: it was astonishing that magazines should still be placed adjacent to coal bunkers.[29]

Signs of war were increasing rapidly. Julian Pauncefote, the British minister in Washington, reported to his government the preparations the Americans were making to defend Jacksonville, Florida; Galveston, Texas; and New York City. He observed that the Newport News Shipbuilding and Dry Dock Company had launched simultaneously the battleships *Kearsarge* and *Kentucky*. They were unusual ships. Each had two 2-story turrets, with the upper level carrying a pair of 8-inch guns and the lower level carrying two 13-inch guns. Sampson had sponsored the unusual arrangement when he was Chief of the Bureau of Ordnance. Pauncefote remarked the battleships were ". . . particularly interesting additions to what has been called a 'fleet of experiments'." [30]

Long believed the emotion in Congress jeopardized McKinley's chances of preserving peace. Senator Henry Cabot Lodge was deluged with letters and telegrams, most urging him to support the President. He was doing so, but he thought that Congress might break away from McKinley and force the President's hand. Unless McKinley acted now, the Republicans faced disaster in the next election. In early April the House debated naval appropriations and whether to add three battleships (one to be named the *Maine*) and six torpedo boats and six torpedo boat destroyers.[31]

In the first week of April, McKinley worked on his message to Congress but delayed its completion, partly to give Americans a chance to leave Cuba, partly because he still hoped for concessions from Spain. To Congress, expecting his message on April 6, the wait was exasperating. On April 10, Lee left Havana; the flag flying from the *Maine* had been hauled down a few days earlier. That same day the Spanish minister brought another message from Madrid. The Queen Regent had proclaimed a cessation of hostilities but left the details to be worked out by General Blanco. The Spanish diplomat wanted to send Madrid new American views, since those of March 29 were unacceptable. After consulting with McKinley, Day replied that the President could not go beyond the terms of March 29. Tomorrow—April 11—the President would send his message to Congress but he would accompany it with the latest communications from Spain.[32]

Congress received McKinley's message. It was a turgid document; even Long, who had heard parts of it in preparation, believed it lacked force and was weak in logic. McKinley surveyed past negotiations and efforts to bring peace to the island. The court of inquiry which investigated the *Maine* "commands the unqualified confidence of the Government." It could not fix responsibility for the loss of the ship on any individual. But the real issue was that the destruction of the ship showed that Spain could not even assure safety of an American naval vessel visiting Havana on a legitimate mission of peace. He asked Congress for authority to end the warfare on the island and to secure for it a stable government. For these purposes he wanted the power to use American military and naval forces.[33]

For two weeks Congress wrangled over whether to recognize a Cuban revolutionary government. Lee, just arrived in Washington, appeared before the Committee on Foreign Relations. He said the Spanish had recently placed two rows of mines at the mouth of the harbor; he had no information that mines had been planted before the arrival of the *Maine;* he was certain that the ship had been destroyed by a submarine mine exploded by Spanish officers who knew their business; and he was sure that General Blanco had nothing to do with it. Lee had seen the officers of the court of inquiry nearly every day, but had not known what the verdict would be. All his information came from divers, and what he learned he had sent to the Department of State. In its report, the Committee on Foreign Relations declared that the

Maine had been destroyed by a mine positioned under the ship in a Spanish harbor—near a buoy which had been selected for the vessel by Spanish authorities. There was a minority report, but the difference between it and the majority position was whether to recognize immediately the Republic of Cuba.[34]

On April 19, Congress passed a joint resolution recognizing the independence of Cuba (but not the existence of a Cuban government) and authorizing the President to force Spain to relinquish Cuba. The next day McKinley signed the resolution. The two countries broke off diplomatic relations on April 21, and the North Atlantic Squadron, now under Sampson, took up the blockade of Havana and other principal Cuban ports. For the first time in half a century, the United States faced a foreign enemy.[35]

CHAPTER 7

Reexamination

American battle deaths during the Spanish-American War were astonishingly light. The Navy lost ten men, the Army 369. Total combat fatalities were only about 100 more than the number from the *Maine*. During the war Sigsbee commanded the *St. Paul,* an ocean liner which had been armed and converted to an auxiliary cruiser and used primarily for scouting. When peace returned he was given command of the *Texas,* a second-class battleship which had a turret arrangement similar to that of the *Maine*. Sigsbee returned to Havana late in 1898. It was a tense time, for the Spanish were evacuating Cuba. Some officers felt that Sigsbee was risking assassination by going ashore, but he refused to be deterred. He was right, for nothing happened. In March, 1899, the *Texas* was inspected and several deficiencies observed; the ship was dirty and rusty, and the boats not properly outfitted. The incident did not affect Sigsbee's subsequent career. He was advanced in seniority for extraordinary heroism and from 1900 to 1903 served as the Navy's chief intelligence officer. In 1903 he was promoted to rear admiral and, before he retired in 1907, commanded the South Atlantic Squadron and the second division of the North Atlantic Squadron. He died in New York City on July 19, 1923.[1]

The three members of the court of inquiry and the judge advocate also achieved flag rank. Sampson commanded the North Atlantic Squadron during the Spanish-American War. By ill luck, he was some miles away when the squadron defeated the Spanish at the battle of Santiago. Never robust, Sampson ended the war a sick man, exhausted by his responsibilities and troubled by controversy. Chadwick became president of the Naval War College and commanded the South Atlantic Squadron before retiring in 1906. He wrote some volumes, still useful, on Spanish-American diplomatic relations and on the war itself. Potter held several important sea and shore assignments before retiring in 1912. Marix won recognition during the war for conspicuous bravery. He became a rear admiral in 1908 and retired two years later. Sampson died in 1902, Potter in 1917, and Chadwick and Marix in 1919. All but Sampson lived to see the emergence of the United States as a modern naval power.[2]

75

Doubts about the cause of the destruction of the *Maine* continued during and after the war. Despite repetition, it is necessary to make Sigsbee's position clear. He was aware that many people did not believe the Spanish had sunk the ship. In the third installment of his "Personal Narrative of the 'Maine'," appearing in the *Century Magazine* of January 1899, he gave the reasons for his belief. In essence he argued that Spain was unfriendly to the United States; the *Maine* was not welcome because the Spanish feared its presence would lead to disorder; the ship was taken by a Spanish pilot to a special buoy which "was apparently reserved for some purpose not known"; at that mooring the battleship was, according to the court of inquiry, blown up by an external explosion. Therefore a mine must have been placed at that location either before or after the *Maine* arrived.

Sigsbee also explained how as many as a dozen dissidents could have planted a mine after the *Maine* arrived. It would have been easy to make a device, ballast it to almost float, and carry it slung below a lighter. Of course, the lighter would have to be specially prepared; its bottom pierced by tubes through which slings carrying the mine would be passed, and through which wires would be unreeled to carry the electrical charge for the detonation. These changes would not have been apparent as the lighter approached the *Maine*. At a given moment the lighter would release the mine and continue on its way; there would be no movement to betray the action. Soon the lighter could anchor or make fast to a wharf. The wires could be taken ashore if desired, or the lighter could be used as the firing station. In either case disposing of the evidence was easy. Of course, Spanish regulations concerning the private possession of explosives were very strict, so perhaps the government-controlled mine was the most likely possibility. It didn't really matter, however, because Spain was responsible for the safety of vessels visiting her ports.[3]

The most serious contemporary attack on the mine theory came from the pages of *Engineering,* a highly reputable British professional journal. John T. Bucknill, a lieutenant colonel in the Royal Engineers, had been secretary of a joint Admiralty-War Office committee which, from 1874 to 1876, had carried out experiments with explosives against the double bottom of the HMS *Oberon*. Bucknill was an expert on mines and their effects. After carefully studying the testimony he concluded that the findings of the American court of inquiry were absurd. Modern analysis does not bear out Bucknill's arguments in some respects; he was, however, a technically qualified individual raising serious questions.

He began with some observations about harbors and the technique of mine defense. Havana had a long narrow entrance admirably suited for defense by mines. With this natural advantage, Bucknill found it incredible that anyone could argue that the best way to defend Havana by mines was to place them inside the harbor. He was equally caustic about a mine planted in anticipation of the arrival of the *Maine* or after the ship had been moored. Bucknill argued that only a large mine could have driven the bottom plating 30 feet above its normal position. To plant such a weapon would require a large working party. By his reading of the testimony, Bucknill believed that the Spanish could have known of the *Maine*'s arrival perhaps 18 hours before the event. In that time the Spanish could not have planned and executed a scheme of laying, undetected, a large mine 300 feet from the wharves and 400 yards from the German training ship *Gneisenau*. He thought it would have been more difficult to lay the mine after the ship arrived because of the alertness of Sigsbee and his crew. Bucknill dismissed the possibility of a large drifting mine. He pointed out that the court of inquiry located the point of the mine explosion on the bottom of the ship. The water was so shallow, however, that a mine drifting so deep as to hit the ship's bottom ran a serious risk of dragging and catching on the harbor floor. He placed no stock in the statement that the mooring was seldom used. The court, he observed, did not consider the matter even though it examined Captain Frank Stevens, who was said to have made the allegation.

From the testimony and from his professional background, Bucknill analyzed the wreckage as best he could. In his experience, a large mine capable of causing such damage would have caved in the bottom of the ship and produced "dome-shaped" damage—not the sharp angular upward thrust which had actually occurred. He did not place much reliance on the testimony of Converse. The American based part of his explanation on the statement by others that an explosion lifted the forward body of the ship; a magazine explosion would not have had this effect, but a mine would have provided the necessary upward force. Bucknill agreed that a magazine explosion would not have lifted the ship, but no one had proved that this was what had happened. Certainly the forward decks had been raised but that was a very different thing. The absence of a column of water was another point Bucknill marshalled against the possibility of a mine.

From his analysis, Bucknill concluded that there had been two detonations. He suspected that spontaneous combustion in the coal bunker caused the first explosion in or near the 6-inch reserve magazine; the second was caused by some of the slow-burning powder in the 10-inch magazine. It was the second explosion that had done the damage, destroying the sides, pushing the main deck upward, and driving the double bottom downward. The afterpart of the ship would have moved forward to fill the void, forcing the keel upward in the inverted V. He could not be precise on the details but he was convinced there was no mine.[4]

Rear Admiral George W. Melville, Chief of the Bureau of Steam Engineering in 1898, delivered another attack upon the mine hypothesis. He had a long and distinguished career. Born in New York City in 1841, he graduated from the Brooklyn Polytechnic Institute and was working in an East Brooklyn engineering works when the Civil War broke out. He enlisted as third assistant engineer. After the war, he remained in the Navy and took part in Arctic exploration. His heroism in the ill-fated *Jeannette* expedition of 1879–1881 brought him world fame. In 1887 he was selected over 44 engineers to become Chief of the Bureau of Steam Engineering. By building up a small staff of highly skilled assistants, he prepared plans for many of the Navy's propulsion plants, ending the practice of buying such plans from private contractors. He was able, pugnacious, and irascible. In 1898 he had not hesitated to declare that an accident had destroyed the *Maine*. In 1902, Melville answered a request from former Speaker Thomas B. Reed, now retired from public life, for his views. In 1911 when the *Maine* was being raised, Melville decided to publish his letter. The former Engineer-in-Chief of the Navy—retired for some years—showed his article to George von L. Meyer, Secretary of the Navy. Meyer had no objection to its publication and the letter appeared in the June 1911 issue of *The North American Review*.[5]

Melville's letter was marred by several errors but these did not invalidate his general reasoning. He began from the premise that Spain did not want war; that correspondence published after the nation's defeat showed that officials in Madrid and Havana saw only catastrophe for them in a struggle with the United States. In Melville's view the visit of the *Vizcaya* to New York was one more indication that the Spanish did not want war: otherwise they would not have placed a valuable unit of their fleet in the hands of a potential enemy. He observed that no one had come forward since the tragedy to accuse any individual, to claim a part in the conspiracy, or to say that he was a member of the working party which laid the mine. He believed American experience with Spanish mines during the war was significant. At Guantánamo, two American ships had struck mines: neither exploded. He gave no credit to the theory that a shock from a mine explosion could detonate the magazines.

Naval ships had hit rocks, wharves, piers, and each other; yet the magazines never detonated. As for the *Maine,* the complexity of the damage and the opacity of the water made it difficult to know what happened. He thought, however, that raising the battleship would provide the answer.[6]

Sigsbee and Chadwick were convinced that, if the *Maine* were raised, an examination of the wreck would confirm the findings of the court of inquiry. Writing some years after the war, Chadwick gave his reasons. He had seen the Spanish cruisers driven ashore in flames during the battle of Santiago. Their magazines exploded, blew out the sides of the ships, but did not drive the bottoms upward. Chadwick thought that Russian experiences during the Russo-Japanese War also supported the court. The Russians lost two battle-ships to mines which detonated the magazines. What Chadwick did not realize, however, was that the Russians were using a volatile and unstable smokeless powder. In contrast the *Maine* had been carrying the far more stable black and brown powders.[7]

Eventually something would have to be done about the wreck. It was occupying valuable harbor space and the buildup of silt around the hull promised to create a shoal. Further pressure came from various patriotic groups, many of which wanted souvenirs of the ship. Finally responding to public opinion, Congress in March 1910, June 1910, and March 1911, appropriated a total of $650,000 to remove the *Maine,* recover an estimated 70 bodies still in the ship, and transport them and the mast to Arlington Cemetery. The Army Corps of Engineers was to do the work. Congress did not specifically call for a new investigation.[8]

Brigadier General William H. Bixby, Chief of Engineers, selected three officers to form the *Maine* board to plan and supervise the effort. All were experienced. Colonel William M. Black had taken part in the Cuban and Puerto Rican campaigns and in work on the Panama Canal. Major Mason M. Patrick had been an engineering instructor at West Point, the chief engineer of the Army of Cuban Pacification, and was an expert on river and harbor projects. Captain Harley B. Ferguson was a West Point graduate who, at the time of his selection, was district engineer at Montgomery, Alabama. He acquired engineering experience in Cuba and in China during the Boxer Rebellion. Upon him would fall most of the responsibility for work at the site.[9]

Among Black's first moves was to get Cuban permission to work in the harbor. The Cuban government assured him that he would be welcome and would help in every way possible. On August 29, 1910, Black, Patrick, and Ferguson held their first meeting as the *Maine* board. The same day Black gave President William Howard Taft the board's views on how it would proceed. Ferguson was soon in Havana, working out the preliminary arrangements. One thought occurred to Black in late September: perhaps the Spanish should be asked if they wanted to send a representative. Taft endorsed the proposal but exploratory conversations at Madrid revealed that the Spanish had no such desire. To them the matter would only reopen old and painful wounds.[10]

Taft received a detailed plan for the project on October 10, 1910. The board proposed to construct a cofferdam around the *Maine,* pump out the water, expose the hull, cut away and remove the most damaged parts, and refloat the remainder. The cofferdam was to consist of twenty steel cylinders of interlocking steel sheet piling, driven 38 feet into the harbor floor. Each cylinder was to be 50 feet in diameter. They would be filled with clay and gravel, and connected to each other by sheet metal walls. Taft approved the plan on October 13, and in early December, tugs, launches, dredges, barges, and scows surrounded the hulk and the pile drivers began their work.[11]

Although it was the Army's assignment to remove the *Maine,* the Navy was involved. The Department furnished Black with plans of the ship, lists of equipment (such as ordnance and ammunition), and weights of various components which were believed still on board. The Department also intended that its board of inspection and survey, whose duty it was to examine the Navy's ships, would look at the *Maine* when it was exposed. So that the Navy would have a representative at the site, Rear Admiral Richard M. Watt, Chief of the Bureau of Construction and Repair, sent a naval constructor to Havana. He would advise the Army on matters dealing with the structure of the ship, prepare a record of the condition of the *Maine* for later use by the board of inspection and survey, handle the removal of effects recovered from the wreck, and select items for distribution among thousands of claimants for relics.

William B. Ferguson, the naval constructor whom Watt selected, held impressive credentials: Phi Beta Kappa at the University of North Carolina,

NA, RG. 38, E.242

Early stage of the salvage of the Maine. The cofferdam is completed and pumping has just begun. The intact after superstructure is hidden behind the large body of wreckage in the center. The wreckage above the water to the left of the pole carrying cables in the foreground is the top of the inverted V of the keel. Photograph taken in June, 1911.

an honor graduate at the Naval Academy, and graduate work in engineering at the Massachusetts Institute of Technology. He was also the brother of Harley B. Ferguson, the Army's engineer in charge of the work on the *Maine*. When William Ferguson arrived on June 7, 1911, the cofferdam was completed and pumping out the water had begun. The water level was reduced at the rate of one foot every four hours but the pumping stopped when the water inside the cofferdam was about five feet below sea level. The reason for not going further was to inspect for leaks which, so far, were small. The plan called for removing the rest of the water in easy stages. Ferguson heard that July 1 might be the earliest day that the wreck would be completely uncovered. In his own view July 15 might be more realistic. As work went on, both dates proved wildly optimistic.[12]

Difficulties grew quickly when pumping was resumed. As the water level inside dropped, the pressure from the outside increased. Some of the cylinders showed signs of shifting and significant leakage occurred. Even at this stage it was easy to see that the damage to the *Maine* was greater than anyone thought. Barnacles encrusting the wreck, thick layers of silt covering the decks, severe corrosion of other areas—all combined to make the work difficult. To Bixby, who visited the site in June 1911, the deterioration was so great he doubted if the origin of the explosion could ever be determined. William Ferguson photographed the wreck from various angles and annotated the prints with overlays. He painted marks on the hull which, by indicating the keel and frame numbers, showed how the explosion had wrenched the ship, and he made models in an effort to explain what had happened. Working conditions were appalling—over everything hung the stench of the corroded ship, dying marine life, and filthy mud.[13]

The Army engineers were methodically dismantling and stripping the ship. They used the recently introduced oxyacetylene torches to cut free the bent superstructure and folded decks; these were dumped at sea off Morro Light. At frame 41, about halfway between the bow and stern, they began to seal off the after portion of the *Maine* with a concrete and wooden bulkhead. As yet it had not been necessary to cut the ship in two and the forward part was undisturbed. But as summer went on, it became clear that the Army engineers would have to cross-connect the cylinders of the cofferdam with heavy timbers to prevent further movement inward. Some of the forward part of the wreckage, of critical importance to an investigation by the board of inspection, might have to be cut away. Ferguson informed Watt of the problem.

NA 77–RMN–453

Model for 1911 investigation. A 1/48 scale model built by Naval Constructor William B. Ferguson for his analysis of the wreckage for use by the board of inspection and survey. Background is a portion of the Maine's hull.

Watt turned to Rear Admiral Washington L. Capps. He was a naval constructor and Watt's immediate predecessor as Chief of the Bureau of Construction and Repair. Watt asked Capps to go to Havana to inspect the wreck and verify the identification of certain parts should the Army have to remove them. Capps arrived on September 20. For some days Capps and Ferguson clambered over the *Maine*. The water was pumped down to very low levels, several feet of the forward wreckage were cleared away for better photographs, and mud removed from some of the inner bottom. On October 2, Capps left, taking back to Washington photographs and two models of the forward wreckage.[14]

As it turned out, the Army engineers were able to erect the bracing so there was no need to disturb the crucial area. By early November it was clear that it was time for the Navy's board of inspection to take up its task. Taft was personally interested in the *Maine*. On a tour through the Midwest, Meyer raised the question of the board's composition. Taft gave Meyer instructions (these have not been found) as to the scope of the investigation. Taft also specified that an Army officer be a member of the board: he preferred Colonel Black. The board, consisting of Rear Admiral Charles E. Vreeland as senior member, Chief Constructor Richard M. Watt, Colonel William M. Black, Commander Joseph Strauss (an ordnance expert), and Commander Charles F. Hughes as member and recorder, arrived in Havana November 20, 1911. In technical competence the Vreeland board was far superior to the Sampson court of 1898. Until they left for Washington on December 2, the members met at the Plaza Hotel, frequently visiting the wreck, and studying the material which Ferguson had prepared.[15]

With the Navy out of the way, the Army engineers could concentrate on their task. They completed the bulkhead and cut away the forward wreckage, which made it possible to float the *Maine*. Releasing the remaining portion from the suction of the mud was difficult. The problem was solved by cutting holes in the bottom of the ship, through which jets of water were used to break the mud seal. The holes were plugged with flood cocks which could be used later for sinking the ship. On February 13, 1912, the cofferdam was flooded and the *Maine* floated. On March 16, escorted by United States Navy ships and gunboats of the Republic of Cuba, the hulk was towed to sea. Short and stubby, the concrete and wooden bulkhead clearly evident, and the conning tower lashed upside down on the starboard side as a counterbalance, the hulk moved uneasily through the sea. Four miles off the coast of Cuba, the *Maine* was sunk with great ceremony in about 600 fathoms

The last of the Maine. Flying a large ensign, the salvaged after portion of the ship is sunk off Cuba at 5:30 p.m., March 16, 1912.

of water. Two important relics had already gone to the United States as memorials to the ship; the foremast to Annapolis and the Naval Academy, the mainmast to Arlington National Cemetery.[16]

The Army Corps of Engineers returned to the immense task of removing the cylinders and grading the harbor bottom in the area to a depth of 37½ feet. Much of the heavy wreckage remaining was deeply embedded in the mud, but parts protruded above the agreed-upon depth. By using small charges of dynamite, the engineers removed the projections and tamped into the bottom pieces of armor, barbettes, and the finally discovered forward 10-inch turret. Not until December 20, 1912, was the Havana office of the *Maine* board closed.[17]

The Vreeland board found that the general condition of the wreck was not very different from that described by the Sampson court. The damage was, however, more severe than expected. The board made two important observations. One concerned the area where the keel had been driven into the shape of an inverted V. In the words of the board:

> The condition of the vertical keel and flat keel at frame 18 was ascribed by the court of inquiry of 1898 to the direct effect of an explosion exterior to the ship in that vicinity. Because of its better opportunity for a detailed examination of this wreckage, now fully exposed, the board concludes that the external explosion was not in the vicinity of frame 18. The board believes that the condition of the wreckage . . . can be accounted for by the action of gases of low explosives such as the black and brown powders with which the forward magazines were stored. The protective deck and hull of the ship formed a closed chamber in which gases were generated and partially expanded before rupture.

The other observation of the board dealt with damage further aft, in the area between frames 28 and 33. Here, on the port side of the keel, a force apparently had been exerted from the outside inward. Furthermore, some plating—about an area of 100 square feet was ". . . *displaced upwards, inward, and to starboard. . . .*" In conclusion:

> *The board finds that the injuries to the bottom of the Maine above described, were caused by the explosion of a charge of a low form of explosive exterior to the ship between frames 28 and 31 . . . . This resulted in igniting and exploding the contents of the 6-inch reserve magazine, A–14–M, said contents including a large quantity of black powder. The more or less complete explosion*

Evidence that led the 1898 court to the opinion that a mine destroyed the Maine. The man is seated on top of the inverted V of the ship's keel. The pipe passing over the wreckage indicates the centerline of the ship and the original height of the main deck. The stern is off the photograph to the right. Photograph taken July 7, 1911.

of the contents of the remaining forward magazines followed. The magazine explosions resulted in the destruction of the vessel.[18]

To sum up, the Vreeland board believed that a magazine explosion could account for the upraised keel and plating in the vicinity of frame 18—the damage which had baffled the Sampson court. On the other hand, the force from the exploding magazine could not have damaged the plating further aft. The board found no other way to account for this damage except by a mine.

Bucknill was no more satisfied with the new conclusion than he had been with the old. "Plating, keel-plates, bulkheads, frames, decks, guns, a turret, a conning tower, etc. were bent, torn and driven this way and that, but nothing in the report of the second Board warrants the theory of an external explosion." Fourteen years had elapsed since the night the *Maine* was lost, Bucknill remarked, and no one in Havana had yet stepped forward with even a whisper of evidence that a mine had ever been planted in the inner harbor.[19]

Subsequent to the investigations of the court of inquiry of 1898 and the board of inspection of 1911, a great deal of experience has been gained in analyzing ships damaged by external and internal explosions. It seemed to me that a new examination of the evidence in the light of present information might help to solve the question of the destruction of the *Maine*. Fortunately, Naval Constructor Ferguson had taken many photographs of the ship as it was uncovered; these not only showed the entire wreck but the critical areas of damage as well. The National Archives had these photographs as well as Ferguson's reports, drawings, and overlays, although the models which Ferguson made could not be located. Mr. Ib S. Hansen of the David W. Taylor Naval Ship Research and Development Center and Mr. Robert S. Price of the Naval Surface Weapons Center volunteered to look at the evidence. Mr. Hansen and Mr. Price studied the reports of the court of inquiry and the board of inspection and examined carefully the Ferguson material. The Hansen-Price analysis in its entirety is Appendix A, "The U.S.S. *Maine:* An Examination of the Technical Evidence Bearing on its Destruction."

NA, RG. 80, E.19

The keel at the start of the inverted V. The abrupt upward bend of the keel which forms one leg of the V can be seen at the right. The stern is toward the left and the bow toward the right of the picture. The white line running from left to right indicates the keel line. The numbered cards locate the frames. Photograph taken November 26, 1911.

NA, RG. 80, E.19

Evidence that led the 1911 board to conclude that an external explosion initiated events that destroyed the Maine. The view is looking aft. Of great importance to the board was the piece of outer bottom plating prominent in the upper half of the photograph and further identified by the white intersecting lines painted on it. The board reached its conclusion because the plate was bent inward and folded back from its original position at the lower right of the photograph. Because the section shows no marks from an explosion the Hansen-Price analysis concludes that the plate was bent inward by the dynamic effects of the magazine explosion and the sinking of the ship. Photograph taken November 26, 1911.

The Hansen-Price analysis shows that the characteristics of the damage are consistent with a large internal explosion. The analysis concludes that the primary source of the explosion was centered in the 6-inch reserve magazine which caused a partial detonation of the other forward magazines. In this area, the explosion blew out the sides and ruptured the decks. The bottom was driven downwards, although its displacement, because it was supported by water, was less than that of the sides and decks. The forward section was separated from the after section *except* where it was attached by the keel and adjacent bottom plating, mostly on the starboard side. As the forward section turned on its starboard side, the keel at frame 18 was raised upward. At the same time the after section was flooding, inclining downward at that part through which the water was pouring. The movement of the two sections led to the inverted V configuration which so troubled the court of 1898. The Hansen-Price analysis does not support the finding of the 1911 board. That area which attracted the attention of the board showed no evidence of a rupture or deformation which would have resulted from a contact or near contact mine. Th e is no doubt that in one relatively small area the bottom plating was folded inward. But there are several plausible explanations for its cause *other* than an external explosion.

What did happen? Probably a fire in bunker A–16. Fires of this kind had happened before. Instances had occurred in which bituminous coal of the type carried in the *Maine* bunkers had ignited through spontaneous combustion. Such fires were difficult to detect. Often they smoldered deep below the exposed surface of the coal, giving off no smoke or flames, or raising the temperature in the vicinity of the alarm. The bunker on the *Maine* had not been inspected for nearly 12 hours before the explosion; a period which experience had shown was ample time for a bunker fire to begin, heat bulkheads and set fire to contents in adjacent compartments.

In conclusion: There is no evidence that a mine destroyed the *Maine*.

CHAPTER 8

Summary

The following pages summarize some key points. These are: the *Maine*'s visit to Havana considered as part of a larger naval movement aimed at exerting pressure on Spain to end the war in Cuba, the competence of Sigsbee as commanding officer of the ship, the explanations of the court of inquiry of 1898, the board of inspection of 1911, and the Hansen-Price analysis.

Confronted with the Cuban problem, McKinley at the beginning of 1898 had three choices. He could support Spanish efforts to regain control of the island. He could favor the attempt to establish an autonomous government. He could assist the Cubans in their struggle for independence. To each of these policies there were serious objections. It was doubtful if Spain could reassert her authority without taking measures intolerable to American public opinion. The success of autonomy depended upon the ability of local Spanish and Cuban leaders to work together. The January riot in Havana and the revelations from Enrique Dupuy de Lôme's pilfered letter convinced McKinley's advisors—perhaps prematurely—that autonomy was a shadow without substance. As for the island's independence, McKinley apparently believed that the Cubans possessed no organization capable of assuming governmental authority. From this perspective the riot of January 12 left McKinley with no acceptable alternative. The one thing he could not do was permit the war to continue as it had. To do so was dangerous statesmanship, poor politics, bad business and, in the light of Victorian morality, wicked and evil.

A recapitulation of events shows the pressure the McKinley administration was bringing to bear upon Spain. In the summer of 1897 Madrid was warned that the war must end. In October 1897, the *Maine* was at Port Royal, South Carolina, ready to be sent to Havana. In December 1897, Spain was again warned, this time by a message to Congress, and the *Maine* moved to Key West. On January 11, 1898, the Commander-in-Chief of the European Station was ordered to retain men whose enlistments were about to expire. On January 23 the North Atlantic Squadron arrived off Key West and, after being joined by the *Maine* and other vessels, proceeded to the anchorage at

93

the Dry Tortugas. On January 24 the *Maine* was ordered to Havana. Finally, on February 11, the first of a planned series of torpedo boat visits took place. The presence of the *Maine* in Havana—the resumption of "friendly visits"—was not a sign that tensions between the United States and Spain were easing, but that they were increasing.

McKinley was unfortunate in the commanding officer of the *Maine*. Although Sigsbee took proper extra precautions to protect his ship against harm from external sources, there is no evidence he took more than routine measures in Havana to safeguard his ship from an accident. He knew that spontaneous combustion of coal was an ever-present danger. He must have been aware of bunker fires on other ships. He knew that the bunker alarms sounded below the danger point, which was no ground for feeling safe. The important fact was that they were inaccurate. Perhaps it is also significant that the *Kearsarge* and *Texas* while under his command were inspected and found dirty.

The loss of the *Maine* had to be investigated, but it could have been done differently. The Secretary of the Navy could have chosen the members of the court of inquiry. Instead Long decided to rely upon established procedures, a step consistent with the way he viewed his function. He assigned the task to Sicard. When the Commander-in-Chief of the North Atlantic Squadron proposed a list of relatively junior officers, Long—or someone else in Washington—intervened and changed the membership. By Sampson's selection, the court had for its president a senior captain, well-known and respected in the Navy, and an officer who had been a vigorous Chief of the Bureau of Ordnance. The Navy Department answered as best it could requests from the court for plans and for a naval constructor. Long also turned to O'Neil, Chief of the Bureau of Ordnance, for additional advice. Long erred in his failure to go beyond normal procedures for technical advice.

The court of inquiry presented its results in two parts. The proceedings consisted mainly of transcripts of testimony. The findings were the facts as determined by the court. Between the proceedings and the findings was a broad gap. The court left no record of the reasoning which carried it from the often inconsistent witnesses to the conclusion that an external explosion had destroyed the ship. In other respects the court was also deficient. Curiously, the log of the *Maine* was never mentioned. In all probability it was lost with the vessel, but an acknowledgment of the fact would have helped complete the record and fulfill *Navy Regulations*. The court failed to reconcile estimates of the contents of the magazines. It did not explore a significant matter which was part of Sigsbee's defense. This was the alleged fact that the mooring assigned to the *Maine* was seldom used. Even if true, a sinister connotation did not immediately follow. The court could have taken up the subject. Captain Frank Stevens, captain of the *City of Washington* and the individual whom Sigsbee said had made the statement, appeared before the court and was not questioned on this point. Sigsbee's testimony and his later writing can be criticized in detail but to do so would be lengthy and repetitious. His arguments were necessarily vague and speculative.

The Sampson court failed to call for technical experts. The simplest explanation for this omission is that the court felt no need to do so. All members were officers with years of service at sea. With plans of the ship and assistance of the naval constructor they had requested, and with information from the divers, the court might have believed that no one else could do a better job. From this standpoint, bringing in technical advisors would have meant delay, added nothing, and perhaps endangered control of the court over the investigation. Sampson was working under pressure. The possibility of war was imminent and the nation was clamoring for his report. As it was Sampson had fended off Washington attempts to hurry the court.

The court's verdict of an external explosion was one that could be expected. The strained relations between the two nations, the warlike and patriotic atmosphere in Congress and the press, and the natural tendency to look for reasons for the loss that did not reflect upon the Navy might have been predisposing factors in the court's finding. Above all, there was the way in which part of the keel and bottom plating were driven upward to form the inverted V. As the questioning of Converse by Marix revealed, the court was aware of an hypothesis by which an internal explosion accounted for this particular characteristic of the damage. Had the ship blown up in an American or friendly foreign port, and had the same type of damage occurred, it is doubtful that an inquiry would have laid the blame on a mine. The finding of the court of 1898 appears to have been guided less by technical consideration and more by the awareness that war was now inevitable.

The hearings held by the Senate Committee on Foreign Relations contained nothing of technical substance and appears to have had no more justification than to compile a record of Spanish misdeeds. Officers who had not even seen the findings of the court were asked for their opinion. Sigsbee was allowed to relate his theories about the makeshift mine without challenge. He even alluded to his possession of certain information too sensitive to reveal. So far as is known no one took up the matter and asked that Sigsbee testify in secret. By the time the committee held its hearings, the time for rational consideration had passed.

The board of 1911 could do its work free from the risk of war. Moreover, its members were better qualified for their task than were those of the court and they could examine the wreck under the best possible circumstances. The order signed by the Secretary of the Navy stated that assignment clearly: "The Board will make an exhaustive examination of the wreck of the *Maine* and state whether in its opinion there is anything shown, or any new evidence developed, that would indicate the cause of the explosion which destroyed the vessel." The board's report, ordered printed by Congress on December 14, 1911, is difficult to understand, partly because its exhibits were not printed and partly because the reasoning behind its conclusion was not given. The report can be considered in the following order: first, what the report said about the damage done to the keel and bottom plating near frame 18—the inverted V—which the 1898 court said was caused by a mine: and second, the board's own explanation for the loss of the ship.[1]

The board stated that the damage done to the keel and bottom plating near frame 18 "ascribed by the court of inquiry of 1898 to the direct effect of an explosion exterior to the ship" was not caused by a mine. In the board's words: ". . . the condition of the wreckage . . . [in the area of frame 18] can be accounted for by the action of gases of low explosives such as the black and brown powders with which the forward magazines were stored. The protective deck and hull of the ship formed a closed chamber in which the gases were generated and partially expanded before rupture." With these two sentences out of an 11-page report, the board negated and overturned the key evidence upon which the 1898 court based its finding that the *Maine* was destroyed by a mine. The remainder of the report dealt with a description of the wreck and the board's finding.[2]

Secretary of the Navy Meyer's orders calling for an "exhaustive examination" gave full authority to the board to say why it did not believe that the inverted V was caused by a mine, and to offer a description of the forces—even if only a hypothetical explanation—of how this section of the keel and bottom plating were driven upward.

The 1911 board based its finding that a mine destroyed the *Maine* upon an important discovery in the area of the wreck inaccessible to the 1898 court. After some mud was removed, it was discovered that the bottom of the ship had been damaged between frames 28 and 31—about 45 feet aft of the location of the inverted V. One section of plating was bent inward and folded back with one edge remaining attached to the outer bottom. The exposed edge of an adjacent plate was also bent inward slightly. The board stated that a mine caused this damage.

Why the board took this position is not understood. The displacement of the bottom plating could have been accounted for by an internal explosion and the dynamic effects of the ship's sinking. More important, the displaced plating did not exhibit the scars which would be expected from a mine explosion. The 1911 board depended upon Ferguson's photographs and models, the proceedings and finding of the 1898 court, and visits to the wreck. So far as the records show, the 1911 board, as did the 1898 court, carried out its investigation without the advice of any outside experts and without the help of available technical information.

Perhaps, but this is only speculation, the 1911 board was willing on technical grounds to overturn the fundamental conclusion of the 1898 court, though unwilling to raise the question whether there had been a mine at all. Only 13 years had elapsed since the nation had gone to war with the battle cry "Remember the *Maine*." It would have been difficult for the board to raise the issue whether the nation and its constituted authorities had made a grave error in 1898.

It is interesting in this connection to look at the manner by which the French investigated an accident occurring to the battleship *Jena,* lost by a magazine explosion in 1907. In contrast to the two American investigations, the French examination appears to have been particularly exhaustive. However, the French investigation took place under more favorable conditions, for the accident happened in their own country and at a time when the international situation was calm. A summary appears in Appendix C, "Investigation of the Explosion On Board the French Battleship *Jena*, March 12, 1907."

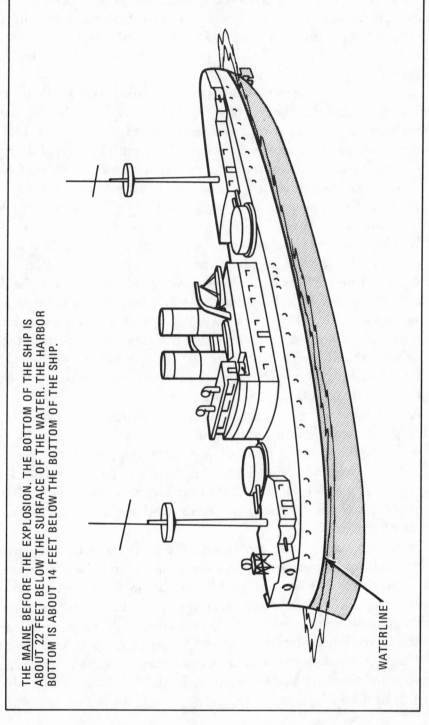

The Explosion of the MAINE (Figure 1 of 6)

THE MAINE BEFORE THE EXPLOSION. THE BOTTOM OF THE SHIP IS ABOUT 22 FEET BELOW THE SURFACE OF THE WATER. THE HARBOR BOTTOM IS ABOUT 14 FEET BELOW THE BOTTOM OF THE SHIP.

WATERLINE

The Explosion of the MAINE (Figure 2 of 6)

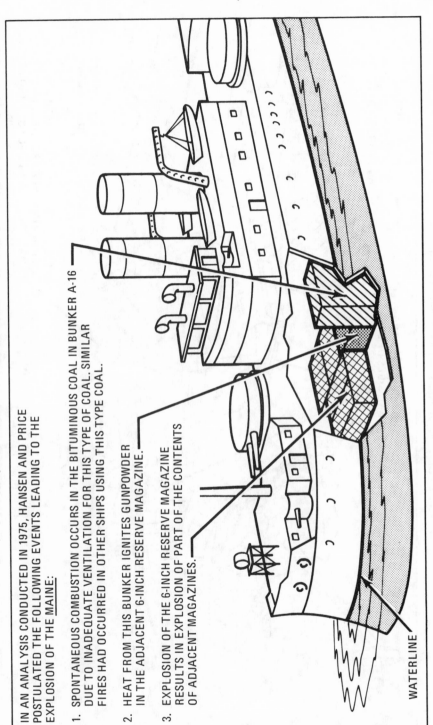

IN AN ANALYSIS CONDUCTED IN 1975, HANSEN AND PRICE POSTULATED THE FOLLOWING EVENTS LEADING TO THE EXPLOSION OF THE MAINE:

1. SPONTANEOUS COMBUSTION OCCURS IN THE BITUMINOUS COAL IN BUNKER A-16 DUE TO INADEQUATE VENTILATION FOR THIS TYPE OF COAL. SIMILAR FIRES HAD OCCURRED IN OTHER SHIPS USING THIS TYPE COAL.

2. HEAT FROM THIS BUNKER IGNITES GUNPOWDER IN THE ADJACENT 6-INCH RESERVE MAGAZINE.

3. EXPLOSION OF THE 6-INCH RESERVE MAGAZINE RESULTS IN EXPLOSION OF PART OF THE CONTENTS OF ADJACENT MAGAZINES.

WATERLINE

The Explosion of the MAINE (Figure 3 of 6)

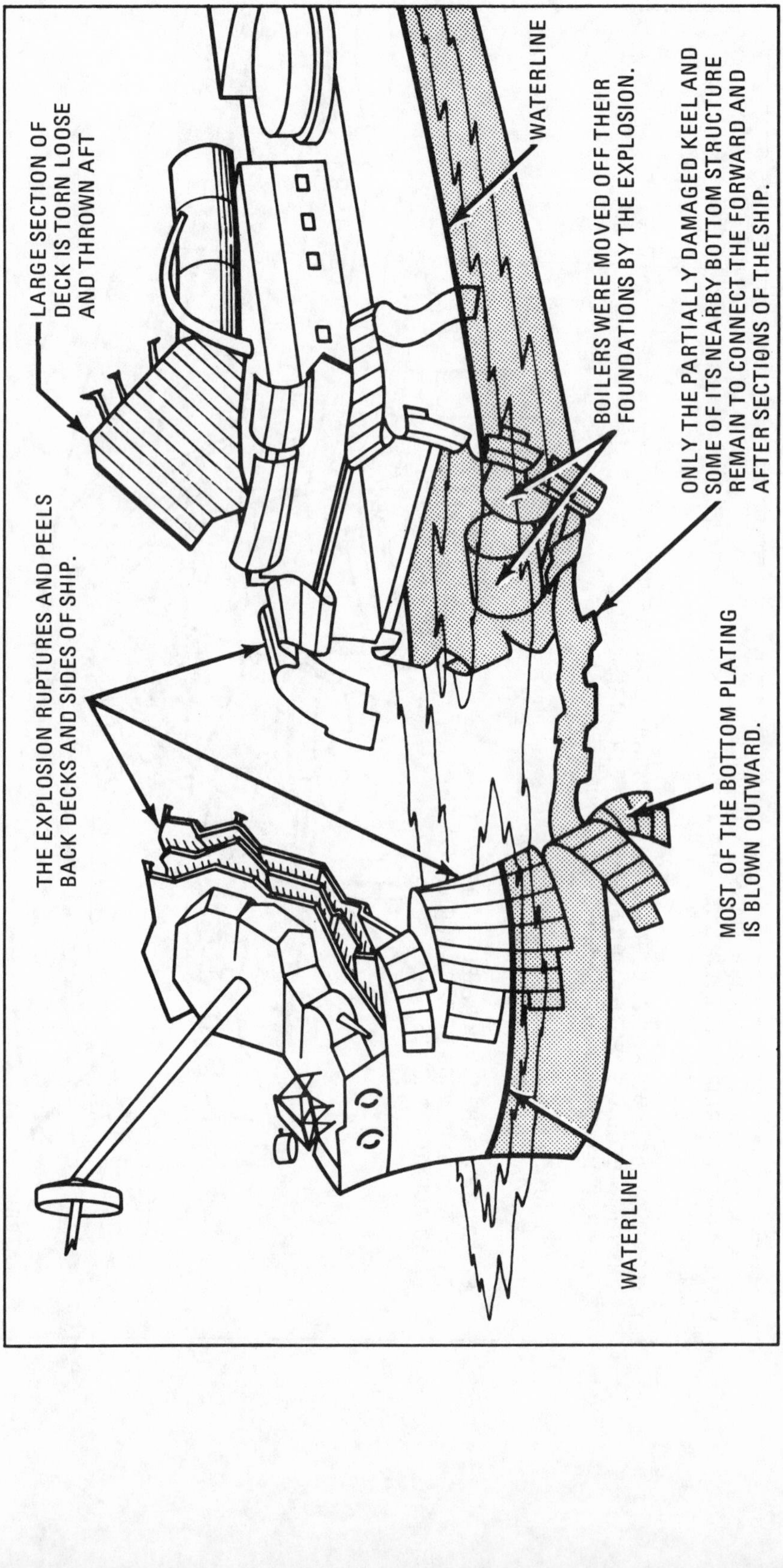

LARGE SECTION OF DECK IS TORN LOOSE AND THROWN AFT

WATERLINE

BOILERS WERE MOVED OFF THEIR FOUNDATIONS BY THE EXPLOSION.

ONLY THE PARTIALLY DAMAGED KEEL AND SOME OF ITS NEARBY BOTTOM STRUCTURE REMAIN TO CONNECT THE FORWARD AND AFTER SECTIONS OF THE SHIP.

THE EXPLOSION RUPTURES AND PEELS BACK DECKS AND SIDES OF SHIP.

MOST OF THE BOTTOM PLATING IS BLOWN OUTWARD.

WATERLINE

The Explosion of the MAINE (Figure 4 of 6)

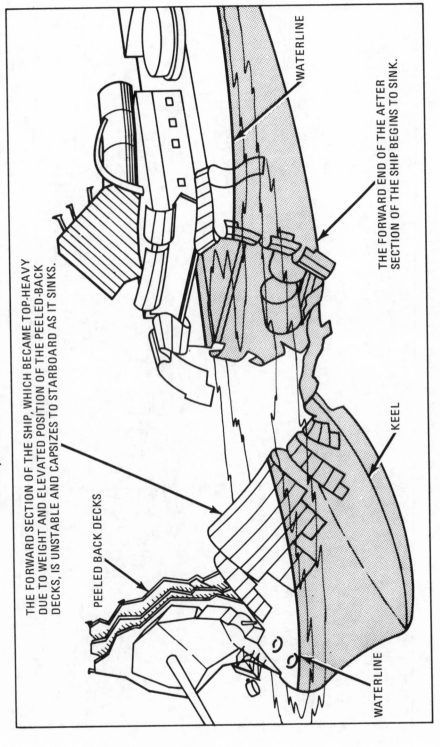

THE FORWARD SECTION OF THE SHIP, WHICH BECAME TOP-HEAVY DUE TO WEIGHT AND ELEVATED POSITION OF THE PEELED-BACK DECKS, IS UNSTABLE AND CAPSIZES TO STARBOARD AS IT SINKS.

PEELED BACK DECKS

KEEL

WATERLINE

WATERLINE

THE FORWARD END OF THE AFTER SECTION OF THE SHIP BEGINS TO SINK.

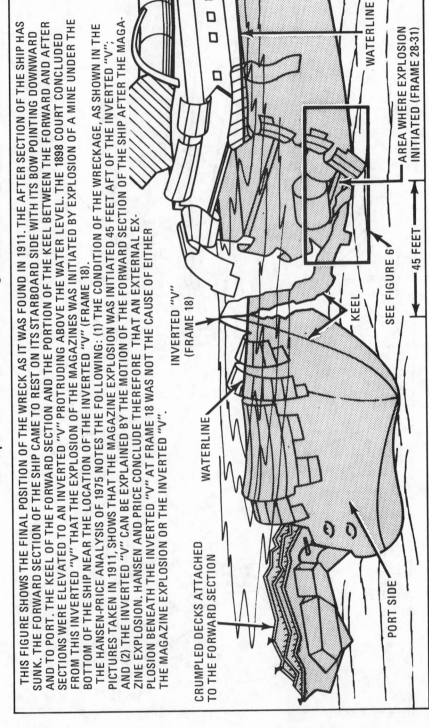

The Explosion of the MAINE (Figure 5 of 6)

THIS FIGURE SHOWS THE FINAL POSITION OF THE WRECK AS IT WAS FOUND IN 1911. THE AFTER SECTION OF THE SHIP HAS SUNK. THE FORWARD SECTION OF THE SHIP CAME TO REST ON ITS STARBOARD SIDE WITH ITS BOW POINTING DOWNWARD AND TO PORT. THE KEEL OF THE FORWARD SECTION AND THE PORTION OF THE KEEL BETWEEN THE FORWARD AND AFTER SECTIONS WERE ELEVATED TO AN INVERTED "V" PROTRUDING ABOVE THE WATER LEVEL. THE 1898 COURT CONCLUDED FROM THIS INVERTED "V" THAT THE EXPLOSION OF THE MAGAZINES WAS INITIATED BY EXPLOSION OF A MINE UNDER THE BOTTOM OF THE SHIP NEAR THE LOCATION OF THE INVERTED "V" (FRAME 18).

THE HANSEN-PRICE ANALYSIS OF 1975 NOTES THE FOLLOWING: (1) THE CONDITION OF THE WRECKAGE, AS SHOWN IN THE PICTURES TAKEN IN 1911, SHOWS THAT THE MAGAZINE EXPLOSION WAS INITIATED 45 FEET AFT OF THE INVERTED "V"; AND (2) THE INVERTED "V" CAN BE EXPLAINED BY THE MOTION OF THE FORWARD SECTION OF THE SHIP AFTER THE MAGAZINE EXPLOSION. HANSEN AND PRICE CONCLUDE THEREFORE THAT AN EXTERNAL EXPLOSION BENEATH THE INVERTED "V" AT FRAME 18 WAS NOT THE CAUSE OF EITHER THE MAGAZINE EXPLOSION OR THE INVERTED "V".

WATERLINE

WATERLINE

AREA WHERE EXPLOSION INITIATED (FRAME 28-31)

SEE FIGURE 6

45 FEET

KEEL

INVERTED "V" (FRAME 18)

WATERLINE

PORT SIDE

CRUMPLED DECKS ATTACHED TO THE FORWARD SECTION

The Explosion of the MAINE (Figure 6 of 6)

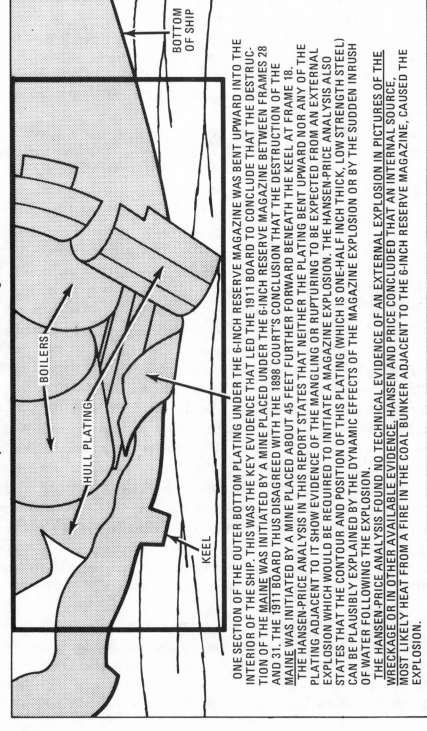

BOTTOM OF SHIP

BOILERS

HULL PLATING

KEEL

ONE SECTION OF THE OUTER BOTTOM PLATING UNDER THE 6-INCH RESERVE MAGAZINE WAS BENT UPWARD INTO THE INTERIOR OF THE SHIP. THIS WAS THE KEY EVIDENCE THAT LED THE 1911 BOARD TO CONCLUDE THAT THE DESTRUC- TION OF THE MAINE WAS INITIATED BY A MINE PLACED UNDER THE 6-INCH RESERVE MAGAZINE BETWEEN FRAMES 28 AND 31. THE 1911 BOARD THUS DISAGREED WITH THE 1898 COURT'S CONCLUSION THAT THE DESTRUCTION OF THE MAINE WAS INITIATED BY A MINE PLACED ABOUT 45 FEET FURTHER FORWARD BENEATH THE KEEL AT FRAME 18.

THE HANSEN-PRICE ANALYSIS IN THIS REPORT STATES THAT NEITHER THE PLATING BENT UPWARD NOR ANY OF THE PLATING ADJACENT TO IT SHOW EVIDENCE OF THE MANGLING OR RUPTURING TO BE EXPECTED FROM AN EXTERNAL EXPLOSION WHICH WOULD BE REQUIRED TO INITIATE A MAGAZINE EXPLOSION. THE HANSEN-PRICE ANALYSIS ALSO STATES THAT THE CONTOUR AND POSITION OF THIS PLATING (WHICH IS ONE-HALF INCH THICK, LOW STRENGTH STEEL) CAN BE PLAUSIBLY EXPLAINED BY THE DYNAMIC EFFECTS OF THE MAGAZINE EXPLOSION OR BY THE SUDDEN INRUSH OF WATER FOLLOWING THE EXPLOSION.

THE HANSEN-PRICE ANALYSIS FOUND NO TECHNICAL EVIDENCE OF AN EXTERNAL EXPLOSION IN PICTURES OF THE WRECKAGE OR IN OTHER AVAILABLE EVIDENCE. HANSEN AND PRICE CONCLUDED THAT AN INTERNAL SOURCE, MOST LIKELY HEAT FROM A FIRE IN THE COAL BUNKER ADJACENT TO THE 6-INCH RESERVE MAGAZINE, CAUSED THE EXPLOSION.

In the light of much greater experience acquired since the court and the board investigated the *Maine,* the Hansen-Price analysis concludes that, in all probability, the damage between frames 28 and 31 was caused by an internal explosion alone. Photographs of this portion of the bottom taken in 1911, and studied by Hansen and Price, show no evidence of the tearing and distortion of plates that would be expected from an external underwater explosion.

In all probability, the *Maine* was destroyed by an accident which occurred inside the ship. Since the accident could have been prevented, it is proper to ask what would have happened if the *Maine* had not exploded. The answer to this question is difficult, for it depends on an assessment of the relations between the United States and Spain before the ship sailed for Havana. If war between the two countries was inevitable before the *Maine* left for the Cuban capital, the destruction of the battleship and the efforts to determine the cause of the disaster are only interesting footnotes to history.

No matter what course McKinley followed he risked war. If he did nothing and the conflict in Cuba continued, congressional sentiment and public feeling might force American military intervention which Spain was bound to resist. If he exerted pressure on Spain to end the fighting, he also ran the danger of war. In this dilemma he chose to act. He warned Spain that fighting on the island must end. He tendered his good offices, but did not become a pawn of Spain by underwriting Spanish efforts to restore peace. The Spanish government in Madrid was weak. Toward the end of 1897 it established an autonomous government in Cuba. Under its terms the inhabitants of the island were to govern their own internal affairs but were to remain under Spanish sovereignty. If autonomy succeeded in winning the support of the civilian population of Cuba, three years of civil warfare would end. The odds against success were great. Years of bitter strife had to be overcome, a deteriorated economy rebuilt, and a population divided by social and racial prejudice brought together.

There were signs of hope. Granting autonomy was itself an indication that a better future for Cuba was possible, for Spain having once ventured along this course could not turn back. Dupuy de Lôme, toward the end of 1897, thought that autonomy was improving the relations between the United States and Spain, for Cuban affairs were no longer attracting American attention to the extent they had a few months earlier. Even the riot of January 12, 1898, in Havana did not necessarily mean the failure of autonomy. The disturbance was not sufficiently dangerous for Lee to call for the *Maine,* even though the ship was available for that purpose; even though he was convinced that autonomy could not succeed; and even though he was eager to introduce a naval presence into the harbor. It was the officials in Washington who were alarmed. It was they who sent the *Maine* to Havana.

Ordering the *Maine* to Havana did not mean that war was inevitable. Probably McKinley was uncertain what he should do. It was essential to prevent the loss of American lives. Nothing could have made his determination clearer than the despatch of a major fleet unit to the Cuban capital. On the other hand, the President, the Assistant Secretary of State, and the Secretary of the Navy, would hardly have sent a battleship into Havana, with its narrow entrance guarded by strong fortifications, if they thought war was imminent. Nor would Spain have sent the *Vizcaya* to New York. The governments of the two countries were trying to establish normal relations, although recognizing that war was a possibility.

Chances for peace dropped after the explosion of the *Maine.* From the debates in the *Congressional Record* and from the pages of the press, a strong sentiment demanded intervention. The court of inquiry carried out its work under these circumstances. Had its members investigated the loss of the battleship with all the resources available to them, they might have reached two possible findings: that the *Maine* was destroyed by an internal explosion, or that the ship was destroyed by causes unknown. In either case, the result would have been the injection of reason into an atmosphere of emotion. At least the United States would not have found itself adopting an official position which was technically unsound and which increasing numbers of people have questioned over the years. And—although the chance was slim—war might have been avoided.

As a result of the war the United States became an imperial power. The sinking of the *Maine* did not create the emotional forces that led to American imperialism: it released them. The United States assumed, particularly in the Philippines, obligations to maintain order and to defend territories remote from its shores. The easiness of victory for a time obscured the responsibilities which had been incurred. Exuberant Americans lionized the victor of the easy battle of Manila and celebrated the triumph which carried the flag to new heights of world prestige. Rudyard Kipling uttered a deep and fervent appeal:

> Take up the White Man's burden—
> Ye dare not stoop to less—

A bitter struggle took place in the Senate over the treaty which ended the war. Opposition stemmed from several motives, but one was misgivings over the role of the United States as an imperial power. Ironically the United States became an imperial nation just as classic imperialism (symbolized by colonial possessions on a map having the same color as the mother country) was ending. Within a few decades an increasing number of Americans recognized the justice of some of the earlier doubts. In 1935 the Commonwealth of the Philippines was established with the intent that after ten years the islands would become independent. Despite the intervention of World War II, the Philippines obtained independence in 1946, although the United States retained extensive privileges.

In the modern technological age, the battle cry "Remember the *Maine*" should have a special meaning for us. With almost instantaneous communications that can command weapons of unprecedented power, we can no longer approach technical problems with the casualness and confidence held by Americans in 1898. The *Maine* should impress us that technical problems must be examined by competent and qualified people; and that the results of their investigation must be fully and fairly presented to their fellow citizens.

With the vastness of our government and the difficulty of controlling it, we must make sure that those in "high places" do not, without most careful consideration of the consequences, exert our prestige and might. Such uses of our power may result in serious international actions at great cost in lives and money—injurious to the interests and standing of the United States.

APPENDIX A

The U.S.S. *Maine:*
An Examination of the Technical Evidence
Bearing on Its Destruction

BY IB S. HANSEN AND ROBERT S. PRICE

Mr. Ib S. Hansen is Assistant for Design Applications in the Structures Department at the David W. Taylor Naval Ship Research and Development Center. After receiving a master's degree in civil and structural engineering in 1946, he was a bridge designer before joining the Naval Ship Research and Development Center in 1960. There he took up the science of structural dynamics and has been concerned with weapons effects and response of ship structures ever since. He has authored more than 50 reports and papers on the subject, has lectured on ship protection at the Navy postgraduate school at the Massachusetts Institute of Technology, and has directed or taken part in numerous field tests of Navy structures and ships exposed to simulated weapons explosions.

Mr. Robert S. Price is a research physicist for the Naval Surface Weapons Center. After receiving a B.S. in chemical engineering from the Michigan Technological University in 1943, he joined the Underwater Explosions Research Laboratory at the Woods Hole Oceanographic Institution. While there, he developed systems for the underwater photography of explosions and submarine models. Since 1947 he has been at the Naval Surface Weapons Center where he developed techniques which extended photographic capability to tests in the ocean at depths of two miles. He participated in several nuclear tests, including one in which he served as project officer for underwater shock wave phenomena. He participated in the analysis of the data from the nuclear submarine *Scorpion* and the interpretation of data gathered from other wrecks. He received the Navy Meritorious Civilian Service Award in 1951 and 1960.

1. INTRODUCTION

At the request of Admiral H. G. Rickover, the undersigned examined the official records of the 1898 and 1911 investigations into the loss of the *Maine*.

The object was to determine if present-day knowledge of explosion phenomena and their effects on ship structures could provide new insight into the question of whether the explosion was initiated externally or internally. Although not exhaustive, the investigation covered the principal technical points on which the boards appear to have based their decisions. Our investigation, described below, has led us to the conclusion that the *Maine* was destroyed by an internally initiated magazine explosion.[1]

2. EVALUATION OF THE EVIDENCE

The evidence from the *Maine* explosion that is available for examination is of three kinds: (1) data from the physical examinations of the wreckage, (2) the recorded statements of witnesses, and (3) other types of evidence. Each of these kinds of evidence is discussed separately below.

2.1 EVALUATION OF WRECKAGE

2.1.1 *Comments on the Evidence.* There were three separate examinations of the wreckage: one performed in connection with the 1898 United States court of inquiry, a second performed by Spanish divers in 1898, and a third performed in connection with the 1911 board of inspection and survey. The description of the wreckage contained in the 1898 court of inquiry report was obtained basically from diver inspections in muddy water. The Spanish divers who investigated the wreck in 1898 were even more handicapped because the Spanish knew less about the ship. Between 1898 and the 1911 dewatering, various salvage operations were carried out. These may have disturbed minor elements of the wreck and the 13 years of immersion allowed powder to dissolve, steel to rust, and wood to rot; but the essential pieces of the wreck remained. The 1911 inspection was made by open-air surveys of the wreckage after it had been dewatered inside a cofferdam. This permitted accurate identification of almost every bit of wreckage, measurement of displacements, and photographic recording. Therefore, despite the time lapse between the explosion and the 1911 inspection, our study of the wreckage has been based on the 1911 data.

The statements in the 1911 report describing the wreckage and the photographs and sketches of the wreckage are generally consistent with one another. The photographs were taken as the dewatering progressed and as the wreckage was dismantled. In some cases wreckage material was removed in the interval between pictures. This was taken into account in the interpretation of the photographs.[2]

2.1.2 *Evidence of a Magazine Explosion.* The general character of the overall wrecked structure of the *Maine,* with hull sides and whole deck structures peeled back, leaves no doubt that a large internal explosion occurred. This is the immediate reaction on seeing the photographs of the wreckage. The impression is verified by the similarity to some later experience. In a recent study of warhead effectiveness, high explosive charges were fired inside destroyer hulks. Allowing for the differences in explosive type, size, and placement, the damage produced was remarkably similar to that found on the *Maine.* The internal explosion on the *Maine* was, without a doubt, a magazine explosion, since only the magazines contained an amount of explosive material sufficient to do the documented damage. The wreckage also leaves no doubt that the explosion was in the forward magazines, since the after magazines were found intact in the less damaged after portion of the ship.

2.1.3 *Magnitude and Location of Magazine Explosion.* It is quite clear that the full contents of all the forward magazines did not explode. This is proven by the fact that unexploded debris of 1-pounder, 6-pounder, 6-inch, and 10-inch ammunition was found widely scattered within and outside the wreck. The evidence was therefore examined to determine what quantities of powder did explode, and to determine the area in which the explosion was centered. This is the area we must examine to find clues for the initiating cause.

The location of the center of the explosion can be determined from the structural damage to the *Maine,* as follows. The direction and manner in which the upper decks were peeled back indicates that the center of the explosion was in the after part of the forward magazine complex. Further, the longitudinal bulkhead between the 10-inch magazine (A–13–M) and the coal bunker (A–15) on the starboard side was still attached to the inner bottom, and part of bulkhead 21 between the forward fixed ammunition room (A–9–M) and the forward 6-inch magazine (A–6–M) was still attached to the starboard side of the hull. (See forward hold plan on page 110.) Similar bulkheads on the port side were completely swept away, indicating that the explosion forces were greater on the port side than on the starboard side. Finally, the damage to the inner bottom was most severe in the region under the 6-inch reserve magazine (A–14–M), which was on the port side around frame 27. Thus, the 1911 conclusion that the center of the explosion was in the 6-inch reserve magazine is sustained by the existing evidence.

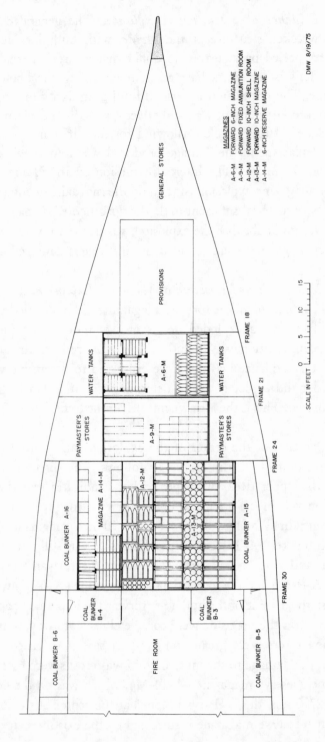

FORWARD HOLD PLAN

MAGAZINES
A-6-M   FORWARD 6-INCH MAGAZINE
A-9-M   FORWARD FIXED AMMUNITION ROOM
A-12-M   FORWARD 10-INCH SHELL ROOM
A-13-M   FORWARD 10-INCH MAGAZINE
A-14-M   6-INCH RESERVE MAGAZINE

DMW 8/19/75

SCALE IN FEET   0   5   10   15

The structural damage details also contain some evidence bearing on the amount of powder that probably exploded. Interpretation of this evidence is made possible on the basis of World War II experience with bomb explosions inside ships of light construction similar to the *Maine*. The extent of damage caused by the bombs has been related to the amount and type of explosive contained in them. Looking for the extent of similar interior blast damage on the *Maine* we find that such damage reached aft to frame 54 but not beyond. Forward of the explosion center, located around frame 27, the interior blast damage reached to the end of the bow. From this it is estimated that 10,000 to 20,000 pounds of powder exploded. The estimate takes into consideration that the *Maine* magazines contained brown prismatic powder rather than high explosive used in the bombs of World War II. It is assumed that black or brown gunpowder is two-thirds as effective in causing structural damage as the same weight of TNT.

The powder content of the forward magazines is estimated to have been:

6-inch reserve magazine (A–14–M)	11,190 pounds
Forward fixed ammunition room (A–9–M)	6,738+ pounds
Forward 10-inch shell room (A–12–M)	2,498 pounds
Forward 10-inch magazine (A–13–M)	39,500 pounds
Forward 6-inch magazine (A–6–M)	12,262 pounds
TOTAL	72,188+ pounds

With the evidence indicating that the explosion was centered in the 6-inch reserve magazine (A–14–M), and that 10,000 to 20,000 pounds of powder exploded, we can conclude that most of the 11,190 pounds in the 6-inch reserve magazine (A–14–M) exploded, possibly together with parts of the contents of adjacent magazines.[3]

2.1.4 *Bottom Damage Below Explosion Center.* The 1911 board stated its conclusion as follows:

> *The board finds that the injuries to the bottom of the Maine, above described, were caused by the explosion of a charge of a low form of explosive exterior to the ship between frames 28 and 31, strake B, port side. This resulted in igniting and exploding the contents of the 6-inch reserve magazine, A–14–M, said contents including a large quantity of black powder. The more or less complete explosion of the contents of the remaining forward magazines followed. The magazine explosions resulted in the destruction of the vessel.[4]*

This finding was based almost entirely on the appearance of the wrecked bottom structure on the port side located approximately between frames 22 and 33. Using the frames and the strakes (the longitudinal

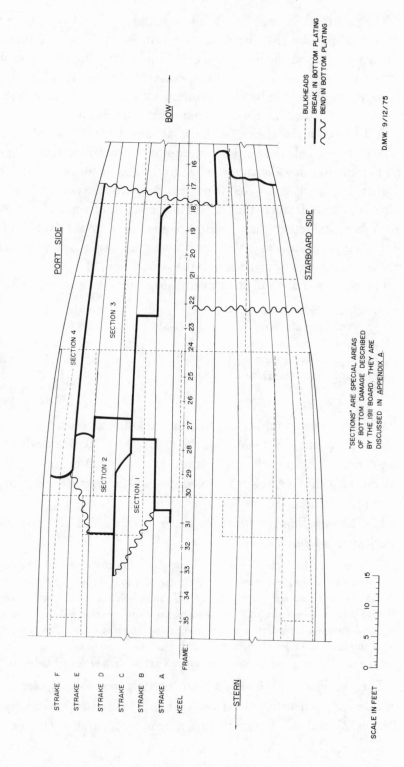

BOTTOM PLATING DAMAGE

"SECTIONS" ARE SPECIAL AREAS
OF BOTTOM DAMAGE DESCRIBED
BY THE 1911 BOARD. THEY ARE
DISCUSSED IN APPENDIX A.

D.M.W. 9/12/75

----- BULKHEADS
▬▬▬ BREAK IN BOTTOM PLATING
〜〜〜 BEND IN BOTTOM PLATING

rows of bottom plating) as references, the 1911 board identified four damaged sections of the bottom. The board reported that bottom section 1 was displaced inward, whereas adjacent sections 2, 3, and 4 were displaced outward. (The sections and strakes are illustrated on page 112.) The inward displacement of section 1 was taken by the board as proof of its conclusion quoted above. We do not believe this conclusion can be drawn from the evidence. In fact, it appears more appropriate to conclude from the total evidence that there was *no* external burst.[5] The arguments for this are as follows:

All of the bottom structure in this area was deflected downward, except (a) the section 1 piece of outer bottom plating (strakes B and C) that was folded inward over the severely crumpled inner bottom, and (b) the adjacent edge of the port garboard strake (strake A), which was bent inward slightly. The inward folded section 1 plating was bent smoothly, not severely mangled, and shows no evidence of the rupture or deformation typical of an external contact or near-contact explosion. The Spanish contact mines of the day contained a charge of 100 to 200 pounds of guncotton. Such a charge would have ruptured and mangled the outer bottom over an area of 15 to 25 feet in diameter and would most likely have ruptured the keel had it exploded at or near the B strake. This location of the charge would have been necessary if the 6-inch reserve magazine was to be ignited by the burst. The keel was not broken in that area, and the outer bottom plating does not exhibit the mangling expected from an outside burst. It also appears that the inner bottom plating was more mangled than the outer bottom plating in the region, which again is contrary to expectations if an external burst had taken place.[6]

If an external burst did not take place in the vicinity of frame 30, the inboard folding of the section 1 portion of the bottom plating in that area must be accounted for in some other way. A simple explanation is not to be found. However, some possible ways in which it could have occurred are as follows. The 6-inch reserve magazine was bounded by transverse bulkheads at frames 24 and 30, and by two longitudinal bulkheads, of which the inboard one was directly over the B strake. There was also a longitudinal web between the inner and outer bottom plating at the B strake. When the magazine exploded, both bottom platings and the bulkheads were ruptured. It appears plausible that the inner bottom around the boundaries of section 1 plating could have ruptured prior to the bulkheads. Then, when the bulkheads were displaced violently an instant later, the attached pieces of the bottom structure were whipped upward. In the process, the inner bottom plating became folded up and the longitudinal web was torn loose and also whipped up.[7]

Another phenomenon which may have contributed to the final position of the section 1 bottom plating is the following. The ruptures in the bottom would have permitted some of the high pressure explosive gases from the magazine to expand into the bottom structure, pushing it sideways, and also below the ship pushing the water aside. The subsequent return rush of the water and rapid flooding into the ship could have caused the unstiffened, unsupported outer bottom plating to be bent inward to its final position.

The inward bending of the edge of the port garboard strake (strake A) of bottom plating can be explained as follows. Before the explosion the edge of strake A was riveted to bottom section 1. When section 1 was whipped upward, by either of the above described mechanisms, the edge of strake A was carried along until the rivets failed. Another effect which could have contributed to the inward bending of both section 1 and strake A was the force of hitting the harbor bottom when the ship sank immediately after the explosion.

Although these explanations of the condition of the plate are conjectural, an occurrence such as the inward folding of section 1 is not unique in the field of structural response to explosive loads. The overall weight of the evidence obtainable from the damaged bottom of the *Maine* points towards the absence of an external burst.

2.1.5 *Damage to Keel and Bow.* The 1898 court of inquiry concluded that the *Maine* explosion was initiated by a mine below the ship in the area near frame 18. The principal evidence advanced to support this was the appearance of the keel in the region of frames 18 to 22, and the position of the bow section, as these were revealed by diver inspections. The keel was bent into an inverted V shape ($\wedge$) with the top of the V above water, and the bow section was turned to port and capsized on its starboard side. These displacements were thought to have been due to an external burst below the keel near frame 18. This location is below the forward 6-inch magazine (A–6–M).[8]

After the wreck was dewatered, the 1911 board concluded that the explosion was not centered at frame 18, but in the 6-inch reserve magazine (A–14–M) near frame 27, and that it was initiated by an external burst below that location. As indicated in the previous sections, our examination of the evidence confirms this location of the explosion center, but not that the explosion was initiated by an external burst. Thus, the evidence in no way supports the 1898 conclusion. The V shape of the keel and the capsizing of the forward section were secondary results of the magazine explosion and have no bearing on whether there was an external burst. They are, nevertheless, on the surface rather surprising phenomena. To complete our discussion of the wreckage evidence, the following explanation is advanced for the positions of the keel and bow.

The explosion destroyed the hull girder by removing the sides, rupturing the decks, and decreasing the spacing between inner and outer bottoms. The forward section was separated from the after section, except where the two were connected by the keel and adjacent bottom plating, mostly on the starboard side. The protective deck was broken at frame 24 by the explosion. Most of the forward portion of this deck was folded upward and forward over the bow, carrying portions of the berth, main, and superstructure decks along. Another phase of the destruction then followed as a result of the sinking motions of the forward and after sections. The repositioning of the protective deck and other weights made the forward section extremely unstable and it capsized onto its starboard side. Although the remaining bottom structure connecting the forward and after sections did contain some unbroken structural members, they alone were not strong enough, without the support of the ship sides and decks, to resist the bending and twisting exerted by the capsizing forward section of the ship. Because of the shape of the remaining portion of the forward section and its top-heavy condition, the after end of the keel of the forward section at about frame 17 was raised well above its normal position. This bent the keel and the attached bottom plating into a vertical position between 21 and 17, as noted in both the 1898 and the 1911 investigations. The after section of the hull was flooded through the hole so that the intact after section of the ship inclined down at its forward end. Since the bottom structure connecting the forward and after sections was probably already on the bottom of the harbor at frame 21, the continued sinking of the after section bent the keel and bottom in the vicinity of frame 35 by pressing the bottom of the ship between frames 35 and 21 against the harbor bottom or by hanging it from the capsized forward section at frame 17.[9]

The precise sequence of events that occurred cannot be established without experiment or further study, but it seems clear that the general mechanism explaining the final gross condition of the forward section of the wreck does not involve an explosion external to the hull.

2.2 EVALUATION OF EYEWITNESS REPORTS OF EXPLOSION PHENOMENA

2.2.1 *General Comments.* Although individual eyewitness reports usually are not reliable, it was quite proper that the 1898 court of inquiry collected such evidence. Nearly every witness before the 1898 court of inquiry was asked to describe, in as much detail as possible, his impressions of the explosion phenomena. The court's conclusion that there were two explosions must have been based on eyewitness descriptions. The 1911 report accepted and restated this conclusion. We think the evidence does not support it.

Eyewitness reports of the explosion phenomena are evaluated in the following to determine what can and cannot be learned from them. The reports fall into two categories, observations from other ships and those made by survivors on board the *Maine*. The reports vary considerably in detail, as can be expected. No one in either group of observers reported seeing any surface phenomena: spray dome or plume, which might have come from an under-water explosion. However, since the night was dark, this is not surprising. No witness gave a clear description of certain rather awe-inspiring phenomena which must have occurred, such as the inversion of the pilot house and conning tower or the movement of the forward 10-inch gun turret over the starboard side of the ship. At least one witness said the bow sank immediately, but whether this was because he saw it sink, or just believed it must have, is impossible to tell. A great many of the observers made contradictory reports, or reported events that were not evidenced in the final condition of the hull. Typical accounts, including those considered to be most consistent and reliable, are discussed in the following.

2.2.2 *Observations from Other Ships.* Most people reported hearing a double explosion. People at the greatest distances indicated the greatest time difference between the two sounds. For example, the master of the ship *Deva*, Captain Frederick G. Teasdale, felt the first shock and ran on deck where he heard what he reported as the main explosion. His position was between one-quarter and one-half mile from the *Maine*.[10] The following explanation of his observation can be made. The shock and sound waves from an explosion travel faster through water than through air. It is to be expected in a case such as the *Maine* magazine explosion that observers at some distance would hear the water sound wave before the arrival of the sound wave through the air. The sensing of two shocks or sounds was a function of where the observer was. At the position of Captain Teasdale, the travel time for an underwater shock is about half a second, and for an air blast, two and one-half to three seconds. Captain Teasdale could probably have reached his deck in two to three seconds. Thus what he heard could well have been one explosion, transmitted first through water, then later through air. Similar explanations for the reported two explosions can be accepted for other remote witnesses and fit present knowledge of explosion phenomena. The fact that two phases were heard by some people does not indicate that there were two explosions.

2.2.3 *Observations By Witnesses On Board the* Maine. The testimony of people on board the *Maine* concerning their impressions of the initial sounds and the initial movements of the ship also varies considerably. In general, they seem to verify the motions which can be expected from an internal explosion. One of the clearest testimonies was that of Naval Cadet Wat T. Cluverius, who was in his quarters (located at frame 57 on the extreme starboard side) at the time of the explosion. He said:

(1) "My first knowledge of anything occurring was a slight shock as if a 6-pounder gun had been fired somewhere about the deck."
(2) "After that a very great vibration in my room, which
(3) was then followed by a very heavy shock, and
(4) still continued vibration and rushing of water through the junior officers' mess room, and the sound as if something breaking up all the time." [11]

Cadet Cluverius' observations were amazingly perceptive. They can be explained as follows. Observation (1) describes the structure-borne shock or sound wave from the explosion; observation (2) describes the structural vibrations transmitted from the dynamically loaded and failing structure near the explosion; observation (3) describes the shock transmitted from the blast-loaded structure nearer his position, which loading occurred later because of the time it takes for the blast wave to travel through the air; observation (4) describes the vibration motions and sounds arising from large structural pieces, e.g., decks falling back on the remaining structure and from the sinking of the ship. Thus, the observations made by Cadet Cluverius appear to describe the sounds and motions to be expected from an internal burst.

Another witness, Lieutenant George F. M. Holman, stated that, "It was precisely similar to many other submarine explosions I have heard, except that it was on a much larger scale." Although this witness had some prior experience with underwater explosions, he could hardly have had much experience with *internal* explosions. He could therefore, not be expected to be able to distinguish between internal and external explosions. It is possible that the 1898 inquiry put too much stock in his words because of his experience with underwater explosions.[12]

None of the witnesses on board described motions which unmistakably can be ascribed to an external explosion. Unfortunately, this absence cannot be taken as positive proof that an external explosion did not occur, for both technical reasons and because of the unreliability of witnesses in such matters. The phenomena occur very rapidly, and even trained observers, who know what to expect, have difficulty in discerning them. The Spanish used a Latimer-Clark mine with a charge of 500 pounds of nitrocellulose in the later mining of the Havana harbor entrance. If such a mine had been exploded on the bottom, about 14 feet below the keel of the *Maine,* at least some of the witnesses should have noticed a very pronounced upward shock motion almost together with the first sound. There is no report of such an upward shock motion, indicating that it is reasonably certain that a large bottom mine was not exploded. If, on the other hand, a contact mine had exploded against the ship, the response of the ship to the underwater shock wave would have been much reduced. This is because the explosion largely vents into the ship, thus reducing the shock in the water. The shock response is also reduced because the angle of attack of the shock wave is 90 degrees (i.e., parallel to the ship bottom) rather than more perpendicular to the ship bottom as would be the case for a bottom mine. The shock response discussed here is the immediate elastic structural response to the underwater shock wave. The longer duration large whipping motions which would result from either a contact or a bottom mine explosion, if the magazine did not explode, would most likely have been obscured, eliminated, or at least greatly modified by the overpowering response to the magazine explosion.

In summary, observations by people on board the *Maine* concerning the initial sounds and ship motions confirm the magazine explosion. They also indicate that a bottom mine explosion in all likelihood did not occur, but they cannot provide positive proof that an external explosion in contact with the ship bottom did or did not occur.

2.3 EVALUATION OF MISCELLANEOUS EVIDENCE

There are several categories of evidence which do not fit into the previously considered categories of "wreckage" and "eyewitness reports." They are, however, valid areas of concern in the total picture of evidence. They are examined in the following sections.

2.3.1 *Absence of Dead Fish After the Explosion.* The 1898 Spanish board of inquiry took up the question of fish kill in some detail. The question was barely touched upon in the American court of inquiry. The Spanish knew, as did the Americans no doubt, that an underwater explosion will kill fish that are within range. A bottom detonation of 500 pounds of high explosive would probably have caused free-swimming fish to surface within a radius of 250 to 300 yards of the ship. A 100-pound contact charge would have injured fish out to a radius of 200 to 250 yards. On the other hand, even a violent deflagration of the powder in one or more of the magazines inside the ship might not harm the fish at a modest distance from the ship. The type of underwater pressure waves generated by slow-burning black or brown powder are relatively innocuous to fish, even when the explosions occur in the water. Dead fish were not noticed after the *Maine* explosion, although much other debris was found. The Spanish took this as evidence of the absence of an external explosion. However, such a conclusion cannot properly be drawn. The only thing that can be said is that either there was no external explosion, or there were no fish nearby, or there were no dead fish found. Underwater explosion tests have often been carried out in modern times with no fish kill resulting, simply because there were no fish within range. Thus, the absence of dead fish is inconclusive evidence, one way or the other. Had the evidence been reversed, that is, if dead fish had been found at some distance from the explosion, then it could have been concluded that in all likelihood an underwater explosion had taken place.[13]

2.3.2 *Absence of Remnants of a Mine or Torpedo Casing.* No remnants of a mine or torpedo casing were reported found. If a sizable mine or torpedo had indeed exploded, some remnants of the casing would have existed.[14] However, the lack of remnants cannot be taken as positive proof that a mine or torpedo was not employed. The pieces could have been buried in the mud and thus not found.

2.3.3 *Feasibility of Placing a Mine Near the* Maine. Either civilian or military persons might have wanted to place a mine under the *Maine*. Although no firm evidence of any intent to place a mine near the *Maine* has ever been produced and verified, the feasibility of such an operation has been examined as follows.

If civilians had attempted it, they would have had to find the right people, the right equipment, and enough explosive to do the job. The problems of manufacturing a functional, watertight mine are much greater than those encountered in making a satchel-bomb, such as might be used by a terrorist gang. During the Vietnam War, the Viet-Cong/North Vietnamese trained underwater sappers for six months or more, depending on the type of target (bridges, ships, etc.) for which they were being trained. In the field the sappers spent as much as a month studying a particular target. Then, several dry runs and inspections were often made before trying to explode a charge. Their swimmers were not able to handle more than 200 pounds of an explosive device at one time, even in water; larger charges were built up of pieces carried in separately. River current was often used to help carry the material into place without vigorous swimming. It is quite evident that the mining of a ship is not a simple task, even when using trained personnel, waterproof high explosives, and sophisticated firing equipment. The availability of such equipment to civilians of Havana in 1898 is highly improbable. Further, it is almost beyond doubt that civilians had inadequate warning time to prepare and place a mine in the harbor before the *Maine* arrived. A covert operation after the ship was moored would have been additionally difficult since the ship was well guarded.

If the *Maine* had been mined by military persons, some of the difficulties would have been reduced. Explosives, complete harbor defense mines, and personnel trained in mine laying could have been available. The force detailed (after the war started) to mine the harbor entrance and control the mines consisted of 39 officers and men. Most of these seem to have been crew for mine and cable-laying boats. There were only two torpedomen and two gunners. So far as is known, these forces were not trained for or supplied with equipment for covert mining or underwater demolition.

If military forces had attempted to mine the *Maine,* they would have employed one of four types of mines, (1) a mine located on the harbor bottom and wired for remote electrical initiation (controlled bottom mine), (2) a buoyant submerged mine moored to an anchor and wired for remote initiation (controlled moored mine), (3) a buoyant submerged mine moored to an anchor and fitted with fuzes that explode when the mine contacts any substantial object (contact mine), and (4) a mine attached to the ship and equipped with a time fuze (limpet mine). The placing of these mines is discussed in the following paragraphs.

A controlled bottom mine could have been placed in the harbor before the ship arrived, although the mooring location of the ship could not have been known with any assurance. Several locations would have had to be mined. Thus, the mining would have involved a considerable effort, and the effort would have been unusual from a military point of view. If a harbor is to be mined, the logical location to place the mines is at the harbor entrance. It is doubtful that a considerable mining effort within the harbor would have gone unnoticed, or could have been concealed during the later inquiries. The covert placing of a bottom mine after the *Maine* was moored would have been difficult. To lay the available Latimer-Clark electrically controlled bottom mine and associated cable is believed to have required the services of a launch and a number of men. It is difficult to see how they could have gone unnoticed by the well-guarded *Maine*. Finally, a bottom mine is believed incapable of igniting a magazine, as further discussed in section 2.3.4.

A controlled moored mine could have been used, with about the same difficulties as indicated above for the controlled bottom mine. The length of the moor would determine whether the mine would be under the ship or collide with the ship side. The mooring length would have to be exactly the right length for the mine to be closely below the ship, and thus be effective in igniting the magazine, as further discussed in section 2.3.4. The right mooring length could hardly have been known before the *Maine* arrived. In fact, the correct mooring length could not have been determined without experimenting to see how far the anchor would sink into the muddy bottom. An effective controlled moored mine would have been even more difficult to place near the *Maine* than a bottom mine.

A moored contact mine would, in all probability, have had to be placed covertly after the arrival of the *Maine*. If it was planted beforehand, it would have been a hazard to innocent vessels in transit through the harbor, or part of the harbor would have been deliberately closed off until the *Maine* arrived. This would have been difficult to conceal. The covert placing of such a mine after the ship was moored would have been just as difficult as placing the previously discussed mine types. The mooring length for this type would also have to be the correct length for the mine to be effective. This, again, would compound the difficulties.

A limpet type mine could conceivably have been placed against the ship bottom. It would have been ineffective if placed against the ship side, as will be outlined in section 2.3.4. It would have had to have some means for attachment such that it would remain under the ship bottom for some time. Also, it would have had to be a rather large charge to accomplish the result noted. The placing of a large limpet mine below the *Maine* would have required several accomplished underwater swimmers and, if a magazine was to be intentionally ignited, a thorough knowledge of the ship would be necessary.

It is difficult to see how such an operation could be carried out in muddy water, with the diving equipment available in 1898, without being noticed by the guarded vessel.

In summary, the difficulties involved in placing a mine of sufficient size and in the right location to explode the *Maine* would have been great. It is most unlikely that civilians were able to do it, and it is very doubtful that military personnel could have accomplished it without the operation being noticed.[15]

2.3.4 *Capability of an External Burst to Ignite the Magazine.* Even if the successful mining of the *Maine* was accomplished, the capability of an external burst to ignite magazine A–14–M is questionable. Direct technical data, empirical or otherwise, to determine without a doubt whether or not such an ignition could occur are not available today. It is known that black and brown powders are sensitive to heat. They have an ignition temperature of about 280 degrees centigrade. But powder is relatively bullet-insensitive and powder magazines are, therefore, not ordinarily required to be of bulletproof construction. Shock sensitivity tests, which have been carried out by dropping a weight on a small amount of explosive, have shown black powder to be slightly more sensitive than TNT and far less sensitive than such explosives as mercury fulminate (used for detonators) and dynamites. The sensitivity of powder to shock, flame, and heat was controlled to some extent on the *Maine* by the storage of powder in copper cans (tanks), by cooling the magazines by natural ventilation, and by incorporating space and proper dunnage in the magazine construction. The copper cans retarded the spread of flame and protected the powder from contact with steel, which might have caused sparks. The construction of the ship, with a double bottom, coal bunkers outboard of the magazines, and with the powder cans in wooden racks, provided considerable mitigation of shock transmitted from an external explosion. That the powder was insensitive to shock, and that the copper cans and ship bulkheads were somewhat effective in limiting the spread of an explosion, is shown by the fact that only a small portion of the total amount of powder available in the forward magazines did explode (see section 2.1.3).[16]

The transmittal into the magazine of shock and thermal effects from an underwater explosion would vary with location, standoff, and size of the burst. The following categories of burst locations are discussed: (1) a burst at some standoff below the ship, such as a bottom mine or a controlled moored mine with a short moor, (2) a burst in contact with the ship bottom or very close to it, such as a moored mine with just the right length of moor, or a limpet mine, and (3) a burst in contact with the ship side or at some standoff from it, such as a moored mine with a long moor. It is a reasonable assumption that the biggest mine that would have been available was of the Latimer-Clark type with 500 pounds of explosive.

A bottom mine would have had the greatest standoff below the ship. The harbor bottom was about 14 feet below the keel. At this standoff even the largest mine, with the 500 pound charge, would most likely not have ignited the magazine. A burst at this standoff would cave in and rupture the ship bottom directly overhead over an area of 25 to 40 feet in diameter. However, the expansion of the gaseous products from the explosion would drive huge quantities of water into the hole. This would tend to quench a fire or powder explosion if initiation was caused beforehand by the shock. This "quenching" effect would also occur for bursts somewhat closer to the ship than the 14 feet to the harbor bottom. If, however, the burst were too close to the ship bottom the immediate "quenching" effect would be reduced, and the effects would be nearly that of a contact burst considered next.

A burst in contact with the ship bottom directly below the magazine will immediately transmit shock and hot gases into the magazine, provided the charge is big enough. A charge of at least 50 to 100 pounds is believed to have been required to transmit substantial shock and heat through the empty double bottom and into the magazine. After the external burst goes off, the magazine would have to explode within a second or two, before the water rushes in through the hole and quenches the conflagration. The 50 to 100 pound charge size required for an underbottom burst to be success-ful, tends to rule out the possibility of a limpet mine. However, the Spanish contact mines of the day contained a charge of 100 to 200 pounds of gun-cotton. Such a mine, moored and exploding close under the magazine, cannot be completely ruled out as the source on the basis of its capability to ignite the magazine.

An external burst against the side of the ship or at some distance from it could arise from a moored mine with a length of moor too long to permit the mine to go under the ship. The possibility of either fire, shock, or hot metal reaching the magazine from such a burst is remote because of the full coal bunker (A–16) positioned between the 6-inch reserve magazine (A–14–M) and the hull plating.

In summary, the mines available in 1898 are believed to have been incapable of igniting the *Maine* magazine if they exploded on the harbor bottom or against the ship side. Only a mine with at least 50 to 100 pounds of explosive bursting on contact, or near contact, with the ship bottom below the magazine, would have had any chance of igniting the magazine. This tends to rule out a limpet mine, but not a Spanish contact mine of the day with 100 to 200 pounds of explosive. However, such a mine would have had to be placed with exactly the right length of moor, and it would have been extremely difficult to place without discovery, as discussed in section 2.3.3. Further, such a burst would have caused the mangling of the ship bottom which is characteristic of an external burst. This type of damage was not found in the examination of evidence from the wreckage (see section 2.1.4). Thus, it is most unlikely that the *Maine* explosion was indeed initiated by a mine.

2.3.5 *Possible Internal Sources of Explosion.* If an external source did not cause the *Maine* explosion, the question immediately arises as to what internal source might have been responsible. Several possible internal sources have been suggested: a bunker fire, crew sabotage, a small arms accident, a bomb planted by a visitor, etc. We consider the first of these the most likely, although there is no way of completely ruling out the others. The feasibility and likelihood of a bunker fire being the source is discussed in the following.

A fire in bunker A–16 adjacent to the 6-inch reserve magazine is a probable source of the explosion because (1) frequent bunker fires did occur on warships of that period, (2) the brand of bituminous coal in the A–16 bunker is known to have caused fires by spontaneous combustion, (3) the coal had been in bunker A–16 since loading at Newport News, Virginia, about three months earlier, (4) the bulkhead between the bunker (A–16) and the 6-inch reserve magazine (A–14–M) was a single steel plate, probably ¼-inch thick, (5) tanks of both brown powder and black saluting powder were stored in the 6-inch reserve magazine right against the bulkhead or at least very close to the bulkhead, and (6) ventilation of the bunkers was natural through a vent pipe to the forward stack. This stack was not in use, thus perhaps making the ventilation insufficient to prevent a rise in bunker temperature.[17]

The longer coal remained in a bunker, the more susceptible it was to spontaneous combustion. *Navy Regulations* required that the bunkers be inspected by the engineering officer before 10:00 a.m. each day. On the *New York* in March of 1897, a bunker fire occurred only three and one-half hours after the last normal inspection. The coal had been loaded on board only 14 days when the fire broke out. The *Maine* had the same brand of coal in bunker A–16, and it had been on board three months. The explosion on the *Maine* occurred nearly 12 hours after the last required inspection time. This would indicate ample time, regardless of the inspection, for the initiation of a bunker fire, heating of the bulkhead, transmission of the heat to nearby powder tanks, and deflagration of the powder.[18]

It is evident that the storage of coal was hazardous. In the years between 1894 and 1908, more than 20 coal bunker fires were reported on United States naval ships. From the facts that extra bulkheads were ordered installed in the *New York* and that new ships had double bulkheads surrounding the magazines, it is evident that a number of people in the United States Navy did not believe that the single bulkhead system on the *Maine* was safe.[19]

3. SUMMARY

1. The object of this examination was to determine if present-day knowledge of explosion phenomena and their effects on ship structures could provide new insight into the question of whether the *Maine* explosion was initiated externally or internally.

2. The analyzed factual knowledge concerning the *Maine* disaster was obtained from the records of the American and Spanish courts of inquiry of 1898, the records from the American board of inspection and survey of 1911, and certain other contemporary technical data. The evidence from the *Maine* explosion is of three kinds: (1) data from examination of the wreckage, (2) the recorded statements of witnesses, and (3) other types of evidence. The analysis of the wreckage made here has been based on the 1911 data, since it has to be considered more reliable than the data obtained from the 1898 inspections.

3. The general character of the overall wreck as revealed in photographs, drawings, and descriptions leaves no doubt that a large internal explosion occurred. The explosion was, without a doubt, a magazine explosion, since only the magazines contained sufficient explosive material to do the documented damage. Examination of the structural details of the wreck show that the explosion was centered in the 6-inch reserve magazine (A–14–M) which is on the port side around frame 27. This location of the explosion center was correctly determined by the 1911 board. From an analysis of the extent of the damage to the ship it is concluded that most of the 11,190 pounds of powder in the 6-inch reserve magazine (A–14–M) exploded, possibly together with parts of the contents of adjacent magazines. This amount is

approximately one-sixth of the total amount of powder in the forward magazine complex.

4. The 1911 board concluded that an explosion exterior to the ship took place, resulting in ignition and explosion of the magazine. This finding was based almost entirely on the appearance of the wrecked bottom structure, which included an inward displaced section below the magazine. This conclusion is believed erroneous because (1) the outer bottom plating and the keel were not mangled within an area of 15 to 25 feet in diameter in the manner to be expected if a charge sufficiently large to ignite the magazine had exploded in contact with the outer bottom, (2) the inner bottom plating was more mangled than the outer bottom plating, contrary to what would be expected if an external burst had taken place, and (3) the inward displacement of one bottom section can be plausibly explained as a result of an internal explosion. Thus, the overall weight of the evidence obtainable from the damaged bottom of the *Maine* strongly points towards the absence of an external burst.

5. The 1898 court of inquiry's conclusion that an external burst took place below the ship near frame 18 was based on the appearance of the keel in that area. It was bent into an inverted V shape (∧) with the top of the V above water. The 1911 board did not agree with this conclusion because it found that the explosion was centered at about frame 27. However, the 1911 board proceeded to find its own explanation for an external burst, as indicated in paragraph 4 above. The evidence does not support the 1898 conclusion: the explosion center was indeed not where the court of inquiry thought, and the inverted V-shape of the keel can be satisfactorily explained as a result of an internal burst alone.

6. The 1898 court of inquiry's conclusion that two explosions took place must have been based on the reports of eyewitnesses who testified that two sounds were heard. The conclusion is likely erroneous. The witnesses probably heard the sound from one explosion, transmitted first through water, then later through air.

7. The recorded observations by people on board the *Maine* concerning the initial sounds and ship motions confirm the magazine explosion. They also indicate that a bottom mine explosion in all likelihood did not occur, but they cannot provide positive proof that an external explosion in contact with the ship bottom did or did not occur.

8. The apparent absence of dead fish in the water around the wreck cannot be taken as positive proof that an external burst did not take place. It means

only that either there was no external explosion, or there were no fish nearby, or there were no dead fish found.

9. The apparent absence of remnants of a mine or torpedo casing cannot be taken as positive proof that a mine or torpedo was not employed. The remnants could have been buried in the mud and thus not found.

10. The mines available in 1898 are believed to have been incapable of igniting the *Maine* magazines if they exploded on the harbor bottom or against the ship side. Only a mine with at least 50 to 100 pounds of explosive bursting in contact, or near contact, with the ship bottom below the magazine, would have had any chance of igniting the magazine. This tends to rule out a limpet mine, but not a Spanish contact mine of the day with 100 to 200 pounds of explosive. However, such a mine would have had to be placed with exactly the right length of moor to bring the mine sufficiently close to the bottom of the ship, and it would have been extremely difficult to place. It is most unlikely that civilians were able to do it, and it is very doubtful that military personnel could have accomplished it without the operation being noticed. Further, such a burst would have caused the mangling of the ship bottom which is characteristic of an external burst, and this type of damage was not found in the evidence from the wreckage. Thus, there is no evidence to indicate that the *Maine* explosion was indeed initiated by a mine. In fact, all the evidence points to the absence of an external burst.

11. Possible internal sources of the *Maine* explosion include a coal bunker fire, crew sabotage, a small arms accident, a bomb planted by a visitor, etc. Although there is no way of completely ruling out any of these, the most likely source is a fire in bunker A–16 adjacent to the 6-inch reserve magazine. This opinion is supported by the facts that frequent bunker fires did occur on warships of that period, the brand of bituminous coal in the A–16 bunker is known to have caused fires by spontaneous combustion, the coal had been in the bunker long enough to ignite spontaneously, and the coal bunker was separated by only a single thickness bulkhead from powder tanks stowed right against the bulkhead or at least very close to the bulkhead in the magazine.

4. CONCLUSION

We have found no technical evidence in the records examined that an external explosion initiated the destruction of the *Maine*. The available evidence is consistent with an internal explosion alone. We therefore conclude that an internal source was the cause of the explosion. The most likely source was heat from a fire in the coal bunker adjacent to the 6-inch reserve magazine. However, since there is no way of proving this, other internal causes cannot be eliminated as possibilities.

SIGNED:

25 November 1975

IB S. HANSEN   ROBERT S. PRICE
David W. Taylor Naval Ship   *Naval Surface Weapons Center*
Research and Development Center

NOTES FOR APPENDIX A

1. The records which Mr. Hansen and Mr. Price examined during the preparation of this analysis included: U.S. Congress, Senate, *Message from the President of the United States Transmitting the Report of the Naval Court of Inquiry Upon the Destruction of the United States Battle Ship Maine in Havana Harbor, February 15, 1898, Together with the Testimony Taken Before the Court*, 55th Congress, 2d session, 1898, Document 207 (hereafter cited as *Court of Inquiry*); Report of the Spanish Naval Board of Inquiry As to the Cause of the Destruction of the U.S.B.S. Maine, in *Report of the Committee on Foreign Relations, United States Senate, Relative to Affairs in Cuba*, 55th Congress, 2d session, April 13, 1898, Senate Report 885; the final report of the 1911 Vreeland board of inspection and survey printed as, U.S. Congress, House of Representatives, *Report on the Wreck of the Maine*, 62d Congress, 2d session, 1911, Document 310 (hereafter cited as *1911 Board*) coupled with Naval Constructor Ferguson's reports from Havana in 1911 found in RG. 38, E. 242, Binder 108, *NA* and the Navy Department file on the 1911 board of inspection and survey: RG. 80, E. 19, File 6658, *NA*, (hereafter cited as *Vreeland Board File*). Also examined were ship's plans of the *Maine* (old): 103–6–12 "Berth Deck, 1897": 103–3–41 "Transverse Bulkheads, 1887": 103–3–43 "Hold and Magazines, 1887": 103–6–7 "Hold Plan, 1897": 103–3–40 "Expansion Plan of Outside Plating, 1887": 103–3–44 "Longitudinal Elevation, 1887": 103–3–49 "Main Deck Plating and Framing, 1887": 103–3–42 "Inboard Longitudinal Elevation": 1–9–22 "Platform Deck Plating and Framing, 1887 with 1892 Notations": 103–3–32 "Platform Deck": 103–3–46 "Sheer, Half Breadth, and Body Plan, 1887": 103–6–14 "Superstructure Deck." All plans within RG. 19, E. 126, *NA*.

2. Photographs and drawings of the wreckage are in Ferguson's reports: RG. 38, E. 242, Binder 108, *NA*. The exhibits which accompanied the report of the Vreeland board of inspection and survey in 1911 were never published but most may be found in *Vreeland Board File*.

3. For a description of unexploded debris, see: *1911 Board*, paragraphs 36 and 43 (pp. 10–11). The estimated contents of the magazines were computed from: Sigsbee to Commandant, Navy-Yard and Station, June 30, 1897 reproduced as Exhibit G in *Court of Inquiry*, pp. 292–293, "Table of Elements for Naval Guns, 1886" on page 47 in J. F. Meigs and R. R. Ingersoll, *Text-Book of Ordnance and Gunnery* (Annapolis: U.S. Naval Institute, 1887), and *Description of Ammunition Used in the Naval Service and Instructions for Preparing Same for Issue*, U.S. Navy, Bureau of Ordnance (Newport, Rhode Island: Naval Torpedo Station Print., 1896), pp. 10, 15, 23, 24. For the extent of damage, see: *1911 Board*, paragraph 26 (p. 8).

4. The conclusion is italicized paragraph 43 (p. 11), *1911 Board*. The 6-inch reserve magazine (A–14–M) had, in addition to 164 charges (7,690 pounds) of brown prismatic powder for the 6-inch guns, 3,500 pounds of black powder stored in bulk containers. The black powder was used to refill blank saluting cartridges for the 6-pounder guns and used for bursting charges in shells.

5. The appearance of the wrecked bottom structure on the port side between frames 22 and 33 is described in *1911 Board*, paragraphs 30–35 (pp. 9–10). Bottom section 1 is described in paragraph 31 and bottom sections 2, 3, and 4 are described within paragraphs 33, 34, and 35. Bottom sections 1 through 4 are outlined on the drawing marked Exhibit G in *Vreeland Board File* and the sections also appear in the photographs forming Exhibits D–1 through D–8 in *Vreeland Board File*.

6. The smoothness of the inward folded section 1 is demonstrated in *Vreeland Board File*, Exhibits D–1, 2, and 3. For descriptions of typical Spanish mines of the 1898 period, see: M. Pluddemann, "Main Features of the Spanish-American War," War Note 2, p. 12, in *Spanish American War Notes 1–8*, Office of Naval Intelligence (Washington: Government Printing Office, 1898); French E. Chadwick, *The Relations of the United States and Spain. The Spanish-American War* 1 (New York: Charles Scribner's Sons, 1911): 80. The Navy Memorial Museum at the Washington Navy Yard has a Spanish mine which is reported to have been removed from Havana Harbor in 1899. Illustrations of the type of damage which might be expected from underwater explosions can be found in A. H. Keil, "The Response of Ships to Underwater Explosions," David Taylor Model Basin Report number 1576, November 1961. That the inner bottom was more mangled than the outer bottom may be seen in Exhibit D–1 in the *Vreeland Board File*.

7. The shape of the longitudinal web, frames 24 to 30, is seen in Exhibit D–1, *Vreeland Board File*.

8. The reference to the inverted V shape is in *Court of Inquiry*, p. 281.

9. The destruction of the hull girder is evidenced in Exhibits D–6 and D–7 of the *Vreeland Board File*. The movement of the protective deck, carrying with it parts of the berth, main, and superstructure decks, is seen in Exhibits C–3, D–9, D–10, D–11, and E of the *Vreeland Board File*. The vertical portion of the keel between frames 17 and 21 and the reversed V shape appear in Exhibits C–4, D–6, D–8, D–10, D–11, and F of the *Vreeland Board File*.

10. Captain Teasdale's description is in *Court of Inquiry*, p. 53.

11. Cluverius' statements are in *Court of Inquiry*, p. 30.

12. Holman's testimony is in *Court of Inquiry*, p. 22.

13. Two articles which concern the effects of underwater explosions upon fish are: Ermine A. Christian, "The Effects of Underwater Explosions on Swimbladder Fish," Naval Ordnance Laboratory Technical Report number 73–103, July 1973, and Carl L. Hubbs and Andreas B. Rechnitzer, "Report on Experiments Designed to Determine Effects of Underwater Explosions on Fish Life," in *California Fish and Game* 38 (July 1952): 333–366.

14. In at least one well-documented case concerning a ship which was torpedoed during World War II, the air flask from the afterbody of the torpedo was found in the wreckage inside the hole which was caused by the explosion of the torpedo against the side of the ship.

15. The difficulties of mining the *Maine* were recognized early. See, for example: J. T. Bucknill, "The Destruction of the Battleship 'Maine'," *Engineering* 65 (May 27, 1898): 650–651. The complexity of Spanish mine laying was observed by Americans during the war. See: *Record of Proceedings of a Court of Inquiry in the Case of Rear-Admiral Winfield S. Schley, U.S. Navy* (Washington: Government Printing Office, 1902), volume 1, p. 934; volume 2, pp. 1350, 1441, 1457–1458. The mining of Havana Harbor during the war is described in Severo Gómez Núñez, *The Spanish American War* 3 (Madrid: n.p., 1900), chapter 3.

16. The sensitivity of black powder is discussed in: *Blasters' Handbook* (Wilmington, Delaware: E. I. Du Pont de Nemours & Co., 1953).

17. Sigsbee testified before the Senate Committee on Foreign Relations on March 31, 1898 and stated that coal bunker A–16 contained New River brand bituminous coal taken on in Newport News three months prior to the explosion: U.S. Congress, Senate, *Report of the Committee on Foreign Relations, United States Senate, Relative to Affairs in Cuba*, 55th Congress, 2d session, April 13, 1898, Senate Report 885, p. 489. Specifically, New River brand coal caused bunker fires on the *New York* in March of 1897 and the *Brooklyn* in May 1898. See F. J. Schell, C. F. Snow, and C. Laird to Commanding Officer, USS *New York* and attachments, March 11, 1897, and W. S. Schley to Secretary of the Navy, May 12, 1898, both in RG. 45, E. 464, File HF, *NA*. The chemical properties of this brand of coal were analyzed at the Washington Navy Yard in 1898.

See: *Reports of the Efficiency of Various Coals 1896 to 1898, Expenses of Equipment Abroad 1902–1903, Recent Analyses of Coal at Navy-Yard, Washington, D.C.* (Washington: Government Printing Office, 1906). The stowage of powder close to the bulkheads is documented in ship's plan 158–7–3 "Stowage of Ammunition" in RG. 19, E. 126, *NA* and from testimony given in *Court of Inquiry*, pp. 143–144. The method of ventilating coal bunkers is detailed in plan 103–7–5 "Ventilating System," RG. 19, E. 126, *NA*. That the forward stack was not in use is in *Court of Inquiry*, p. 280 .

18. Regulations regarding the inspection of coal bunkers are found in *Regulations for the Government of the Navy of the United States, 1896* (Washington: Government Printing Office, 1896), p. 145. A detailed description of the discovery and characteristics of a bunker fire is in W. S. Schley to Commander-in-Chief, North Atlantic Squadron and enclosures, March 11, 1897, RG. 45, E. 464, File HF, *NA*.

19. The retrofitting of extra bulkheads on the *New York* and recognition of the unsafe design of the bunkers and magazines on ships like the *Maine* were in a report submitted by the Board to Investigate the Spontaneous Ignition of Coal to the Secretary of the Navy. It was dated January 27, 1898—less than three weeks before the *Maine* explosion. The report was published in 1906 in *Reports of the Efficiency of Various Coals . . .*, pp. 81–85. James Webb, in "Ventilation of Merchant Ships" appearing in *Transactions of the Institution of Naval Architects* 25 (1884): 276–284, estimated that between the years 1871 and 1881, 231 British merchant ships and warships were lost due to coal gas or spontaneous combustion. Numerous accounts of bunker fires may be found in RG. 45, E. 464, File HF, *NA*.

Addendum to Appendix A

This addendum illustrates by means of damage data from World War II some of the explosion effects to be expected. The samples selected demonstrate and amplify the principal arguments made in the original appendix A. Apart from a desire to clarify, the addendum is also motivated by a desire to provide answers to most of the reviewers and other authors who have raised questions and criticisms of some of the arguments leading to our conclusion.

The appearance of the bow section and the keel, bent into an inverted "V" with its top above the water, was mistakenly taken as proof of a mine explosion by the 1898 court of inquiry. The 1911 inquiry reversed this finding, correctly placing the center of the explosion some 40–45 feet farther aft in the A-14-M magazine. The 1911 board ascribed the keel and bow positions to the effects of the magazine explosion alone, but failed to adequately explain how the bow section ended up in the position it did. Our explanation is without a doubt the correct one, accounting as it does for the movement of the bow section relative to the stern section after the explosion had blown out the ship's sides and decks. Some of the deck structure was folded aft over the bridge, and some was flipped up over the bow, which became unstable and was put in rotating motion by the explosion, finally capsizing and sinking as both ends of the ship flooded. The larger stern section sank more slowly and grounded on the harbor bottom without capsizing. The cause of the "V" was the capsizing of the bow section so that the after end of its keel was brought to the surface. By sheer chance a ribbon of keel remained connected to both the bow and stern sections and formed the second leg of the "V." It is interesting to note that very similar detachments of bow sections occurred several times during World War II when bombs or torpedoes severed destroyer bows. To quote from a Bureau of Ships Damage Report: ". . . the bow section forward of the bridge containing two high mounts is top heavy as evidenced by the immediate capsizing of many bows including that of SHAW." Figures A1 and A2 illustrate the damage to the *Shaw* caused primarily by the explosion of the forward magazine set off by Japanese bombs at Pearl Harbor. The bows of World War II

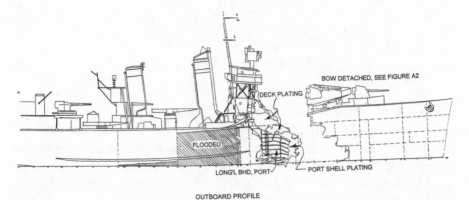

OUTBOARD PROFILE

BUREAU OF SHIPS WAR DAMAGE REPORTS, DEPARTMENT OF THE NAVY

Figure A1—Sketch of Damage to the USS *Shaw*

destroyers were top heavy because of high gun mounts, the bow of the *Maine* was top heavy because of the flipped-up decks, and capsizing occurred in both cases, although the rotation of the bow of the *Maine* was greater because of its shape—it was a ram bow with "reverse" flare (the sides sloped inward).

The 1911 board rested its case on the inward bent plate found in the wrecked bottom structure under the magazine (see photo on page 90

BUREAU OF SHIPS WAR DAMAGE REPORTS, DEPARTMENT OF THE NAVY

Figure A2—The Severed Bow Section of the USS *Shaw* after Dewatering of the Dry Dock

and figure A3). We found that this evidence does not prove an external explosion. Any explosion under the bottom that would have initiated a magazine reaction would have been violent enough to penetrate the outer hull, bottom void, and inner bottom. The best chance for such an initiation would have been with a contact or near-contact charge under the bottom, for in this case the hot and high-pressure explosion gases could impact directly on the contents of the magazine without the effect of intervening water. However, this case can definitely be ruled out because the photographs provide incontrovertible evidence that an external contact or near-contact mine explosion did not occur, for such an explosion would have distinctly mangled the outer bottom. An example of such mangling is the damage from one of the torpedo hits that the *California* received at Pearl Harbor (shown in figure A4). As seen, the edges of the hole are very ragged, and although not clear from the picture, but known from many other results of near-contact explosions, pieces of plating near the center of the damage are usually torn loose and

NA,RG.80, E.19

Figure A3—Detail of Upturned Outer Bottom Plating, Looking Aft beneath the Port Bottom

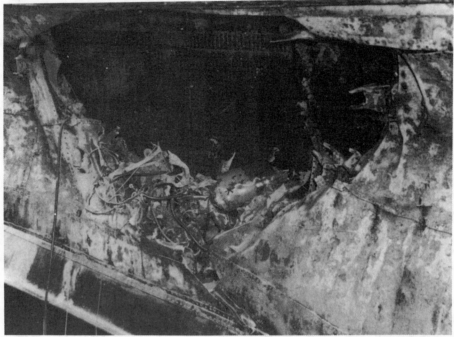

BUREAU OF SHIPS WAR DAMAGE REPORTS, DEPARTMENT OF THE NAVY

Figure A4—Torpedo Damage on the USS *California* at Pearl Harbor

projected inward, causing projectile or fragment damage to inboard structures. This happened to the *California* and to many other ships in World War II. On the *Maine,* the inward bent plate was not mangled, and no projectile or fragment holing was found. Also seen in figure A4 is the remainder of the attacking torpedo. No mine remnants were found in the wreckage of the *Maine.* Although this lack cannot be taken as positive proof that no mine exploded, it does weigh on that side of the case. The lack of mangling of the outer hull appears to have bothered the 1911 board, for why else would they make the statement that "the injuries to the bottom of the MAINE . . . were caused by the explosion of a charge of a low form of explosive exterior to the ship." They probably knew what "torpedo" (contact mine) damage normally looked like. It is a pity they did not explain what they meant by a "low form" of explosive—they may have been thinking of black or brown gunpowder. However, it should be noted that the mangling of plates can be expected to be less pronounced as the distance between the charge and the plate is increased because the intervening water spreads the loading. But as the distance from the hull to the charge is increased, the bigger the charge must be to be capable of initiating a magazine explosion. This would make the area of the local damage larger and, therefore, more likely to be detected. The character of the local damage would include ruptures of the bottom plating directly above the charge, and dishing (inward bowing) of the plating between supporting frames at the edges of the local damage. The photos (page 90 and figure A3) do not show this type of damage. On the contrary, they provide clear evidence that an external noncontact explosion did not take place under the magazine. The outer bottom plating that was smoothly bent inward was folded over the severely crumpled inner bottom. The inner bottom could not be crumpled from an external burst without the outer bottom also being crumpled or dished, and the inner bottom must have been crumpled first, or it would have stopped or hindered the inward motion of the bottom plating. The only explanation is that the magazine explosion must have crumpled the inner bottom first, while the outside water stabilized and impeded the motion of the outer bottom—a sequence that excludes an initial exterior burst. The explanation given in appendix A for the position of the upward bent plating is much more plausible than that given by the 1911 board. That plates exposed to explosions do not always get bent in the direction intuitively presumed has been seen on other occasions. For example, a torpedo hit on the *North Carolina* caused a piece of the outer plating to be bent outward (see figure A5). The explanations

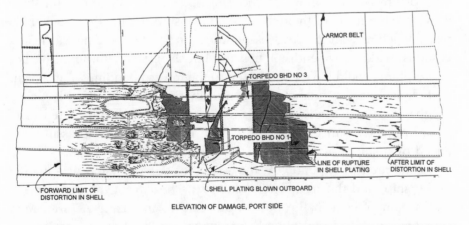

ELEVATION OF DAMAGE, PORT SIDE

BUREAU OF SHIPS WAR DAMAGE REPORTS, DEPARTMENT OF THE NAVY

Figure A5—Torpedo Damage on the USS *North Carolina*, Showing Shell Plating Blown Outboard

BUREAU OF SHIPS WAR DAMAGE REPORTS,
DEPARTMENT OF THE NAVY

Figure A6—Temporary Patch over Torpedo Damage on the USS *Saratoga*, Showing Plating Peeled Back by Action of Sea

for such phenomena are not simple, but obviously the plates follow the laws of physics and move in the direction of the net forces on them, which are the result of the difference in pressures on the two sides of the plates together with the stresses produced in the plates. Finally, the suggestions made in appendix A that the inrush of water through the bottom ruptures could have contributed to the inward bending of an unsupported plate has been labeled ludicrous by one reviewer. To this we can say that it does not take great forces to bend a long unsupported plate. Figure A6 shows an example of a plate bent by just the pressure produced by a ship moving through the water.

As indicated in appendix A, the source of the explosion was internal to the ship, and the most likely cause was heat from the spontaneous combustion of coal in the bunker adjacent to magazine A-14-M. More than one critic has questioned this conclusion, perhaps assuming that bunker fires were characterized by widespread heat and flames, which would be detected before the heat was transmitted to the magazine.

Since this is a misconception, it may be worthwhile to briefly amplify our arguments in this connection. It may be noted that contemporary reports (see notes 17–19 for appendix A) explain that coal fires were not always raging conflagrations. Spontaneous combustion could occur in coal dust collected in corners and cracks. Loading would introduce such dust, and the ship's motions and vibrations would probably add to it. With the proper coal chemistry (which existed on the *Maine*), sufficient quantity, packing density, temperature, etc., spontaneous combustion could occur. Thus, bunker fires might be burning dust in small crevasses, glowing with red-hot intensity sufficiently concentrated to burn holes in steel bulkheads, sometimes without tripping fire alarms and without being detectable by tactile inspection only a few feet away. This was possible because coal is an excellent insulator. The reports also indicate that pockets of glowing coal dust might not necessarily ignite the lump coal surrounding it. Thus, contemporary experience indicates that a bunker fire of sufficient heat could in fact have occurred without detection on the *Maine*.

It has been suggested that we started with a preconception of what happened and proceeded to prove it. To this we can say that neither of us had previously had any thoughts or knowledge of what happened, and as stated in the foreword, at no time did Admiral Rickover pressure us to provide arguments one way or the other. More than ever we are convinced that the evidence strongly supports our conclusion. Explosive damage is almost impossible to erase. Torn edges cannot be smoothed, rivets replaced, or bends straightened. With the amount of clearing and recovery of wreckage done on the *Maine,* any concentrated damage from an exterior burst would have been obvious, especially if the investigators had been looking for it, as we suspect they were. To obtain any more convincing proof of our verdict than that provided in the appendix and this addendum would require experimentation costing millions of dollars, but in the end we are certain that such experimentation would provide the same answer.

Some Aspects of International Law and the Destruction of the *Maine,* February 15, 1898

As part of the research on the loss of the *Maine,* Professor William T. Mallison of George Washington University Law School and Mrs. Sally V. Mallison, research associate in international law, answered several questions about the international law aspects of the disaster. Professor Mallison occupied the Charles H. Stockton Chair of International Law at the Naval War College in the spring of 1975 when this material was written. The questions and the replies have been arranged under the following categories: entry into Havana; a disaster occurring to a naval vessel belonging to one state while visiting the port of another state; investigation of the disaster; a summary of customary international law in 1898; and the *Maine* as a case in international law.

SURVEY OF THE LEGAL QUESTIONS PRESENTED BY ADMIRAL RICKOVER CONCERNING THE SINKING OF THE U.S.S. *MAINE* IN HAVANA HARBOR IN 1898

Note

The present survey is limited to the facts concerning the sinking of the *Maine* in 1898. It does not constitute an adequate basis for analogies or extrapolation concerning the sinking of different warships at different times and places. Because of limitations of time, this legal analysis should not be regarded as providing conclusive answers to the particular questions raised. It is analogous to the survey of a problem typically employed at an early stage by legal specialists.

The present answers are based upon some of the primary source material available in official documents as indicated in the bibliography. In addition a number of reliable secondary authorities have been used. Among the primary authorities which have not been examined are the records of the

Office of the Judge Advocate General as well as the Navy Department records in the National Archives.

I. *The Customary Law Which Provides Context and Background for the Specific Issues Arising out of the Sinking of the* Maine

The principles of customary international law applicable in the case of the *Maine* in 1898 were, in general, the outcome of diplomatic practices which had been accepted by the community of states as law. The dividing line between law and diplomatic practice which had not become law in this situation, as in many others, is far from clear. As a result, the questions to which this survey is directed cannot always be answered with the same precision and specificity with which they are asked. The answers, in many instances, must be based upon general consensus and broad trends, and when conclusions are reached, they are almost invariably subject to some exceptions.

The port of Havana, Cuba, at the time of the sinking of the *Maine,* was a part of Spain's internal waters. As the sovereign of Havana Harbor, the Spanish government had a comprehensive jurisdictional authority recognized in customary law. At the time of its sinking, the U.S.S. *Maine* with its officers and crew comprised a portion of the armed forces of the United States. As such, it was within the jurisdiction of its flag state and immune from the jurisdiction of any foreign state. These apparently opposite principles of customary law are both set forth in the famous opinion of Chief Justice Marshall for the United States Supreme Court in *The Schooner Exchange,* 7 Cranch 116 (U.S. 1812). The court stated, concerning the competency of a state over its internal waters:

> The jurisdiction of the nation within its own territory is necessarily exclusive and absolute. It is susceptible of no limitation not imposed by itself.

The Supreme Court then, in a carefully reasoned decision, reached the conclusion that based upon diplomatic practice and international custom, friendly warships in foreign ports were immune from the jurisdiction of the host state. The court decided:

> It seems, then, to the Court, to be a principle of public law, that national ships of war, entering the port of a friendly power open for their reception are to be considered as exempted by the consent of that power from its jurisdiction.

In the situation under consideration, Spain as the host state in Havana, and the United States as the flag state of the battleship *Maine,* had some divergent interests resulting from the sinking. *The Schooner Exchange* provides a widely accepted starting point for an examination of the customary law applicable to the evaluation of these interests. It should also be noted that there was apparently an informal agreement between the United States and Spain concerning the exchange of mutual friendly visits of warships to each other's ports at the time the *Maine* was destroyed. In addition, there was a Spanish domestic royal order permitting the visit of foreign warships to Spanish ports. It is referred to in the following terms in the report of the Spanish naval board of inquiry:

> The undersigned has heard unofficially the reason of the arrival and stay in these waters of the ironclad in question. For this it was sufficient to call to mind the royal order of August 11, 1882, which permits, in ordinary times of peace, the entrance of foreign squadrons and single vessels into our ports without any other restrictions than those prescribed by the Ordinances of the navy, and that of obedience to the police regulations established in those ports.

This royal order, which is clearly consistent with customary law, is also significant because it appears to indicate that the *Maine* was in Havana consistent with the applicable provisions of Spanish law.

II. *Tentative Answers to the Questions*

In the following answers the term "host state" refers to Spain. In the same way, the term "flag state" refers to the United States as the flag state of the battleship *Maine* before, during, and after its sinking in Havana Harbor.

ENTRY INTO HAVANA

1. *How much advance notice should the host state have been given? If this was not a matter of international law, what was the diplomatic practice at that time?*

The customary law required a reasonable time of advance notice in the circumstances so that the host state had the opportunity to give a considered response. The diplomatic practice was, in most instances, consistent with the customary law. An unduly short notice would probably have been in violation of international law unless it had received the acquiescence of the host state.

In the case of the *Maine*, although the notice was very short, the host state acquiesced. The Spanish naval court of inquiry, as quoted above, considered that the entrance of the *Maine* was consistent with the royal order quoted and therefore lawful.

2. If a ship was going to call at the colony of another state, was the mother country as well as the government of the colony informed? If this was not a matter of international law, what was the diplomatic practice at that time?

Under both the international law and diplomatic practice of the time, the mother country, that is, the host state, had to be informed since the colony was not, in either law or diplomacy, a separate subject of or participant in international law and diplomatic relations. It was a matter of practical necessity to inform the capital of the colony also so that local arrangements, such as for pilotage and mooring, could be made.

3. If a visiting naval vessel without prior permission to enter appeared off the port, but could not present a clean bill of health, could the host state refuse entry? Could the host state insist the ship be quarantined?

Under the customary law of the time, the host state was legally entitled to refuse entry to a warship without a clean bill of health because it had ample jurisdictional authority in law to protect the health of its nationals and of personnel on other ships in the harbor from possible contagion.

The host state could not, consistent with law, have insisted that the ship be quarantined; but it could have legally made quarantine a precondition of entry of a warship into its port.

4. Could the colonial government have refused entry to a foreign naval vessel on the grounds that it (the colonial government) wanted instructions from the mother country?

Yes. Unless the colonial government had been specifically granted power to act on this matter by its home government (the host state), the colonial authorities had no independent legal competence and could only act upon instructions.

5. Was the visiting vessel required to state how long it intended to stay? If this was not a matter of international law, what was the diplomatic practice at that time?

The warship was not required to state how long it intended to stay as a matter of law. As a matter of diplomatic practice, it was probably not unusual at that time for the flag state to indicate the time that it desired its warship to stay in its request for diplomatic clearance for the visit.

6. Assuming that the visiting naval vessel's entry into the host state's harbor was diplomatically or legally improper, did the host state waive its rights to protest against such an entry after the exchange of salutes, visits, etc.?

No. In the assumed facts, the host state does not waive its rights to protest against a legally improper entry since the entry may have been permitted as a diplomatic courtesy rather than as a legal right. If the host granted entry as a matter of diplomatic courtesy, it could have resolved any doubts by making an express reservation of all of its legal rights.

7. *After the first visiting vessel (the Maine) had been in port for over a week, a second visiting vessel (the Cushing) from the same nation as the first appeared off the port. The host state had received no official notice that it was arriving or of its purpose. Could the host state have refused entry to the second vessel?*

Yes. The host state was not under legal obligation to admit any foreign warships into its ports. The host state might, as a diplomatic matter, decide to admit a warship which had arrived without official notice in order to promote good will or for other purposes.

8. *Suppose that the host state learned by newspapers that the second visiting vessel was carrying provisions for the first, could the host state have asked to know what these provisions were?*

In the supposed facts, the host state would have been legally entitled to ask concerning the character of the provisions as a precondition to entry. The flag state would have been equally entitled to decline to answer, and this could have resulted in the exercise of the right to deny entry by the host state.

A Disaster Occurring to a Naval Vessel Belonging to One State While Visiting the Port of Another State

1. *If an internal accident occurred aboard the visiting vessel, but the ship was not destroyed, aground, or deserted, what rights and responsibilities does the host state have?*

In general, the host state had the right to protect itself from the consequences of the accident as well as to take possible precautionary measures to encourage the prevention or minimization of future accidents.

The host state had the responsibility, since the warship was within its internal waters by permission, to render necessary and appropriate humanitarian aid to the victims of the internal accident whether they were crew members of the warship, its own nationals, or the nationals of third states. The host state also had the responsibility to minimize dangers which might arise from the accident including possible hazards to other ships in the port.

2. If an accident of undetermined origin occurred aboard the ship, the vessel was virtually destroyed, no member of the ship's company remained aboard, the vessel rested on the harbor bottom, and no flag was flying, did the host state have the right to board?

As a general principle, the host state had the right to board. This right to board, however, was not a comprehensive right but was limited to the special values or interests of the host state which were affected and which were protected by customary law. Since the ownership of the warship remained in the flag state, the host state, because of its obligations to provide some measure of protection, may protect the warship from any acts of interference which may prejudice the rights of the flag state. For example, the host state, as the territorial sovereign in its port, had the legal authority to prohibit marine salvors who were not authorized by the flag state from boarding the wreck of the warship and taking any steps which might lead to unauthorized salvage operations. In the same way, the host state may, consistent with law and diplomatic practice, maintain a presence on board the surfaced portion of the sunken warship to prevent interference by souvenir hunters, curiosity seekers, and other unauthorized individuals who may act to prejudice the rights of either the flag state or the host state.

3. Was the Maine *legally abandoned?*

No. According to the stated facts, the ship was abandoned in a factual sense for at least a short period of time. It does not follow, however, that the flag state had abandoned its warship in any meaningful sense. The warship, even though it was in the situation postulated no longer an effective unit of the flag state's navy, remained the property of the flag state.

4. Suppose that the above conditions existed (the ship abandoned and resting on the harbor floor) except that the national flag was flying, would this have changed the rights and responsibilities of the host state?

No. While the flying of the national flag is important symbolically, this addition to the fact situation did not change the rights and responsibilities of the host state since, according to the given facts above, the vessel was a sunken warship of the flag state.

5. If the ship was destroyed by the deliberate act of dissident elements in the host state's armed forces, or by insurgents who had been struggling for some years against the host state, what were the rights and responsibilities of the flag state and the host state?

In these postulated facts, it was probable that the legal responsibilities of both the flag state and the host state had been enhanced. The existence of "insurgents who had been struggling for some years" must have been known to the flag state and this knowledge would appear to have placed a higher duty upon the flag state, through the captain, officers, and crew of its warship, to take more than routine security measures to protect the ship.

In an analogous way, the legal responsibility incurred because of the failure of protection by the host state would have been greater where the act of destruction is carried out by its own armed forces (although dissident) or by known insurgents.

The situation of increased responsibility of the host state would have accorded it greater rights to take security measures. In the same way, the flag state would have had increased rights to protect the security of its warship beyond those which would exist in a factually peaceful situation.

6. *Suppose the ship was deserted, resting on the bottom, and the captain of the vessel wished to board. The host state had placed some small boats around the hulk. The captain, not in uniform, was stopped and refused permission to board. The captain went to the host state's naval authorities, who explained to him that the problem was only one of identification and that he needed a pass. They granted him a pass. By accepting it, was the captain yielding any of the rights of his own state to that of the host state?*

No. Since the facts state that the pass was given only for purposes of identification, and it should be assumed that it was accepted on the same premise, the captain had yielded none of the flag state's rights. If the captain, because of poor judgment, attempted to yield his state's rights, his state could effectively disavow his act.

INVESTIGATION OF THE DISASTER

1. *Did the host state have the right to conduct an investigation?*

Yes. The right of the host state to conduct an investigation was, however, not an unlimited one. Its investigation, in order to comply with the limitations of customary law, should have been restricted to those subjects concerning which it had legitimate values to protect. Such interests included the protection of persons in the locality from the consequences of the accident. The host state, as the sovereign, was entitled to sufficient information to attempt to discover the cause or causes of the destruction of the *Maine* as a lawful objective in itself and so that it could better fulfill its obligation of protection to visiting warships in the future. Among the matters which it would have been legally improper for the host state to have investigated would be the particular characteristics of the armament of the warship as well as any secret codes remaining on the wreck and other analogous matters which were significant military or diplomatic interests of the flag state.

2. *Did the host state have the right to examine the hulk?*

Yes, subject to the limitations described in the answer to the question above. There can be no doubt that this right exists as a matter of law because the hulk is located in the internal waters of the host state and may for a variety of reasons, including for example being a hazard to navigation, be a matter of great concern to the host state.

3. *Did it have the right to participate in a joint investigation with the flag state?*

No. A joint investigation conducted by the host and flag states with each state emphasizing those aspects of the inquiry which are of more legitimate interest and concern to it, and conducted in an atmosphere of mutual trust and cooperation, is the type of investigation which is most likely to be successful in ascertaining actual causes. Following the sinking of the *Maine* in Havana Harbor, the Spanish government proposed such an investigation, but it was rejected by the United States. Since a joint investigation is dependent upon mutual agreement to conduct such an investigation, there is no customary law principle which accords a right of either state to participate in a joint investigation with the other. So far as is known, there was no bilateral agreement in existence between Spain and the United States which would grant the right to participate in such an investigation.

4. *Suppose the flag state conducted its own investigation, did the host state and its local representatives have a right to be kept informed of the progress of the investigation?*

Assuming the flag state was conducting its investigation, there was no right of the host state and its colonial officials to information on the progress of the investigation.

Assuming the host state was conducting its investigation, there was no right of the flag state and its local consular representative to information on the progress of the investigation.

There was no principle of customary law compelling either state to inform the other of the progress of its investigation. Since each investigation was to some extent limited in law by the rights of the other state to also conduct an investigation, it is clear, as a practical matter, that each investigation could be conducted more efficiently if there was a sharing of the respective information obtained.

5. *Suppose the host state conducted its own investigation. It had given hospital treatment to survivors and allowed burial of the fatalities in established churchyards. Could the host state have examined or in any way have taken testimony from the survivors of the ship or other citizens of the same nation as the visiting vessel and who might have had pertinent knowledge?*

The host state did not have authority to examine or take testimony from the naval survivors of the warship. They were ashore only because of the exigencies connected with the sinking and remained a jurisdictionally immune portion of the armed forces of the flag state.

The host state probably had the legal authority to take testimony from civilian nationals of the flag state who were located within the territory of the host state without violating international law. Since such civilians were afforded the protection of the host state's laws, it would probably be maintained that they were obligated to comply with reasonable obligations which were imposed upon them by the same laws.

The *Maine* as a Case in International Law

1. *Has the loss of the* Maine *set any precedents in international law?*

Yes, to some degree. Among the acts which have some authority as precedents in international law is the jurisdictional authority of each state involved in the fact situation to conduct its own independent investigation.

In addition, the position of the United States following the sinking of the *Maine* was that the host state was responsible not because it was alleged to have caused the sinking, but because it failed in its general duty of protection of a foreign flag state visiting warship. To some extent the Spanish government agreed with this position as a part of its effort to avoid war with the United States. Such agreement, for whatever reasons, adds a precedent of some value to the legal principle of the host state's responsibility to protect visiting warships from externally caused injury.

While these were precedents of some unascertainable degree of authority in 1898, critics could attempt to downgrade their importance because of the great disproportion between the effective naval power of the United States and Spain in the Caribbean which was shortly established beyond any doubt in the ensuing Spanish-American War.

PARTIAL BIBLIOGRAPHY FOR APPENDIX B

Colombos, John C., *The International Law of the Sea,* 6th rev. ed. (London: Longmans, 1967).

Ferguson, Jan Helenus, *Manual of International Law* 1 (London: W. B. Whittingham & Co., 1884).

McDougal, Myres Smith, and William T. Burke, *The Public Order of the Oceans* (New Haven: Yale University Press, 1962).

Moore, John Bassett, *A Digest of International Law* (Washington: Government Printing Office, 1906).

Oppenheim, Lassa F. L., *International Law* 1 (London: Longmans, Green, and Co., 1905–1906).

U.S. Congress, Senate, *Message from the President of the United States Transmitting the Report of the Naval Court of Inquiry Upon the Destruction of the United States Battle Ship Maine in Havana Harbor, February 15, 1898, Together with the Testimony Taken Before the Court,* 55th Congress, 2d session, 1898, Document 207.

U.S. Congress, Senate, *Report of the Committee on Foreign Relations, United States Senate, Relative to Affairs in Cuba,* 55th Congress, 2d session, April 13, 1898, Senate Report 885 which includes Report of the Spanish Naval Board of Inquiry as to the Cause of the Destruction of the U.S.B.S. Maine.

U.S. Department of State, *Papers Relating to the Foreign Relations of the United States . . . 1898* (Washington: Government Printing Office, 1901).

U.S. Naval War College, *International Law Topics and Discussions. 1914.* (Washington: Government Printing Office, 1915).

Weems, John Edward, *The Fate of the Maine* (New York: Henry Holt and Company, 1958).

Wharton, Francis, ed., *A Digest of the International Law of the United States, Taken from Documents Issued by Presidents and Secretaries of State, and from Decisions of Federal Courts and Opinions of Attorneys-General,* 3 volumes (Washington: Government Printing Office, 1887).

Investigation of the Explosion
On Board the French Battleship *Jena*
March 12, 1907

On March 12, 1907, the French battleship *Jena* (*Iéna*) was in drydock at Toulon. The ship was laid down at Brest in 1898 and completed in 1901. She had a waterline length of 400.75 feet, a beam of 68 feet, a maximum draft of 27.5 feet, and a displacement of 12,000 tons. At 1:45 p.m. a series of explosions occurred in the after part of the ship. The first explosion was not severe, but within minutes a second detonation followed, which was extremely violent, blowing out a large portion of the ship's bottom and throwing parts of the ship a distance of 500 yards. Over 100 men were killed.

The French examined the loss of the *Jena* with great care. Both the Senate and Chamber of Deputies established commissions. The three-volume report of the Senate commission was exhaustive and included testimony of hundreds of survivors, witnesses, chemists, and engineers. The commission set forth its philosophy at the outset: "It must be said that it is our duty to ban hypothesis as a means of establishing the truth . . . . We intend rather to allow our cautious reserve to bow only to the authority of fact indisputably established by positive and direct proof." It examined the characteristics of the gunpowder issued to the ships, the instructions of the Army and Navy governing the use of explosives, and other accidents in which gunpowder had been involved. The commission's report contained drawings to illustrate the location of the magazines and show how the explosion of a single piece of ammunition could account for the complete destruction of the ship. Further, a scale model of the *Jena*'s after magazine was constructed and loaded with the explosives which were suspected of causing the disaster, and experiments were conducted in an effort to reproduce the circumstances under which the explosion occurred.

The French, along with other major military nations, were developing smokeless gunpowder in the last half of the nineteenth century. In 1884, the French adopted type B smokeless powder, a cellulose nitrate explosive not unlike guncotton in composition. The new powder reduced the telltale smoke and the residue created by the normally incomplete combustion of black and brown powders previously used. The smokeless powder was more efficient and, when properly manufactured and stored, burned evenly, possessed good ballistic qualities, and had a low combustion temperature. However, when stored in a warm or damp atmosphere, it tended to decompose chemically and became subject to spontaneous combustion. Further, it tended to deteriorate and become unstable with age.

Consequently, the age of the powder and the way the magazines were cooled were important subjects for investigation. About 86 percent of the powder on board the *Jena* was six years old and required great care. At its best, the cooling system was inadequate. It consisted of two machines to chill the air and a distribution system which circulated it through several compartments. The machines were located too far from the magazines; by the time the air reached them, it was only a degree or two cooler than the atmosphere in the magazines. Every commanding officer of the ship had complained about inadequate cooling. At the time of the explosion, part of the system was dismantled because it was useless and taking up space.

The commission concluded that spontaneous combustion in a single item of ammunition was responsible for setting a fire which then exploded an adjacent black powder magazine. It recommended that the Navy cool its magazines to below 77° F. and immediately dispose of over-age powder.

The Senate commission did not confine itself to events that took place on board ship. It criticized design practices by which magazines were placed next to compartments which usually had high temperatures. It reported that in some instances hot steam lines passed directly through the magazines.

The commission also took up the manufacture of gunpowder. In France the manufacture of explosives was a state monopoly under the Army. The *Service des poudres et salpêtres* made powder for the Army and the Navy. The arrangement was unsatisfactory, for the Army tended to ignore the special requirements for naval service while the Navy failed to protect its own interests by rigorous inspection.

The commission established by the Chamber of Deputies proposed the same recommendations as those of the Senate commission. However, the former reached no conclusion as to the cause of the accident. Half the commission believed that type B powder was at fault, the other half believed that spontaneous combustion of that powder was unlikely in this instance, and suspected that ignition of black powder initiated the disaster. One theory was that the malfunctioning of an electrical pump, the shaft of which passed through the compartment in which the black powder was stored, was the cause of the initial explosion.

Although the Chamber of Deputies commission came to no conclusion on the case of the destruction of the *Jena,* its revelations forced the resignation of the Minister of the Navy.

Despite the thoroughness of the investigation, the French continued to have difficulty with their smokeless powder. Their cooling machinery was unable to lower magazine temperatures to the recommended standard. Relations with the Army over the production of powder also continued to be unsatisfactory. On September 25, 1911, while anchored at Toulon, the battleship *Liberté* blew up with a loss of 204 lives. The cause of the explosion was found to be spontaneous combustion of type B powder, probably manufactured in 1905.

A recapitulation of the *Maine* investigation is necessary in order to make a comparison with that of the *Jena.* It is significant that, in the first days after the *Maine* explosion, many officers believed that an accident destroyed the battleship. They held this belief because more than once ships were almost lost because of fires in bunkers located adjacent to magazines. The court of inquiry reached the conclusion that the *Maine* had been lost by a mine, not by an accident. Except in minor instances, the court in seeking testimony and advice did not go beyond the witnesses immediately available to it. Thus the only witness considered as an expert in underwater explosions was an officer who had served for several years at the Navy's torpedo station, and who was commanding a cruiser in Havana while the court was in session.

Nor did the court go beyond the *Maine* to examine officers of other ships on their experience with bunker fires, or to investigate whether a bunker fire could have occurred between the time of the last inspection and the explosion. Further, the court gave none of the reasoning which led to its conclusion; nor did it publish many of the drawings which were used during the interrogation of survivors and divers. Finally, the findings of the court of inquiry were barren of technical conclusions. The court, since it held that a mine set off the magazines, should have made some recommendation about the construction and location of magazines. As far as the court was concerned, the loss of the *Maine* was an event from which the Navy could derive no lessons.

The other two investigations made by the United States can be dismissed briefly. The Senate Committee on Foreign Relations was clearly determined to support uncritically the court of inquiry. It made no effort to hear qualified technical opinion. The board of inspection of 1911 conducted its investigation free from the possibility of war and saw the wreck under the best possible conditions. With less excuse than the court of 1898, it found a mine as the cause of the loss of the *Maine*.

At first glance, a comparison of the investigations of the *Jena* and *Maine* disasters appears unrewarding, for the circumstances surrounding the events differed so greatly. The *Maine* exploded at a time when relations between the United States and Spain were tense. The *Jena* explosion occurred in a French naval dockyard and had no international implications. But the stated purpose of each investigation was to determine facts. The critical state of the relations between the United States and Spain was all the more reason why greater effort should have been made to ascertain the origin of the *Maine* disaster.

PARTIAL BIBLIOGRAPHY FOR APPENDIX C

Earle, Ralph, "The Destruction of the Liberté," U.S. Naval Institute *Proceedings* 37 (December 1911): 1275–1282.

Hovgaard, William, *Modern History of Warships* (London: E. & F. N. Spon, Ltd., 1920), pp. 428–430.

"Naval Notes" in *Journal of the United Service Institution* 51 (January–June 1907): 607–608.

No. 1304, Chambre des Députés, Session Extraordinaire de 1907, *Rapport fait Au nom de la Commission chargée de procéder a une enquête parlementaire sur les causes de la catastrophe de "L'«léna»"* . . . par M. Henri Michel, Député (Paris: Imprimerie de la Chambre des Députés, Motteroz et Martinet, 1907).

No. 244, Sénat, année 1907, *Rapport fait Au nom de la Commission chargée de procéder à une enquête sur la catastrophe de "l'Iéna" et sur les accidents dont la marine nationale a souffert dans ces dernières années* . . . Tome I, II, III.

"Professional Notes: Ship's Magazines," in U.S. Naval Institute *Proceedings* 38 (March 1912): 353–358. (Mentions the *Jena, Liberté,* and *Maine.*)

"Professional Notes: The Catastrophe of the Liberté," in U.S. Naval Institute *Proceedings* 37 (December 1911): 1457–1459.

"Professional Notes: The Destruction of the Iena," in U.S. Naval Institute *Proceedings* 33 (March 1907): 849–853.

"Ships: The French Naval Disaster," in *Journal of the American Society of Naval Engineers* 19 (1907): 571–574.

Wilson, Herbert W., *Battleships in Action* 1 (London: Sampson Low, Marston & Co., Ltd., nd.): 300–303.

Notes for Chapters

CHAPTER 1

1. Navy Department, Office of the Chief of Naval Operations, Naval History Division, *Dictionary of American Naval Fighting Ships* 1 (Washington: Government Printing Office, 1959), Appendix 1, "Battleships 1886–1948," p. 189; T. A. Brassey, ed., *The Naval Annual, 1899* (Portsmouth, England: J. Griffin and Co., 1899), p. 381; William Hovgaard, *Modern History of Warships* (London: E. & F. N. Spon, Ltd., 1920), pp. 204–205; George F. W. Holman, "The Destruction of the *Maine*," *The American-Spanish War: A History by the War Leaders* (Norwich, Connecticut: Charles C. Haskell, 1899), pp. 93–94.

2. Two good articles on armor and gun forgings are in the *Transactions of the Society of Naval Architects and Marine Engineers*. Russell W. Davenport, "Production in the United States of Heavy Steel Engine, Gun and Armor Plate Forgings," is in volume 1 (1893): 70–89, and Charles O'Neil, "The Development of Modern Ordnance and Armor in the United States," is in volume 10 (1902): 235–267. Two useful articles on the development of naval engineering in the United States appeared in the *Journal of the American Society of Naval Engineers*. The articles, with pages referring to the *Maine*, are: C. W. Dyson, "A Fifty Year Retrospect of Naval Marine Engineering," 30 (May 1918): 265–266; and Herbert M. Neuhaus, "Fifty Years of Naval Engineering in Retrospect," part 1: 1888–1898, volume 50 (February 1938): 7–9.

3. Charles D. Sigsbee, "Personal Narrative of the 'Maine'," part 1, *Century Magazine* 57 (November 1898): 76–77.

4. Sigsbee, "Personal Narrative of the 'Maine'," part 2, *Century Magazine* 57 (December 1898): 212; Lewis R. Hamersly, *The Records of the Living Officers of the U.S. Navy and Marine Corps*, 7th ed. (New York: L. R. Hamersly, 1902), p. 95. For Sigsbee's work in oceanography, see his *Deep Sea Sounding and Dredging: A Description and Discussion of the Methods and Appliances Used on Board the Coast and Geodetic Survey Steamer, "Blake"* (Washington: Government Printing Office, 1880). A picture of one of the "appliances" is in Vincent T. Miscoski, "U.S. Naval Oceanography . . . a look back," United States Naval Institute *Proceedings* 94 (February 1968): 51. Reference to a rheostat is in Sigsbee to the Western Electric Co., January 20, 1892, Box 2, Folder 38, Charles D. Sigsbee Papers, New York State Library, Albany, New York, (hereafter this collection will be cited as *Sigsbee Papers*). For an interesting analysis of the effect of stagnation on the officer group, see: Peter Karsten, "No Room for Young Turks?" United States Naval Institute *Proceedings* 99 (March 1973): 37–50.

5. Reference to the *Kearsarge* is in a letter from Admiral David Dixon Porter to the Naval Examining Board, November 22, 1886, in U.S. Naval Examining Boards: Charles D. Sigsbee file, Record Group 125: Records of the Office of the Judge Advocate General (Navy), Entry 58: "Records of Proceedings of Naval and Marine Examining Boards," United States National Archives and Record Service, Washington, D.C. (hereafter this repository will be cited as *NA*).

6. These incidents are summarized in the *New York Herald*, February 16, 1898. The East River incident is described in Arthur M. Johnson, "The Battleship *Maine* and Pier 46, East River," United States Naval Institute *Proceedings* 81 (November 1955): 1295. Evidence of criticism is in Box 1, Folder A, *Sigsbee Papers*.

7. On precautions, see: the testimony of Sigsbee; Lieutenant Commander Richard Wainwright, the executive officer; and Lieutenant John J. Blandin, officer of the deck on February 15, 1898; all in:

U.S. Congress, Senate, *Message from the President of the United States Transmitting the Report of the Naval Court of Inquiry Upon the Destruction of the United States Battle Ship Maine in Havana Harbor, February 15, 1898, Together with the Testimony Taken Before the Court*, 55th Congress, 2d session, 1898, Document 207, pp. 13–14, 25–26, 113 (hereafter cited as *Court of Inquiry*). On Sigsbee's surmise, see his article, "My Story of the 'Maine'," *Cosmopolitan Magazine* 53, (July 1912): 150. Sigsbee wrote about the disaster in the following accounts: "Personal Narrative of the 'Maine'," 3 parts, *Century Magazine* 57 (November, December 1898 and January 1899): 74–97, 241–263, 373–394; "My Story of the 'Maine'," *Cosmopolitan Magazine* 53 (July, August 1912): 148–159, 372–383; *The "Maine". An Account of Her Destruction in Havana Harbor* (New York: Century, 1899). For a popular account, see: John Edward Weems, *The Fate of the Maine* (New York: Henry Holt, 1958).

8. Richard T. Loomis, "The White House and Crisis Management," United States Naval Institute *Proceedings* 95 (December 1969): 64. For an excellent study of the Army, see: Graham A. Cosmas, *An Army for Empire: The United States in the Spanish-American War* (Columbia, Missouri: University of Missouri Press, 1971), pp. 1–4, 107–110, 117–124, 134–138, 295–314.

9. Long to Sicard, August 21, 1898, quoted in *Army Navy Journal* 35 (August 27, 1898): 1079; Alfred T. Mahan, *Lessons of the War with Spain* (Boston: Little, Brown and Co., 1899), p. 157; John D. Long, *The New American Navy* 1 (New York: The Outlook Co., 1903): 123–124.

CHAPTER 2

1. The *Virginius* incident is in French E. Chadwick, *The Relations of the United States and Spain. Diplomacy* (New York: Charles Scribner's Sons, 1909), pp. 314–347 and in Hugh Thomas, *Cuba: The Pursuit of Freedom* (New York: Harper and Row, 1971), pp. 262–263. For a survey of American attitudes after 1895, see Philip S. Foner, *The Spanish-Cuban-American War and the Birth of American Imperialism 1895–1902* 1 (New York: Monthly Review Press, 1972): 168–176.

2. For a text of the proclamation, see: James D. Richardson, comp., *A Compilation of the Messages and Papers of the Presidents* 14 (New York: Bureau of National Literature, 1897): 6023–6024. For a strongly critical view of Cleveland, see: Foner, *The Spanish-Cuban-American War* 1: 177–188. For a favorable view, see: Allan Nevins, *Grover Cleveland, A Study in Courage* (New York: Dodd, Mead & Co., 1932), pp. 713–719. On suspending courtesy calls, see: Julius W. Pratt, "The Coming War With Spain," in Paolo E. Coletta, ed., *Threshold to American Internationalism, Essays on the Foreign Policies of William McKinley* (New York: Exposition Press, 1970), p. 45 and Lawrence S. Mayo, *America of Yesterday as Reflected in the Journal of John Davis Long* (Boston: The Atlantic Monthly Press, 1923), pp. 153–154. On the North Atlantic Squadron, see: John L. Offner, "President McKinley and the Origins of the Spanish-American War," (Ph.D. dissertation, Pennsylvania State University, 1957), p. 179.

3. Foner, *The Spanish-Cuban-American War* 1: 185–194.

4. H. Wayne Morgan, *America's Road to Empire: The War With Spain and Overseas Expansion* (New York: John Wiley and Sons, 1965), pp. 23, 32; Offner, "President McKinley and the Origins of the Spanish-American War," pp. 151–158; Ernest R. May, *Imperial Democracy: The Emergence of America as a Great Power* (New York: Harcourt, Brace & World, 1961), pp. 120–136; Gerald G. Eggert, "Our Man in Havana: Fitzhugh Lee," *The Hispanic American Historical Review* 47 (1967): 463–485; Nevins, *Grover Cleveland*, p. 719.

5. For the college, see: Henry P. Beers, "The Development of the Office of the Chief of Naval Operations," part 1, *Military Affairs* 10 (Spring 1946): 48–51; Rear Admiral Austin M. Knight and Lieutenant William D. Puleston, "History of the Naval War College," typewritten ms. (Newport, Rhode Island: Naval War College, 1916), p. 11, Naval War College Archives (hereafter this collection will be cited as *NWCA*). For Taylor, see: Lewis R. Hamersly, *The Records of the Living Officers of the United States Navy and Marine Corps*, 7th ed. (New York: L. R. Hamersly, 1902), p. 22.

6. "Situation in case of War with Spain," November 1896, UNOpB Box 21, *NWCA*.

7. Henry C. Taylor, "Synopsis of War College Plan for Cuban Campaign in a War with Spain." The document appears to be in Taylor's handwriting. Lieutenant William W. Kimball had proposed a purely naval war with Spain. See his "War with Spain—1896," date June 1, 1896. For changes in the November plan, see: "Corrections in paper on 'Situation in case of War with Spain'," December 13, 1896. The changes refer to scheduled events and not to principles. All documents are from UNOpB Box 21, *NWCA*.

8. For the Army, see: Graham A. Cosmas, *An Army for Empire: The United States in the Spanish-American War* (Columbia, Missouri: University of Missouri Press, 1971), p. 5.

9. "Plan of Operations Against Spain, December 12, 1896," War Plan Portfolios, Box 11, General Board Records, Operational Archives, Naval History Division, U.S. Navy, Washington, D.C. Members of the board were: Admiral F. M. Ramsay, Chief of the Bureau of Navigation; Admiral F. M. Bunce, Commander-in-Chief, North Atlantic Squadron; Admiral W. T. Sampson, Chief of the Bureau of Ordnance; Commander Henry C. Taylor, President of the Naval War College; and Commander Richard Wainwright, Chief Intelligence Officer. Taylor's dissent, undated, and Herbert's note, dated March 2, 1897 are integral parts of the folder containing the plan. Reference to these plans is in John A. S. Grenville, "American Naval Preparations for War with Spain, 1896–1898," *Journal of American Studies* 2 (April 1968): 33–47.

10. "Plan of Campaign Against Spain and Japan, June 30, 1897," War Plan Portfolios, Box 11, General Board Records, Operational Archives, Naval History Division, U.S. Navy, Washington, D.C. Members of the board were: Admiral Montgomery Sicard, Commander-in-Chief, North Atlantic Squadron; Admiral A. S. Crowninshield, Chief of the Bureau of Navigation; Captain C. F. Goodrich, President of the Naval War College; Commander Richard Wainwright, Chief Intelligence Officer.

11. Donald Bruce Johnson and Kirk H. Porter, comps., *National Party Platforms 1840–1972* (Urbana: University of Illinois Press, 1973), pp. 99–100, 108.

12. Fred L. Israel, ed., *The State of the Union Messages of the Presidents 1790–1966* 2 (New York: Chelsea House, 1966), pp. 1826–1831.

13. Margaret Leech, *In the Days of McKinley* (New York: Harper & Brothers, 1959), p. 115.

CHAPTER 3

1. John L. Offner, "President McKinley and the Origins of the Spanish-American War," (Ph.D. dissertation, Pennsylvania State University, 1957), p. 58; Philip S. Foner, *The Spanish-Cuban-American War and the Birth of American Imperialism 1895–1902* 1 (New York: Monthly Review Press, 1972): 202. For the address, see the *Washington Post*, March 5, 1897, second part, p. 3.

2. John D. Long, *The New American Navy* 1 (New York: The Outlook Co., 1903): 134.

3. Foner, *The Spanish-Cuban-American War* 1: 215–216; Ernest R. May, *Imperial Democracy: The Emergence of America as a Great Power* (New York: Harcourt, Brace & World, 1961), p. 125; Margaret Leech, *In the Days of McKinley* (New York: Harper & Brothers, 1959), pp. 148–149; H. Wayne Morgan, *America's Road to Empire: The War With Spain and Overseas Expansion* (New York: John Wiley and Sons, 1965), pp. 5–9. For a view that McKinley favored intervention, see Morgan, p. 25.

4. Ship strength from: Report of the Secretary of the Navy, November 15, 1897 in *Annual Reports of the Navy Department for the Year 1897* (Washington: Government Printing Office, 1898), p. 3. Personnel strength is from David F. Boyd, "The Causes of the Spanish-American War and the Naval and Combined Operations in the Atlantic, Including the Transfer of the Oregon," ms. (Newport, Rhode Island: Naval War College, 1928–1929), *NWCA*.

5. The quotation is from C. F. Goodrich to Long, February 11, 1898 in Gardner Weld Allen, ed., *Papers of John D. Long 1897–1904* (Boston: The Massachusetts Historical Society, 1939), pp. 48–49.

6. Charles Oscar Paullin, *Paullin's History of Naval Administration 1775–1911* (Annapolis: U.S. Naval Institute, 1968), p. 375; Stephen B. Luce, *Text-Book of Seamanship, the Equipping and Handling of Vessels Under Sail or Steam. . . .* (New York: D. Van Nostrand Co., 1898), pp. 158–161.

7. On relations between line officers and engineers, see two articles in the *Journal of the American Society of Naval Engineers:* R. E. Bassler, "The Origin of Engineering Duty Only," 65 (November 1953): 771–790 and Robert B. Madden, "The Bureau of Ships and Its E. D. Officers," 66 (February 1954): 9–41.

8. For a condescending view of Long, see Paullin, *History of Naval Administration*, pp. 427–428. Quotation is from Lawrence S. Mayo, *America of Yesterday as Reflected in the Journal of John Davis Long* (Boston: The Atlantic Monthly Press, 1923), p. 157; Elting E. Morison, ed., *The Letters of Theodore Roosevelt* 1 (Cambridge: Harvard University Press, 1951): 603.

9. Leech, *In the Days of McKinley*, p. 137. On Roosevelt and the engineer controversy, see: Roosevelt to Long, December 9, 1897, in Morison, *The Letters of Theodore Roosevelt* 1: 726–740.

10. Letters relating to the bunker fires are as follows: *Olympia:* C. J. MacConnell to Commanding Officer, November 11, 1895; *Wilmington:* C. C. Todd to Secretary of the Navy, June 9, July 4, 23, August 3, 1897; *Petrel:* W. H. Emory to Secretary of the Navy, January 12, 1896; *Indiana:* R. D. Evans to Commander-in-Chief, North Atlantic Squadron, May 19, 1896; *Cincinnati:* M. L. Dohuson to Secretary of the Navy, December 10, 1895; *New York:* Charles Laird, F .J. Schell, and C. F. Snow to Commanding Officer, March 11, 1897, all in Record Group 45: "Naval Records Collection of the Office of Naval Records and Library," Entry 464: "Subject File," File HF: "Fires Explosions, Etc.," *NA* (hereafter documents from this source are cited by RG number, E number, and *NA*. A list is provided on page 159 which outlines and describes the record groups and their subordinate entries). On the *Oregon* and the coal study, see: Roosevelt to Secretary, November 26, 1897 in RG. 80, E. 124, "Letterbook 2"; and J. C. Colwell to Sir John Surston, December 18, 1897, RG. 45, E. 301, both from *NA*.

11. Roosevelt refers to his conversation in his letter to Lodge, September 21, 1897, Morison, *The Letters of Theodore Roosevelt* 1: 685. Quotations are from: Roosevelt to President, September 20, 1897, RG. 80, E. 124, "Letterbook 2," *NA*.

12. Roosevelt to Lodge, September 21, 1897, Morison, *The Letters of Theodore Roosevelt* 1: 685–686.

13. May, *Imperial Democracy*, pp, 125–126, 161; Foner, *The Spanish-Cuban-American War* 1: 216–217; Leech, *In the Days of McKinley*, p. 149; Lee to Day, November 2, 1897, in U.S. Congress, Senate, *Report of the Committee on Foreign Relations, United States Senate, Relative to Affairs in Cuba*, 55th Congress, 2d session, April 13, 1898, Senate Report 885, p. 552.

14. Ciphered telegram: Long to Kimball, October 8, 1897, RG. 45, E. 19, *NA;* A. S. Crowninshield to Sigsbee, October 21, 1897, Folder 65, *Sigsbee Papers;* Charles D. Sigsbee, "Personal Narrative of the 'Maine'," part 1, *Century Magazine* 57 (November 1898): 74–76.

15. Lt. J. C. Colwell, "Special Report No. 1, November 2, 1897," in RG. 45, E. 301, *NA*. The United States did buy the cruisers and named them the *New Orleans* and *Albany*, see: Fred T. Jane, *All the World's Fighting Ships* (London: William Clowes and Sons, 1901), p. 327.

16. On repairs, see: Marix and Holman, each to Commanding Officer, U.S.S. *Maine*, October 18, 1897; Sigsbee to Commander-in-Chief, U.S. Naval Forces, North Atlantic Station, October 28, 1897. On drydocking, see: Roosevelt to the Chiefs of the Bureaus of Construction and Repair, Steam Engineering, Ordnance, and Equipment, December 3, 1897 and form signed by A. W. Stahl, Naval Constructor to Chief of the Bureau of Construction and Repair, December 21, 1897. All of the preceding documents are from RG. 19, E. 74, Box 442, *NA*. Reference to plans are in Long to Dayton, Commanding Officer, *Detroit*, December 3, 1897 and December 7, 1897, Microcopy M625, Reel 225, *NA* (hereafter the microfilmed documents of the U.S. National Archives are cited by M number [or T number] and R [reel] number, *NA*. The list on page 161 outlines and describes the microcopies used and their subordinate reels of film.). Sigsbee wrote of his time at Norfolk and arrival at Key West in "Personal Narrative," part 1 (November 1898): 76, 79.

17. Roosevelt to Commander-in-Chief, North Atlantic Squadron, January 3, 1898, RG. 313, E. 47, Box 1, *NA*.

18. Fred L. Israel, ed., *The State of the Union Messages of the Presidents 1790–1966* 2 (New York: Chelsea House, 1966), pp. 1861–1869.

CHAPTER 4

1. A useful table of distances is in French E Chadwick, *The Relations of the United States and Spain. The Spanish-American War* 1 (New York: Charles Scribner's Sons, 1911), opposite page 1. For Key West, see: Chadwick, p. 5. Chadwick was a prominent American naval officer who fought in the war.

2. Charles D. Sigsbee, "Personal Narrative of the 'Maine'," part 1, *Century Magazine* 57 (November 1898): 79. One of the letters from Lee to Sigsbee, dated January 22, 1898, has been found in the Albert Gleaves Papers, Naval Historical Foundation, Library of Congress, Washington, D.C. For coal, see: Sigsbee's testimony: U.S. Congress, Senate, *Report of the Committee on Foreign Relations, United States Senate, Relative to Affairs in Cuba,* 55th Congress, 2d session, April 13, 1898, Senate Report 885, p. 489.

3. Extracts of letters, Lee to Day, November 27, December 1, 15, 22, 1897 in Box 35, William R. Day Papers, Manuscript Division, Library of Congress (hereafter cited as *Day Papers*).

4. For a brief summary of the provisions of autonomy, see: Elbert J. Benton, *International Law and Diplomacy of the Spanish-American War* (Baltimore: The Johns Hopkins Press, 1908), pp. 66–68; Adee to the President, November 28, 1897, George B. Cortelyou Papers, Manuscript Division, Library of Congress.

5. The text of the message is in: *Appendix to the Report of the Chief of the Bureau of Navigation, 1898* (Washington: Government Printing Office, 1898), p. 21. That it was a precautionary measure is in: Report of the Secretary of the Navy, November 15, 1898, *Annual Reports of the Navy Department, 1898* (Washington: Government Printing Office, 1898), p. 3. Long describes its importance in his: "The Navy Department in the War," in *The American-Spanish War: A History by the War Leaders* (Norwich, Connecticut: Charles C. Haskell, 1899), p. 340, and in his *The New American Navy* 1 (New York: The Outlook Co., 1903): 146. Numerous references to German activity and Haiti during this period are in: M17, R–68, and M17, R–53, both of *NA*.

6. For the importance of these riots, see: Ernest R. May, *Imperial Democracy: The Emergence of America as a Great Power* (New York: Harcourt, Brace & World, 1961), p. 135; John L. Offner, "President McKinley and the Origins of the Spanish-American War," (Ph.D. dissertation, Pennsylvania State University, 1957), p. 185; H. Wayne Morgan, *America's Road to Empire: The War With Spain and Overseas Expansion* (New York: John Wiley and Sons, 1965), p. 38. For the messages, see: Lee to Day, January 12, 13, 14, 15, 1898, U.S. Department of State, *Papers Relating to the Foreign Relations of the United States . . . 1898* (Washington: Government Printing Office, 1901), pp. 1024–1025 (hereafter cited as *Foreign Relations 1898*); Adee to Day, January 12, 1898, RG. 59, E. 311, "Volume 9, Part II," *NA.*

7. Untitled note by Moore, September 13, 1897, Box 1, John Bassett Moore Papers, Manuscript Division, Library of Congress.

8. Memorandum submitted to President McKinley on January 14th, RG. 59, E. 311, "Volume 9, Part II," *NA;* Margaret Long, ed., *The Journal of John D. Long* (Rindge, New Hampshire: Richard R. Smith, Inc, 1956), p. 213.

9. Margaret Long, *The Journal of John D. Long,* p. 213; Roosevelt to Long, January 14, 1898, Elting E. Morison, ed., *The Letters of Theodore Roosevelt* 1 (Cambridge: Harvard University Press, 1951): 759–763.

10. Woodford to the President, January 17, 1898, Box 185, John Bassett Moore Papers, Manuscript Division, Library of Congress.

11. The American version of the meeting is in: Interview with Spanish Minister, January [no date], 1898, Box 35, *Day Papers.* The despatches of Dupuy to Madrid are in *Spanish Diplomatic Correspondence and Documents, 1896–1900* (Washington: Government Printing Office, 1905). For Dupuy's favorable estimate, see numerous despatches to Madrid from November 25, 1897 to January 5, 1898, pp. 40–62. He refers to the abrupt change of sentiment in despatch no. 40, Dupuy to Minister of State, January 14, 1898, p. 64. He refers to his knowledge of North Atlantic Squadron maneuvers in despatch no. 33, Dupuy to Minister of State, December 16, 1897, p. 52. His account of his meeting with Day is in despatch no. 46, Dupuy to Minister of State, January 20, 1898, p. 67.

12. Day to Lee, Lee to Day, January 22, 1898, *Foreign Relations 1898*, p. 1025.

13. Lee to Day, December 22, 1897, January 12, 15, 1898, Box 35, *Day Papers*.

14. Memorandum of Interview with Spanish Minister, January 24, 1898, Box 35, *Day Papers;* Day to Lee and Day to Woodford, both January 24, 1898, in *Foreign Relations 1898*, pp. 1025, 1028. The *Washington Evening Star*, January 24, 1898, states that Miles and McKenna were present when the decision was made. Long gives a bland account of the meeting in: Margaret Long, *The Journal of John D. Long*, pp. 213–214. For Dupuy's version, see despatch no. 48 and despatch no. 49, Dupuy to Minister of State, January 24, 1898, *Spanish Diplomatic Correspondence and Documents, 1896–1900*, p. 68.

15. For congressional political reaction, see: The *Washington Evening Star*, January 24, 25, 1898.

16. When the possibility of replacing the *Maine* at Havana with another ship occurred, Lee requested a first-class battleship "just to let these people see our Navy is not composed of 'rotten hulks'. . . ." See extract of letter, Lee to Day, February 5, 1898, Box 35, *Day Papers*. For Sigsbee's views, see: "Personal Narrative," part 1 (November 1898): 97.

17. Sicard to the Secretary of the Navy, January 23, 1898, RG. 313, E. 47, Box 4, *NA;* French E. Chadwick, *The Relations of the United States and Spain. Diplomacy* (New York: Charles Scribner's Sons, 1909), p. 532; Sigsbee, "Personal Narrative," part 1 (November 1898): 79–81; Sigsbee to wife, January 20, 1898, Box 1, *Sigsbee Papers*.

18. Crowninshield to Commander-in-Chief, North Atlantic Squadron, January 17, 1898, RG. 313, E. 47, Box 6; Long to Sigsbee, January 16, 1898, RG. 45, E. 19, both *NA;* Sigsbee to Commanding Officer, Torpedo Boat *Cushing*, undated, but probably January 20, 1898, in Albert Gleaves Papers, Naval Historical Foundation, Library of Congress.

19. Sigsbee, "Personal Narrative," part 1 (November 1898): 81–82. The orders to Havana were repeated in a memorandum from C. H. West, Commander and Chief of Staff, to Lieutenant Gleaves of the *Cushing*, January 24, 1898, in the Albert Gleaves Papers, Naval Historical Foundation, Library of Congress; Chadwick, *The Relations of the United States and Spain. The Spanish-American War* 1: 6.

20. Sigsbee, "Personal Narrative," part 1 (November 1898): 82–85; Deposition of Julian Garcia Lopez, Report of the Spanish Naval Board of Inquiry as to the Cause of the Destruction of the U.S.B.S. Maine, U.S. Congress, Senate, *Report of the Committee on Foreign Relations, United States Senate, Relative to Affairs in Cuba*, 55th Congress, 2d session, April 13, 1898, Senate Report 885, p. 610 (hereafter the translation of the Spanish inquiry into the destruction of the *Maine*, which forms a segment of U.S. Senate Report 885, will be cited as *Spanish Inquiry*); Sigsbee to Long, January 26, 1898, M625, R–225, *NA*.

21. Lawrence S. Mayo, *America of Yesterday as Reflected in the Journal of John Davis Long* (Boston: The Atlantic Monthly Press, 1923), p. 156; Sigsbee to Long, January 26, 1898, M625, R–225, *NA;* Lee to Day, January 26, 1898, Box 35, *Day Papers; Washington Evening Star*, January 31, 1898.

22. For the Lee-Day messages, January 24, 25, 1898, see: *Foreign Relations 1898*, p. 1026; Lee to Day, January 26, 1898, Box 35, *Day Papers*.

23. Luis Pastor y Lauden to Excellency, January 25, 1898, handwritten collection "War with U.S.A." (Guerra con EE. UU.), volume 1, Spanish Naval Museum Archives. At my request, the Spanish government searched its archives for material concerning the *Maine*. This body of selected material is hereafter cited as *Spanish Documents*.

24. Crowninshield to Dewey, January 27, 1898, *Appendix to the Report of the Chief of the Bureau of Navigation, 1898*, p. 22; Chadwick, *The Relations of the United States and Spain. The Spanish-American War* 1: 8–9.

25. Dupuy to Day, January 29, February 5, 1898, Box 8, *Day Papers;* Sigsbee, "Personal Narrative," part 1 (November 1898): 92–93; Philip S. Foner, *The Spanish-Cuban-American War and the Birth of American Imperialism 1895–1902* 1 (New York: Monthly Review Press, 1972): 232–236.

26. Ciphered telegrams, Long to *Maine*, January 25, 1898; Roosevelt to Sigsbee, undated, both in RG. 45, E. 19, *NA;* Moret, Colonial Minister, Madrid, to Secretario Gobierno general, Habana, January 26, 1898, *Spanish Documents*, Spanish Military History Service; Sigsbee, "Personal Narrative," part 1 (November 1898): 89–90; 91–92.

27. Sigsbee to the Secretary of the Navy, February 8, 1898, Box 10, *Day Papers*.

28. Long to Sicard, January 22, 1898, RG. 313, E. 47, Box 1, *NA;* Day to Lee, February 4, 1898, Lee to Day, February 4, 1898, *Foreign Relations 1898,* pp. 1027–1028; Lee to Day, February 5, 1898, Box 35, and Crowninshield to Assistant Secretary of State, February 5, 1898, Box 8, both of *Day Papers.*

29. Extracts of letters, Lee to Day, November 27, December 1, 22, 1897, January 12, 15, 1898, February 2, 1898, Box 35, *Day Papers;* Lee to Gleaves, January 29, 1898, M625, R–225, *NA;* Sigsbee to the Secretary of the Navy, January 26, 1898, Box 10, *Day Papers;* Sigsbee to Long, February 1, 3, 9, 1898, M625, R–226, *NA;* ciphered telegrams, Long to *Maine,* February 10, 1898, Long to Naval Station, February 10, 1898, both in RG. 45, E. 19, *NA.* The extract of the letter from Lee to Day, February 2, 1898, is misdated 1897 in the *Day Papers.*

30. Navy Department, Office of the Chief of Naval Operations, Naval History Division, *Dictionary of American Naval Fighting Ships* 1 (Washington: Government Printing Office, 1959), Appendix 4, "Torpedo Boats and Destroyers, 1887–1958," p. 273.

31. Rafael Montoso to Gobernador General de esta Isla, February 10, 1898, and endorsement, *Spanish Documents,* Spanish Military History Service. For customary international law, see: Appendix B, "Some Aspects of International Law and the Destruction of the *Maine,* February 15, 1898."

32. Ciphered telegram, Long to *Ericsson,* February 11, 1898, RG. 45, E. 19, and Log of the U.S.S. *Cushing,* RG. 24, E. 118, both of *NA.* Gleaves later wrote that the *Cushing* had been sent to Havana on special duty to communicate with Sigsbee and then return immediately to Key West. See: Chadwick, *The Relations of the United States and Spain. The Spanish-American War* 1: 7.

33. Gleaves' account, written years later, is in: Chadwick, *The Relations of the United States and Spain. The Spanish-American War* 1: 9. Sigsbee's account of sending the first message is best told in his "My Story of the 'Maine'," *Cosmopolitan Magazine* 53 (July 1912): 150.

CHAPTER 5

1. Margaret Long, ed., *The Journal of John D. Long* (Rindge, New Hampshire: Richard R. Smith, Inc., 1956), pp. 214–215; H. Wayne Morgan, *America's Road to Empire: The War with Spain and Overseas Expansion* (New York: John Wiley and Sons, 1965), pp. 45–46; John D. Long, "The Navy Department in the War," *The American-Spanish War: A History by the War Leaders* (Norwich, Connecticut: Charles C. Haskell, 1899), pp. 341–342. On Crowninshield's absence, see Long to Secretary of State, March 1, 1898, and enclosure, Box 9, *Day Papers.*

2. Log of the U.S.S. *Ericsson,* Log of the U.S.S. *New York,* both in RG. 24, E. 118, *NA.*

3. Log of the *Fern,* RG. 24, E. 118, *NA.* Photographs of the *Maine* wreck are in: Exhibit I, *Court of Inquiry;* Sigsbee to Secretary of the Navy, February 16, 1898, RG. 24, E. 88, Box 180, *NA;* Charles D. Sigsbee, "Personal Narrative of the 'Maine'," part 2, *Century Magazine* 57 (December 1898): 245–246, 248; The Spanish Naval Headquarters in Havana submitted names to Madrid for awards for assisting the *Maine* crew. As seen in: Admiral Vicente Manterola to the Ministerio de Marina, April 6, 1898, January 18, 1899, *Spanish Documents.* The April 6 letter is from: handwritten collection "War with U.S.A.," volume 1, Spanish Naval Museum Archives and the January 1899 letter is from: *Maine* awards, El Viso del Marques Archives, Spain. Several examples of Spanish activities are given as sworn testimony, see: *Spanish Inquiry,* pp. 565–635.

4. Moret to Gobernador general de Cuba, February 16, 1898, *Spanish Documents,* Spanish Military History Service; Ciphered telegram, Sigsbee to Secretary of the Navy, February 17, 1898, RG. 45, E. 40, *NA.*

5. Margaret Long, *The Journal of John D. Long,* pp. 215–216; Lawrence S. Mayo, *America of Yesterday as Reflected in the Journal of John Davis Long* (Boston: The Atlantic Monthly Press, 1923), pp. 163–164.

6. *Washington Evening Star,* February 16, 17, 18, 1898; *Washington Post,* February 17, 1898; *New York Herald,* February 17, 1898; *Harper's Weekly* 42, February 26, 1898; Fletcher to Gleaves, February 17, 1898, Box 8, Albert Gleaves Papers, Naval Historical Foundation, Library of Congress.

7. O'Neil to Sicard, February 18, 1898, RG. 313, E. 47, *NA.*

8. *Washington Evening Star,* February 18, 1898. For a biographical note on Alger, see: Austin M. Knight, "Professor Philip Rounseville Alger, U.S. Navy. An Appreciation," United States Naval Institute *Proceedings* 38 (March 1912): 1–5.

9. Roosevelt to O'Neil, February 28, 1898, Roosevelt to Long, February 16, 1898, Roosevelt to Diblee, February 16, 1898 in Elting E. Morison, ed., *The Letters of Theodore Roosevelt* 1 (Cambridge: Harvard University Press, 1951): 785–786, 773–774, 774–775.

10. Roosevelt to Long, February 19, 1898 in Morison, *The Letters of Theodore Roosevelt* 1: 779–780; Roosevelt to Lodge, February 24, 1898, RG. 80, E. 124, "Letterbook 3," *NA.*

11. *Regulations for the Government of the Navy of the United States, 1896* (Washington: Government Printing Office, 1896), pp. 397–398.

12. Long to Sicard, February 16, 1898, RG. 313, E. 47, Box 1, *NA.*

13. Sicard to Secretary of the Navy, February 16, 1898, M625, R–226, *NA.* Biographical data are in: Lewis R. Hamersly, *The Records of the Living Officers of the United States Navy and Marine Corps,* 7th ed. (New York: L. R. Hamersly, 1902), pp. 168, 291, 306, and 95.

14. Hamersly, *Records of the Living Officers,* 7th ed. (1902), pp. 10, 155, 168, 97; Sigsbee, "Personal Narrative," part 1 (November 1898): 76; John D. Long, *The New American Navy* 1 (New York: The Outlook Co., 1903): 142.

15. Two letters: Sicard to Sampson, February 19, 1898, both are in *Court of Inquiry,* pp. 285–287.

16. *Spanish Inquiry,* pp. 565–579, 602–603, 632–633.

17. Elbert J. Benton, *International Law and Diplomacy of the Spanish-American War* (Baltimore: The Johns Hopkins Press, 1908), pp. 77–81, and Horace Edgar Flack, *Spanish-American Diplomatic Relations Preceding the War of 1898* (Baltimore: The Johns Hopkins Press, January–February 1906), pp. 41–47; Blanco to the general commander of the navy of the station, February 17, 1898, *Spanish Inquiry,* p. 608; Sigsbee, "Personal Narrative," part 3, *Century Magazine* 57 (January 1899): 380; Day to Lee, February 19, 1898, *Spanish Inquiry,* p. 621; Peral's report is in *Spanish Inquiry,* pp. 578–579, 596.

18. *Spanish Inquiry,* pp. 599–601, 603–604, 615–617, 633; Sigsbee, "Personal Narrative," part 3 (January 1899): 300.

19. Roosevelt to Long, February 19, 1898, Roosevelt to Cowles, February 23, 1898, both in Morison, *The Letters of Theodore Roosevelt* 1: 780, 782.

CHAPTER 6

1. *Court of Inquiry,* pp. 9–19, 102–103.

2. On torpedoes, see: *Court of Inquiry,* p. 103.

3. Lewis R. Hamersly, *The Records of the Living Officers of the United States Navy and Marine Corps,* 7th ed. (New York: L. R. Hamersly, 1902), p. 322; On drawings, see: Sigsbee to Bureau of Navigation, February 22, 1898, and a telegram and letter from Hichborn to Key West, both dated February 23, 1898, RG. 19, E. 74, *NA.*

4. *Court of Inquiry,* pp. 43, 46–47, 97.

5. *Court of Inquiry,* p. 111.

6. *New York Times,* February 2, 18, 19, 20, 21, 23, 25, 1898; William Hovgaard, *Modern History of Warships* (London: E. & F. N. Spon, Ltd., 1920), p. 225; Richard K. Morris, *John P. Holland, 1841–1914: Inventor of the Modern Submarine* (Annapolis: United States Naval Institute, 1966), p. 82.

7. On political strength, see: John L. Offner, "President McKinley and the Origins of the Spanish-American War," (Ph.D. dissertation, Pennsylvania State University, 1957), pp. 116, 217–219. For a very perceptive analysis of prominent figures who opposed intervention and the war, see: Robert L. Beisner, *Twelve Against Empire: The Anti-Imperialists, 1898–1900* (New York: McGraw-Hill, 1968); Charles O'Neil Diary, February 18, 1898, Box 2, Charles O'Neil Papers, Naval Historical Foundation, Library of Congress (hereafter cited as *O'Neil Papers*). For the Senate, see: *Congressional Record,* 55th Congress, 2d session, 1898, volume 31, part 2, pp. 1819, 1873, 1877.

8. Lawrence S. Mayo, *America of Yesterday as Reflected in the Journal of John Davis Long* (Boston: The Atlantic Monthly Press, 1923), pp. 165–166; *Washington Post*, February 20, 1898; *Washington Evening Star*, February 22, 1898.

9. Lee to Assistant Secretary of State, February 22, 1898, Box 9, *Day Papers;* A. Maurice Low to Long, February 26, 1898, Gardner Weld Allen, ed., *Papers of John D. Long 1897–1904* (Boston: The Massachusetts Historical Society, 1939), p. 59, For examples of stories, see: Charles M. Pepper, *Washington Evening Star*, February 19, 23, 1898, and Sylvester Scovel, *Washington Post*, February 20, 1898.

10. Margaret Long, ed., *The Journal of John D. Long* (Rindge, New Hampshire: Richard R. Smith, Inc., 1956), pp. 216–217; Charles O'Neil Diary, February 25, 26, 1898, *O'Neil Papers;* Roosevelt to Dewey, February 25, 1898, Elting E. Morison, ed., *The Letters of Theodore Roosevelt* 1 (Cambridge: Harvard University Press, 1951): 784–785.

11. Charles O'Neil Diary, February 27, 1898, *O'Neil Papers.* The meeting of February 28 is in: Margaret Long, *The Journal of John D. Long,* p. 220 and Mayo, *America of Yesterday,* pp. 170–171. Both accounts are not identical. Both are drawn from the original journal in the possession of the Massachusetts Historical Society. The original journal has the reference to the February 27 meeting.

12. Hamersly, *Records of the Living Officers of the U.S. Navy,* 6th ed. (1898), p. 73. For his position on gunnery innovations, see: Elting E. Morison, *Admiral Sims and the Modern American Navy* (Boston: Houghton Mifflin Co., 1942), pp. 119–120.

13. On Munroe, see: telegram, Munroe to Dickens, February 16, 1898, Munroe to Perkins, February 17, 1898, Dickens to Munroe, February 17, 1898, Perkins to Long, February 18, 1898, all from RG. 45, E. 464, File HF, *NA.* For Munroe's distinguished career, see his obituary in: *The Journal of the American Chemical Society* 61 (January–June 1939): 1301–1316. His obituary contains over five pages listing his publications. The caliber of Munroe's former scientific investigation for the Navy can be seen in a report concerning the cause of an explosion aboard the *Atlanta* on May 12, 1891. See: L. A. Beardslee, A. S. Crowninshield, F. L. Fernald, John L. Borthwick, Charles Munroe to Henry Erben, Commandant of the New York Navy Yard, October 27, 1891, in RG. 80, E. 18, Box 110, File 6552, *NA.* On the weakness of the court membership, see: *Washington Evening Star*, February 28, March 1, 1898.

14. Sicard to Secretary of the Navy, February 26, 1898, M625, R–226, *NA.* Fernald's obituary is in: *Transactions of the Society of Naval Architects and Marine Engineers* 29 (1921): 378–380. For Hoover's orders and biographical data, see: RG. 19, E. 88, File 5/A–56 to 13/A–29, *NA.* Writing in 1903, Long believed that "the mystery of her loss yet remains to be solved, but the facts will some day come to light, and it will probably be found that, so far as the Spanish government itself was concerned, it was innocent of the design, though it is possible that some of its subordinates or possibly some insurgent Cuban foreseeing the effect, may have been responsible for the fact." John D. Long, *The New American Navy* 1 (New York: The Outlook Co., 1903): 144.

15. *Court of Inquiry,* p. 204; *Regulations for the Government of the Navy of the United States, 1896* (Washington: Government Printing Office, 1896), p. 400.

16. Long to Sicard, March 4, 1898, Sicard to Long, March 4, 1898, RG. 313, E. 47, Box 1, *NA;* Sampson's views on the *Iowa* are in: ciphered telegram, Lee to Assistant Secretary of State, March 9, 1898, T20, R–132, *NA.*

17. Charles O'Neil Diary, March 6, 7, 1898, *O'Neil Papers; Annual Reports of the Navy Department for the Year 1897* (Washington: Government Printing Office, 1898), p. 275; Margaret Long, *The Journal of John D. Long,* p. 221; Mayo, *America of Yesterday,* p. 172; Margaret Leech, *In the Days of McKinley* (New York: Harper & Brothers, 1959), p. 168; Long to Sicard, March 14, 1898, RG. 313, E. 47, Box 1, *NA.*

18. Woodford to Sherman, March 13, 14, 1898, Box 35, *Day Papers;* Roosevelt to Secretary of the Navy, March 16, 1898, M625, R–409, *NA.*

19. Roosevelt to Chadwick, March 19, 1898, RG. 80, E. 124, "Letterbook 3," *NA;* Sampson to Long, March 16, 1898, Allen, *Papers of John D. Long,* pp. 71–72.

20. *Court of Inquiry,* pp. 242–244, 247, 271; *Who Was Who In America* 1 (Chicago: A. N. Marquis Co., 1942): 253.

21. *New York Times,* March 12, 1898; *Court of Inquiry,* pp. 257–260.

22. Sigsbee to wife, March 15, 1898, Box 1, Folder 23, *Sigsbee Papers.*

23. Ciphered telegram, Sicard to Secretary of the Navy, March 17, 1898, RG. 45, E. 40, *NA; Washington Post,* March 18, 1898; *Washington Evening Star,* March 19, 1898; Day to Woodford, March 20, 1898, Box 34, *Day Papers.*

24. *Washington Post,* March 24, 25, 26, 1898; Cortelyou Diary, March 25, 1898, Box 52, George B. Cortelyou Papers, Manuscript Division, Library of Congress.

25. *Court of Inquiry,* pp. 279–281.

26. Cortelyou Diary, March 25, 26, 27, 1898, Box 52, George B. Cortelyou Papers, Manuscript Division, Library of Congress. The President's message is in *Court of Inquiry,* pp. 3–5.

27. Day to Woodford, March 26, 1898, Woodford to Day, March 27, 1898, Day to Woodford, March 28, 1898, all from *Foreign Relations 1898,* pp. 704, 712–713.

28. For the testimony of Bradford, Barker, and Sigsbee, see: U.S. Congress, Senate, *Report of the Committee on Foreign Relations, United States Senate, Relative to Affairs in Cuba,* 55th Congress, 2d session, April 13, 1898, Senate Report 885, pp. 469–494.

29. Luis Polo de Bernabé to Secretary of State, March 28, 1898, Box 9, *Day Papers; Spanish Inquiry,* pp. 630–636.

30. Two letters from Pauncefote to the Marquis of Salisbury, March 14, 1898, Sanderson to Pauncefote, March 15, 21, 26, 1898, Nugent to Salisbury, March 26, 1898. Pauncefote to Salisbury: Reference:— F.O. 5. 2361. X/J. 7672; Sanderson to Pauncefote and Nugent to Salisbury: Reference:—ADM 1 7386 AvB. X/J. 7658. From the British Public Record Office. These documents were obtained for me by Rear Admiral L. R. Bell Davies, Royal Navy, Commander, British Navy Staff, Washington, D.C.

31. Margaret Long, *Journal of John D. Long,* p. 221; John A. Garraty, *Henry Cabot Lodge, A Biography* (New York: Alfred A. Knopf, 1953), pp. 188–189; *Congressional Record,* 55th Congress, 2d session, 1898, volume 31, part 4, p. 3458.

32. Day to Lee, April 9, 1898, Box 8 and Interview with Spanish Minister, April 10, 1898, Box 35, both from *Day Papers;* Charles O'Neil Diary, April 6, 10, 1898, *O'Neil Papers.*

33. Mayo, *America of Yesterday,* pp. 176–178; *Congressional Record,* 55th Congress, 2d session, volume 31, part 4, pp. 3699–3702.

34. For Lee's testimony, see: U.S. Senate, *Affairs in Cuba,* Report 885, pp. 534–538. For the report, see: pp. v–xxiii.

35. Mayo, *America of Yesterday,* pp. 182–183; Leech, *In the Days of McKinley,* p. 190.

CHAPTER 7

1. Battle death toll was furnished by the Office of the Secretary of Defense; Sigsbee's account of his return to Havana in 1898 is in his "My Story of the 'Maine'," *Cosmopolitan Magazine* 53 (July 1912): 158–159, 380; Criticism about the condition of the *Texas* is in Charles H. Allen, Acting Secretary of the Navy, March 29, 1899 and John D. Long, January 31, 1900, both to U.S. Naval Examining Board in Charles D. Sigsbee file, RG. 125, E. 58, *NA.* Sigsbee's career after 1900 is from: *Who Was Who In America* 1 (Chicago: A. N. Marquis Co., 1942): 1125.

2. The postwar careers of Sampson, Chadwick, Potter, and Marix are from: *Who Was Who In America* 1: 1075, 206, 987, 777. Chadwick's books are: *The Relations of the United States and Spain. Diplomacy* (New York: Charles Scribner's Sons, 1909) and *The Relations of the United States and Spain. The Spanish-American War,* 2 volumes (New York: Charles Scribner's Sons, 1911).

3. Charles D. Sigsbee, "Personal Narrative of the 'Maine'," part 3, *Century Magazine* 57 (January 1899): 391–394.

4. J. T. Bucknill, "The Destruction of the United States Battleship 'Maine'," *Engineering* 65 (May 28, June 3, June 10, June 17, June 24, 1898): 650–651, 687–691, 716–717, 752–754, 782–783.

5. Lewis R. Hamersly, *The Records of the Living Officers of the U.S. Navy and Marine Corps,* 7th ed. (New York: L. R. Hamersly, 1902), pp. 93–95; George W. Grupp, "Rear Admiral George Wallace Melville As a Man and Engineer-in-Chief of the Navy," United States Naval Institute *Proceedings* 74 (May 1948): 613–617; *Washington Post,* February 17, 1898; Meyer to Melville, March 9, 1911, George von L. Meyer Papers, Massachusetts Historical Society.

6. Melville's letter was published in his article, "The Destruction of the Battleship 'Maine'," *The North American Review* 193 (June 1911): 831–849.

7. On Sigsbee's view, see his "My Story of the 'Maine'," *Cosmopolitan Magazine* 53 (July 1912): 381–382; for Chadwick's see: *The Relations of the United States and Spain. Diplomacy,* pp. 561–563.

8. The provisions of the acts are found in: U.S. Congress, House of Representatives, *Raising Wreck of Battleship "Maine",* 62d Congress, 1st session, July 28, 1911, Document 96, pp. 3–5.

9. Brief biographies of Black and Patrick are in: *Who Was Who In America* 1: 101, 941; a biography of Harley B. Ferguson is in *Who Was Who In America* 5 (Chicago: Who's Who, Inc., 1973): 229. Harley B. Ferguson died in 1968.

10. On permission from Cuba, see: Black to Bixby, August 20, 1910, RG. 77, E. 103, Box 1262, File 33774 "Maine," *NA.* On the first meeting of the *Maine* board, see: Black to H. B. Ferguson, August 20, 1910, Box 1, Folder 4, in the Harley B. Ferguson Papers, Southern Historical Collection, University of North Carolina Library, Chapel Hill (hereafter cited as *Harley B. Ferguson Papers*). For Taft's approval, see: Taft to Bixby, August 29, 1910 and for the preliminary suggestion to invite the Spanish, see: Robert Shaw Oliver, Assistant Secretary of War, to the Secretary of State, September 30, 1910, both in RG. 77, E. 103, Box 1262, File 33774 "Maine," *NA.* For Taft's endorsement of the invitation, see: Taft to P. C. Knox, Secretary of State, October 11, 1910, and for the details of the tendering and rejection of the invitation, see: Confidential letter, A. Campbettlumes (?), American Chargé d'Affaires ad-interim, Madrid, to Secretary of State, November 2, 1910, both in RG. 59, "Decimal File, 1910–1924," Box 7497, File 811.304 M/28, *NA.*

11. J. T. Bucknill, "The Raising of the Wreck of the U.S. Battleship 'Maine'," *Engineering* 93 (March 15, 1912): 365–367.

12. The request by the Army for the weights and contents of the *Maine* are in H. B. Ferguson to Black, August 16, 1910, Box 1, Folder 4, *Harley B. Ferguson Papers.* The eventual reply is in: Acting Chief of the Bureau of Construction and Repair to Chief of Engineers, U.S. Army, September 21, 1910, RG. 38, E. 242, Binder 108, *NA.* Major Black recommended a naval constructor be secured to help identify wreckage and advise on structural details in: Black to Bixby, March 27, 1911 and the earliest indication of the intent of the Navy to inspect the wreck is in Robert Stocker, Board of Inspection and Survey, to H. B. Ferguson, April 1, 1911, both from Box 1, Folder 7, *Harley B. Ferguson Papers.* The request for William B. Ferguson's orders is in Chief of the Bureau of Construction and Repair to Chief of the Bureau of Navigation, May 22, 1911, RG. 24, E. 88, Box 172, File 1050–81 to 1055–86, *NA;* William B. Ferguson's background is from his obituary in *Transactions of the Society of Naval Architects and Marine Engineers* 61 (1953): 771; William B. Ferguson to Board of Inspection and Survey, June 7, 1911, RG. 38, E. 242, Binder 108, *NA.*

13. The immense task of building the cofferdam is well documented in Harley B. Ferguson's daily reports in boxes 5 and 6 of the *Harley B. Ferguson Papers.* The work of naval constructor William B. Ferguson is equally well documented in RG. 38, E. 242, Binder 108, *NA.* For Spanish newspaper clippings, see: Henry C. Ide to State Department and enclosures, February 9, 1911, RG. 59, "Decimal File, 1910–1924," Box 7497, File 811.304 M/28, *NA;* Bixby's opinion is in the *Havana Post,* June 27, 1911 and his telegram to the *St. Louis Post-Dispatch,* July 6, 1911 in RG. 77, E. 103, Box 1263, File 52736 "Maine," *NA.*

14. That the Army might have to remove critical wreckage is in: "Unofficial Memo," W.B.F. to Board of Inspection and Survey, August 23, 1911, RG. 38, E. 242, Binder 108, *NA.* Capps' orders to Havana are in: Acting Secretary of the Navy to W. L. Capps, September 12, 1911, RG. 24, E. 88, Box 508, File 2711–132, *NA.* For the Army's instructions regarding Capps' visit, see: "Personal Letter," Bixby to H. B. Ferguson, September 17, 1911, Box 1, Folder 9, *Harley B. Ferguson Papers.* A brief description of Capps' work in Havana is in W. B. Ferguson to Board of Inspection

and Survey, October 4, 1911, RG. 38, E. 242, Binder 108, *NA*. Washington Lee Capps' eminent career is recorded in his obituary in *Transactions of the Society of Naval Architects and Marine Engineers* 43 (1935): 308–311.

15. Meyer to Secretary of War, November 9, 1911, "Official Communication from July 12, 1911 to December, 1911," George von L. Meyer Papers, Massachusetts Historical Society. The minutes of the daily sessions of the board of inspection and survey upon the *Maine* are in: "Record of Proceedings of a Board Convened at Havana, Cuba, By Order of the Secretary of the Navy, to Inspect and Report on the Wreck of the 'Maine' (old)," in RG. 80, E. 19, Box 233, File 6658, *NA*.

16. Official accounts of the final sinking of the *Maine* are: "Paraphrased Telegram," Beaupre to Secretary of State, March 11, 1912; C. Marsh, Commanding Officer, U.S.S. *North Carolina* to Secretary of the Navy, March 16, 1912; and radiogram, Marsh to Secretary of the Navy, March 16, 1912, all in RG. 80, E. 19, Box 233, File 6658, *NA*.

17. The last stages of removing the wreckage are in the miscellaneous reports of F. A. Pope to *Maine* Board, October, November, December, 1912, Folders 15 and 16, *Harley B. Ferguson Papers*.

18. The findings of the Vreeland board were published in: U.S. Congress, House of Representatives, *Report on the Wreck of the Maine*, 62d Congress, 2d session, December 14, 1911, Document 310. The quotations are from paragraphs 37, 40, and 43 (pp. 10, 11).

19. J. T. Bucknill, "The U.S. Battleship 'Maine'," *Engineering* 93 (June 21, 1912): 827–829.

CHAPTER 8

1. Secretary of the Navy G. v. Meyer to Rear Admiral Charles E. Vreeland, November 10, 1911, RG. 80, E. 19, File 6658, *NA*.

2. U.S. Congress, House of Representatives, *Report on the Wreck of the Maine,* 62d Congress, 2d session, December 14, 1911, Document 310, paragraph 37 (p. 10).

List of Abbreviations of Sources
Used in Notes

Court of Inquiry	U.S. Congress, Senate, *Message from the President of the United States Transmitting the Report of the Naval Court of Inquiry Upon the Destruction of the United States Battle Ship Maine in Havana Harbor, February 15, 1898, Together with the Testimony Taken Before the Court,* 55th Congress, 2d session, 1898, Document 207.
Day Papers	William R. Day Papers, Manuscript Division, United States Library of Congress, Washington, D.C.
E.	Entry
Foreign Relations 1898	U.S. Department of State, *Papers Relating to the Foreign Relations of the United States . . . 1898* (Washington: Government Printing Office, 1901)
Harley B. Ferguson Papers	Harley B. Ferguson Papers, Southern Historical Collection, University of North Carolina Library, Chapel Hill
M———	Microfilm copy: "M" series
NA	United States National Archives and Record Service, Washington, D.C.
1911 Board	U.S. Congress, House of Representatives, *Report on the Wreck of the Maine,* 62d Congress, 2d session, 1911, Document 310.
NWCA	United States Naval War College Archives, Newport, Rhode Island
O'Neil Papers	Charles O'Neil Papers, Naval Historical Foundation, Library of Congress, Washington, D.C.
R———	Reel
RG.	Record Group
Sigsbee Papers	Charles D. Sigsbee Papers, New York State Library, Albany, New York
Spanish Documents	Historical documents furnished through the courtesy of the Spanish government
Spanish Inquiry	Report of the Spanish Naval Board of Inquiry as to the Cause of the Destruction of the U.S.B.S. Maine in: U.S. Congress, Senate, *Report of the Committee on Foreign Relations, U.S. Senate, Relative to Affairs in Cuba,* 55th Congress, 2d session, April 13, 1898, Senate Report 885.
T———	Microfilm copy: "T" series
Vreeland Board File	Documents within Record Group 80, Entry 19, File 6658, United States National Archives and Records Service, Washington, D.C.

List of the Record Groups
of the United States National Archives
and their Subordinate Entries
as Employed in the Documentation
of this Work

Record Group 19: Records of the Bureau of Ships
    Entry 74: "General Correspondence 1887–1895"
    Entry 88: "Correspondence ('A' Documents) 1896–1925"
    Entry 126: "Plans of Ships and Shore Establishments 1794–1910"

Record Group 24: Records of the Bureau of Naval Personnel
    Entry 88: "General Correspondence 1889–1913"
    Entry 118: "Logs of United States Naval Ships and Stations 1801–1946"

Record Group 38: Records of the Office of the Chief of Naval Operations
    Entry 242: "Reports of Inspections of Naval Vessels 1893–1946"

Record Group 45: Naval Records Collection of the Office of Naval Records and Library
    Entry 19: "Translations of Messages Sent in Cipher"
    Entry 40: "Translations of Messages Received in Cipher"
    Entry 301: "Letters Sent by Naval Attachés of the United States in London"
    Entry 464: "Subject File"

Record Group 59: Records of the Department of State
    Entry 311: "Reports of Clerks and Bureau Officers"
    Unnumbered: "Decimal File 1910–1944"

Record Group 77: Records of the Office of the Chief of Engineers
    Entry 103: "General Correspondence 1894–1923"

Record Group 80: General Records of the Department of the Navy
    Entry 18: "General File 1885–1897"
    Entry 19: "General File 1897–1926"
    Entry 124: "Letters Sent and Memoranda Issued"

Record Group 125: Records of the Office of the Judge Advocate General (Navy)
    Entry 58: "Records of Proceedings of Naval and Marine Examining Boards"

Record Group 313: Records of Naval Operating Forces
    Entry 47: "Correspondence with Bureaus of the Navy Department 1897–1899"

List of Microfilm Copies
of the United States National Archives
and their Subordinate Reels
as Employed in the Documentation
of this Work

Microcopy M17: General Records of the Department of State
  Reel 53: "Registers of Miscellaneous Communications Received, 1860–1906: January 1, 1897–December 31, 1899"
  Reel 68: "Registers of Miscellaneous Communications Sent, 1840–1906: January 1, 1897–December 31, 1899"

Microcopy M625: Area File of the Naval Records Collection 1775–1910
  Reel 225: "Area 8: November 1897–January 1898"
  Reel 226: "Area 8: February 1898"
  Reel 409: "Area 11: 1866–1910"

Microcopy T20: Despatches from U.S. Consuls in Havana 1783–1906
  Reel 132: "February 1, 1898–December 11, 1902"

Note on Sources

During the study of the loss of the battleship *Maine* it became evident that published accounts of the disaster were superficial. Indeed, most writers have treated the subject as merely a single mysterious incident which contributed to the causes of the Spanish-American War. It was apparent that such accounts were based upon information extracted from standard published primary and secondary sources. The following paragraphs are an effort to indicate the most valuable sources cited in this monograph and to point out some of the other sources which were consulted and used for background.

PUBLISHED SOURCES

The keystone of any investigation into the loss of the *Maine* is necessarily the testimony and findings of the 1898 court of inquiry. They were published as: U.S. Congress, Senate, *Message from the President of the United States Transmitting the Report of the Naval Court of Inquiry Upon the Destruction of the United States Battle Ship Maine in Havana Harbor, February 15, 1898, Together With the Testimony Taken Before the Court,* 55th Congress, 2d session, 1898, Document 207. A spot-check comparison with the original typescript document in National Archives Record Group 125, Entry 30, revealed that the published text is most likely a true and complete version. The 1898 court testimony could not be assessed without applying the contemporary procedures for inquiries as set forth in *Regulations for the Government of the Navy of the United States 1896* (Washington: Government Printing Office, 1896). In 1911 the findings of the Vreeland board of inspection and survey upon the wreck of the *Maine* were published without exhibits as: U.S. Congress, House of Representatives, *Report on the Wreck of the Maine,* 62d Congress, 2d session, December 14, 1911, Document 310. The translated Report of the Spanish Naval Board of Inquiry as to the Cause of the Destruction of the U.S.B.S. Maine is located within U.S. Congress, Senate, *Report of the Committee on Foreign Relations, United States Senate, Relative to Affairs in Cuba,* 55th Congress, 2d session, April 13, 1898, Senate Report 885. A spot-check comparison with the original handwritten Spanish document in National Archives microcopy M59: Notes from the Spanish Legation in the United States to the Department of State 1790–1906, Reel 29: "October 7, 1897–July 27, 1899" indicated minor irregularities in translation and printing.

American diplomatic despatches have been arranged in chronological order in: U.S. Department of State, *Papers Relating to the Foreign Relations of the United States . . . 1898* (Washington: Government Printing Office, 1901). Spanish diplomatic correspondence of the period may be found in: *Spanish Diplomatic Correspondence and Documents, 1896–1900* (Washington: Government Printing Office, 1905). The *Congressional Record* provides information about the activities of Congress for this time. The *Appendix to the Report of the Chief of the Bureau of Navigation, 1898* (Washington: Government Printing Office, 1898) has selected messages and orders issued prior to and during the war with Spain. The *Annual Reports of the Navy Department* are standard sources for general information about the Department or Bureaus during any specific year. The years 1897 and 1898 were utilized for this study.

A number of personal accounts of the disaster were written by the persons involved. Charles D. Sigsbee's three works supply a number of obscure details as well as reveal his personality. Though overlapping on many specifics, each work has its unique points: "Personal Narrative of the 'Maine',", three parts, *Century Magazine* 57 (November, December, 1898 and January 1899); "My Story of the 'Maine'," *Cosmopolitan Magazine* 53 (July and August, 1912). Sigsbee's book, *The "Maine". An Account of Her Destruction in Havana Harbor* (New York: Century, 1899) includes Ensign W. V. N. Powelson's official report as "Appendix E" which Sigsbee believed was a true and accurate account of the

163

technical evidence suggesting a mine destroyed his ship. Shortly after the war the former navigator of the *Maine* wrote a useful chapter: "The Destruction of the *Maine*" for the book *The American-Spanish War: A History by the War Leaders* (Norwich, Connecticut: Charles C. Haskell, 1899). In the same volume appears a chapter by Secretary of the Navy John D. Long, "The Navy Department in the War". In it he steadfastly denies that the Navy Department knew of the findings of the Sampson court prior to Marix's arrival in Washington on March 24, 1898. An account by Cadet W. T. Cluverius appeared as "A Midshipman on the *Maine*" in the United States Naval Institute *Proceedings* 44 (February 1918). His article is flawed by errors and appears to have been written much later than "only a few months" after the disaster as the article claimed. One striking departure from the usual Navy opinion of the time was George Melville whose critical letter was published as "The Destruction of the Battleship 'Maine'," in *The North American Review* 193 (June 1911).

For glimpses of the mood in Washington, the *Washington Post* proved particularly helpful for it frequently published material obtained from sources close to the Navy Department. The *Washington Evening Star* gave a less restrained view of events. In the same direction, the *New York Herald* provided interesting, though not completely reliable, investigative reports. On the whole, the three newspapers reviewed had a remarkably accurate account of the facts of the explosion and subsequent investigation. The *Army Navy Journal* contains a few communications between Key West and Washington which are not published elsewhere and it regularly published selected messages transmitted to and from the Navy Department. Most of the material can be located in archival sources however. *Harper's Weekly* and *Scientific American* provide straightforward news accounts of the explosion.

An understanding of key testimony given during the 1898 Sampson inquiry and a reconstruction of the explosion of the ship as demonstrated in Appendix A, the Hansen-Price analysis, required detailed technical information about the *Maine*'s ammunition. J. F. Meigs and R. R. Ingersoll, *Text-Book of Ordnance and Gunnery* (Annapolis: U.S. Naval Institute, 1887) provided a general picture of the guns, types of ammunition, and practices observed in the decade before the disaster. However, *Description of Ammunition Used in the Naval Service and Instructions for Preparing Same for Issue*, U.S. Navy, Bureau of Ordnance (Newport, Rhode Island: Navy Torpedo Station Print., 1896) gave a more specific and highly technical description of the type of munitions on the *Maine* at the time of the explosion. A separate booklet of ordnance blueprints also accompanies this text. *Reports of the Efficiency of Various Coals 1896 to 1898, Expenses of Equipment Abroad 1902–1903, Recent Analyses of Coal at Navy-Yard, Washington, D.C.* (Washington: Government Printing Office, 1906) is apparently an obscure printing of three separate and only vaguely related reports. However, the *Maine*'s brand of coal is listed in the tables and the report of Roosevelt's spontaneous combustion investigation of January 27, 1898 is printed fully. J. T. Bucknill, "The Destruction of the United States Battleship 'Maine'," *Engineering* 65 (May 28, June 3, June 10, June 17, June 24, 1898) and his "The Raising of the Wreck of the Battleship 'Maine'," in *Engineering* 93 (March 15, 1912) remain as the most competent contemporary criticisms of the disaster and the official investigations. One noteworthy German-language article, Hermann Gercke, "Der Untergang der 'Maine'," *Marine-Rundschau* (Januar bis Juni, Berlin: 1898) attacked the problem in a manner similar to Bucknill's concurrent *Engineering* articles.

American foreign policy is placed in general context in Richard W. Leopold, *The Growth of American Foreign Policy* (New York: Alfred A. Knopf, 1962) and specifically outlined throughout the McKinley administration in Paolo E. Coletta, ed., *Threshold to American Internationalism, Essays on the Foreign Policy of William McKinley* (New York: Exposition Press, 1970). International law and diplomacy is dealt with in: French E. Chadwick, *The Relations of the United States and Spain. Diplomacy* (New York: Charles Scribner's Sons, 1909), Elbert J. Benton, *International Law and Diplomacy of the Spanish-American War* (Baltimore: The Johns Hopkins Press, 1908), and Horace Edgar Flack, *Spanish-American Diplomatic Relations Preceding the War of 1898* (Baltimore: The Johns Hopkins Press, January–February 1906). Philip S. Foner, *The Spanish-Cuban-American War and the Birth of American Imperialism 1895–1902*, two volumes (New York: Monthly Review Press, 1972) is a detailed but partisan and predictable interpretation of events.

A general background to the period is in: H. Wayne Morgan, *America's Road to Empire: The War with Spain and Overseas Expansion* (New York: John Wiley and Sons, 1965) and Ernest R. May,

Imperial Democracy: The Emergence of America as a Great Power (New York: Harcourt, Brace & World, 1961). Robert L. Beisner, *Twelve Against Empire: The Anti-Imperialists 1898–1900* (New York: McGraw-Hill, 1968) is a good study of prominent Americans who opposed expansion. Warm portraits of two presidents and their administrations are in Allan Nevins, *Grover Cleveland, A Study in Courage* (New York: Dodd, Mead & Co., 1932) and Margaret Leech, *In the Days of McKinley* (New York: Harper & Brothers, 1959). A scholarly examination of the McKinley administration is John L. Offner, "President McKinley and the Origins of the Spanish-American War," (Ph.D. dissertation, Pennsylvania State University, 1957). Graham A. Cosmas, *An Army for Empire: The United States in the Spanish-American War* (Columbia, Missouri: University of Missouri Press, 1971) depicts the role of the Army in the war and the reforms which followed. Similarly, John D. Long, *The New American Navy,* two volumes (New York: The Outlook Co., 1903) depicts the success of the Navy.

French E. Chadwick, *The Relations of the United States and Spain. The Spanish-American War,* two volumes (New York: Charles Scribner's Sons, 1911) details especially the Navy's role in the war. A most comprehensive bibliography has been published in Thomas E. Kelly III, *The US Army and the Spanish-American War Era, 1896–1910,* two parts (Carlisle Barracks, Pennsylvania: U.S. Army Military History Research Collection, 1974). Hugh Thomas, *Cuba: The Pursuit of Freedom* (New York: Harper & Row, 1971) presents a broad and moderate treatment of the island's history and is useful for background.

The standard biographical collections had information on a few key individuals, but for other figures the appropriate edition of Lewis R. Hamersly, *The Records of the Living Officers of the U.S. Navy and Marine Corps* (New York: L. R. Hamersly) and the obituaries in the United States Naval Institute *Proceedings* and the *Transactions of the Society of Naval Architects and Marine Engineers* were essential.

Recent writings about the destruction of the *Maine* include the factual article appearing in the current edition of *Enciclopedia General Del Mar* (Madrid-Barcelona: Ediciones Garriga, S.A., n.d.) and the recent José Manuel Allendesalazar, *El 98 de Los Americanos* (Madrid: Editorial Cuadernos Para El Dialogo, S.A., 1974). In both of these examples of current Spanish treatment of the *Maine* problem there was disappointment that the authors did not make greater use of Spanish archives but rather employed well-used American sources. John Edward Weems, *The Fate of the Maine* (New York: Henry Holt, 1958) is a generally accurate and readable book written in the journalistic style. Though there is a minimum of documentation, Weems was able to interview several survivors of the disaster. As far as could be ascertained, there are now no survivors still living. L. VanLoan Naisawald, "Destruction of the USS *Maine*—Accident or Sabotage?" appeared in the Comments and Discussion section of the United States Naval Institute *Proceedings* 98 (February 1972, pp. 98–100) and hypothesizes that the explosion was caused by methane gas escaping from a coal bunker. The author incorrectly assumes that the existence and proper control of this gas was unknown to the Navy in 1898. Richard M. Basoco, "What Really Happened to the *Maine?*" *American History Illustrated* 1 (June 1966) restates the question and attempts to assign some significance to the incredible testimony given before the 1898 court by local civilians who claimed to overhear a Spanish plot to destroy the battleship. Walter Scott Merriwether, "Remembering the *Maine,*" United States Naval Institute *Proceedings* 74 (January 1948) is an anecdotal story about American newsmen trying to cable news about the *Maine* passed the Havana censor. Arthur Johnson, "The Battleship Maine and Pier 46, East River," United States Naval Institute *Proceedings* 81 (November 1955) gives the story of the East River collision. John M. Talyor, "Returning to the Riddle of the Explosion that Sunk the Maine," appeared in the *Washington Star-News* September 1, 1974 and it was Taylor's thought-provoking questions which must be acknowledged as the instigator of this entire monograph.

UNPUBLISHED SOURCES

For the purpose of easy location, "entry" numbers have been used when referring to documents within the collections of the National Archives. The entry numbers are further identified by title on page 159. Although these numbers were in common use at the National Archives during, and many years prior to the research upon the subject of the *Maine* in this monograph, the Archives staff indicates that the entries in many cases are only preliminary and are subject to change in the future. In this event the full titles would be sufficient to locate the documents cited.

In assessing the value of the records consulted at the United States National Archives and Record Service in Washington, D.C. perhaps Record Group 45: Naval Records Collection of the Office of Naval Records and Library, Entries 19 and 40: "Translations of Messages Sent in Cipher" and "Translations of Messages Received in Cipher" proved most helpful in documenting the events surrounding the despatch and sinking of the *Maine*. Although this record group is often used, the ciphers provide a concise record of the most important communications sent and received by the Secretary of the Navy during this crisis. The telegrams proved especially useful since the exact time of day they were sent or received was noted on each document. During critical days, the exact daily sequence of the messages was very important. Within this same record group, Entry 464: "Subject File", is File HF— two boxes of letters dealing with fires and explosions on board ships. There is some peripheral data about the *Maine* in this file, however, the letters dealing with bunker fires on board other ships were far more revealing. Though an apparently arbitrary collection and probably far from comprehensive, File HF has documents which would be impossible to track down and locate within the general correspondence files of the Navy Department and the bureaus.

The various general correspondence files were rewarding in several cases where specific information or orders were required and could be traced by index. However, use of these files is a painstaking and frequently fruitless task. Most notable in the general file letters is Record Group 80: Records of the Navy Department, Entry 19: "General File 1897–1926," File 6658. This is the original file, the report, and most of the exhibits to the 1911 Vreeland board of inspection and survey.

In Record Group 19: Records of the Bureau of Ships, Entry 126: "Plans of Ships and Shore Establishments 1794–1910," are the assorted and nearly complete, detailed plans to the *Maine*. Access to the plans are through a series of several hundred file cards. The researcher requires some knowledge of naval architecture to understand the cards and read the ship's plans. Care should be taken to call for plans which show the ship during its later period of construction or post-commissioned state. Within Record Group 24: Records of the Bureau of Naval Personnel is Entry 118: "Logs of United States Naval Ships and Stations 1801–1946." The last log of the *Maine* in the collection ends March 31, 1897. The ship's log is a very precise, efficient document which records the movements of the ship, the weather, and none but the most important and prescribed events in a brief, standard manner. Thus the log affords no great insight into internal shipboard activities.

Roosevelt's letterbooks of correspondence with various persons during this time offer a good look at the chief concerns of the Assistant Secretary and are in Record Group 80, Entry 124: "Letters Sent and Memoranda Issued." Most revealing, however, are Admiral Sicard's official correspondence located in an unlikely place—Record Group 313: Records of Naval Operating Forces, Entry 47: "Correspondence with Bureaus of the Navy Department 1897–1899." Within Record Group 38: Records of the Office of the Chief of Naval Operations, Entry 242: "Reports of Inspection of Naval Vessels 1893–1946" are the reports of the board of inspection and survey. Binder 108 deals with the raising of the *Maine* and the work of Naval Constructor William B. Ferguson at the site.

The microfilmed records at the National Archives are convenient. Within microcopy M17: General Records of the Department of State are two reels, 53 and 68, which reproduce the registers of communications received and sent during the Spanish-American War years. Microcopy T20: Despatches from U.S. Consuls in Havana 1783–1906, reel 132, has many of Consul General Fitzhugh Lee's communications during the *Maine* crisis. Microcopy M625: Area File of the Naval Records Collection 1775–1910 is a reproduction of an arbitrary collection of documents. The documents are arranged by "area" or geographic location from which they were sent to the Navy Department. They are further arranged in chronological order. Area 8 included Cuba and area 11 Washingon, D.C.

The Naval War College at Newport, Rhode Island contains, in addition to an excellent library, an archival collection which includes a number of documents pertaining to plans for a war with Spain. The U.S. National Archives and the Operational Archives of the Naval History Division, U.S. Navy, have others. Manuscripts which were written as War College exercises at the time should be noted: David F. Boyd (a *Maine* survivor), "The Causes of the Spanish-American War and the Naval and Combined Operations in the Atlantic, Including the Transfer of the *Oregon*," (Newport, Rhode Island: Naval War

College, 1928–1929). Here too is Austin M. Knight and William D. Puleston, "History of the Naval War College," (Newport Rhode Island: Naval War College, 1916). On the history of the college is Ronald Spector, "Professors of War: The Naval War College and the Modern American Navy," (Ph.D. dissertation, Yale, 1967).

The Nimitz Library of the United States Naval Academy at Annapolis, Maryland currently has nothing in the manner of primary sources dealing with the *Maine*. However, the Naval Academy Museum has two documents. One is a 21-page handwritten "Personal Reminiscence" by John Hood and the other, a February 25, 1898 letter of Carl Jungen to "Friend." Neither document is particularly informative beyond the published sources but both serve to demonstrate the solidarity demonstrated by *Maine* officers in supporting the findings of the Sampson board.

In Spain, the Military History Service, archives of the Spanish Naval Museum and the archives of El Viso del Marques have documents pertaining to the *Maine*. The British Public Record Office has files dealing with British observations of American preparations for war as well as a few routine reports about the sinking of the battleship.

Personal papers were of great value to this study. The Charles D. Sigsbee Papers at the New York State Library, Albany were most interesting and included a variety of both personal and official correspondence spanning Sigsbee's lifetime. Within the papers is a folder of handwritten reports submitted by the *Maine*'s officers. Generally dated February 16, 1898, the day after the explosion, they indicate that the observations expressed in testimony before the Sampson board were generally consistent with their observations as recorded very shortly after the disaster.

At the Massachusetts Historical Society in Boston are the papers of John D. Long, George von L. Meyer, and Henry Cabot Lodge. The Long papers treating the subject have been thoroughly published among three books: Margaret Long, ed., *The Journal of John D. Long* (Rindge, New Hampshire: Richard R. Smith, Inc., 1956); Gardner Weld Allen, ed., *Papers of John D. Long 1897–1904* (Boston: The Massachusetts Historical Society, 1939); Lawrence S. Mayo, *America of Yesterday as Reflected in the Journal of John Davis Long* (Boston: Atlantic Monthly Press, 1923). The Lodge correspondence also has been published. The George von L. Meyer papers were of limited use for this purpose. The Library of Congress has some Meyer papers but these deal with his diplomatic career.

At the Library of Congress, within the collections of the Naval Historical Foundation, are the Charles O'Neil Papers and the Albert Gleaves Papers. O'Neil's papers, especially his diary, proved useful and the Gleaves papers explained the role of the torpedo boats in the *Maine* incident. Papers dealing with George W. Melville, Montgomery Sicard, Henry C. Taylor, Alfred Thayer Mahan, William S. Sims, Joseph Strauss, William S. Cowles, and the Wainwright Family were searched but they were found to contain nothing of great relevance to the *Maine*.

Within the Manuscript Division of the Library of Congress, the papers of William R. Day, John Bassett Moore, and George Cortelyou were of particular value when examining the political and diplomatic aspects of the despatch of the ship. The Taft and McKinley presidential papers contained nothing of importance on the *Maine*. The Theodore Roosevelt Papers were checked but, like the Long and Lodge correspondence, these have been extensively published. Elting E. Morison's, *The Letters of Theodore Roosevelt*, 8 volumes (Cambridge: Harvard University Press, 1951–1954) was most helpful.

The Harley B. Ferguson Papers are in the Southern Historical Collection at the University of North Carolina Library, Chapel Hill. These consist of Ferguson's official papers pertaining to his work during the Boxer Rebellion and hundreds of his daily reports concerning work upon the *Maine* cofferdam from 1910 until 1912. There are also several volumes of photographs.

PHOTOGRAPHIC COLLECTIONS AND MUSEUMS

Photographs of the wreck of the *Maine* and related subjects exist in considerable quantity. Because of the brief period of its service, however, photographs of the *Maine* afloat are less common. The Naval Historical Center in Washington, D.C. has a fine selection of photographs dealing with the battleship afloat and with the personalities involved.

The Library of Congress has, perhaps, the largest collection of photographs dealing with the *Maine*. Although they have been published, a series of images by the Detroit Publishing Company offers a unique view of shipboard life during the 1890s and within the set are several interior views of the *Maine* and her crew. Particular attention should be given a group of stereograph views of the wreck obviously taken while the Sampson court was still in session. The Library also has numerous photos of *Maine* memorial services and a large collection of presidential portraits. Because the copyright date is included on the photos, many of them can be accurately dated.

The National Archives has a number of photos of the ship and also a complete set of Corps of Engineers photographs taken during the cofferdam building in 1911. There are well over 500 images in this set, portions of which can be found in RG. 38, E. 242, *NA,* the Harley B. Ferguson Papers, Southern Historical Collection, University of North Carolina Library, Chapel Hill, and the collections of the Army Corps of Engineers Museum, Fort Belvoir, Virginia. The Archives set is the largest and presumably only complete set. Within the Audio-Visual Archives of the National Archives may be found the silent motion picture "The Last Rites of the *Maine*" (#18.7: Pathé, 1912).

Relics of the *Maine* can be found in memorial parks, cemeteries, museums, and even homes across the United States. Perhaps best known is the ship's mainmast and the memorial dedicated to the *Maine*'s dead buried in Arlington National Cemetery. The foremast is in Annapolis at the Naval Academy. The Navy Memorial Museum at the Washington Navy Yard has a small collection of souvenirs in addition to a small gun pedestal, a winch, and a 6-inch gun from the battleship. The Smithsonian Institution has an unusual collection of relics including a corroded typewriter, dumbbells, and cigars—all removed from the ship in 1911. They also boast the prized nameplates from the stern as well as the ship's bugle. Most worthy of study, however, is the magnificent 1/48 scale model of the ship on long-term loan from the Navy Department. Presumably this model was built before the *Maine* was finished and placed in commission. The Army Corps of Engineers Museum at Fort Belvoir, Virginia has the ship's wheel.

Index

169

The Contributors

Adm. H. G. Rickover graduated from the Naval Academy in 1922. From 1922 to 1924 he served in the destroyer *La Vallette* (DD-315), and from 1924 to 1927 in the battleship *Nevada* (BB-36). He took postgraduate work at Columbia University, receiving his master of science degree in electrical engineering in 1929. He began his submarine service in the *S-9* late in 1929, attended submarine school at New London from January to June 1930, and upon graduation was assigned to the *S-48*, first as engineer and then as executive officer. He qualified for submarine command in 1931. Leaving the ship in 1933, he next served in the office of the inspector of naval material. From 1935 to 1937 he was assistant engineer on the battleship *New Mexico* (BB-40), winning an outstanding reputation by raising the ship to first place in engineering efficiency for two consecutive years. In 1937 he reported as commanding officer of the minesweeper *Finch* (AM-9) of the Asiatic Fleet. That same year he was designated an engineering-duty-only officer. In 1939 he reported to the electrical section of the Bureau of Ships in Washington, becoming head of the section in March, 1941. In July, 1945, he reported on Okinawa as commander of the ship-repair base, almost as World War II ended.

Returning to Washington, he was sent in 1946 to Oak Ridge, Tennessee, a major installation of the Manhattan Project that had developed the atomic bomb. In 1949 he became head of the joint Navy–Atomic Energy Commission naval nuclear propulsion program. There, superb engineering led to the development of new materials and components, and the prototype reactor for the submarine *Nautilus* generated the first atomic power in the quantity and with the reliability to drive machinery in June, 1953. On January 17, 1955, the *Nautilus* sent her historic message "Underway on nuclear power." When Admiral Rickover retired on January 31, 1982, the navy had in operation thirty-three ballistic-missile submarines, eighty-eight attack submarines, one deep-submergence research vehicle, four aircraft carriers, and nine cruisers powered by nuclear-propulsion plants for which he was responsible for the design and development. He was also responsible for the design and development of Shippingport, the world's first full-scale atomic power plant. Admiral Rickover died in 1986.

In addition to *How the Battleship* Maine *Was Destroyed,* Admiral Rickover wrote *Education and Freedom* (1959), *Swiss Schools and Ours: Why Theirs are Better* (1962), *American Education: A National Failure* (1963), and *Eminent Americans: Namesakes of the Polaris Submarine Fleet* (1972).

Francis Duncan served in the U.S. Naval Reserve from 1943 to 1946 and took part in the Philippine and Okinawa operations. He attended the University of Chicago, receiving his master's degree and doctorate in history. From 1947 to 1950 he was an instructor of history at Wayne University in Detroit. His career in government began in 1950 with service in the Air Force Office of Intelligence. In 1957 he became a program analyst at the Atomic Energy Commission and in 1962 joined the commission's history office. He is coauthor with Richard G. Hewlett of *Atomic Shield,* volume 2 of *A History of the Atomic Energy Commission* (1969), and *Nuclear Navy 1946–1962* (1974). He contributed to *How the Battleship* Maine *Was Destroyed* (1976) and is the author of *Rickover and the Nuclear Navy: The Discipline of Technology* (1990). He received the David D. Lloyd Prize in History for 1970 and the Theodore and Franklin D. Roosevelt Naval History Prize for 1991.

Dr. Duncan has retired from government service and remains a consultant on history to the Department of Energy. He is a member of the U.S. Naval Institute, the Naval Submarine League, the Naval Historical Foundation, the Society for History in the Federal Government, and the American Association for the Advancement of Science.

Dana Wegner received his bachelor's degree at Elmhurst College in Elmhurst, Illinois, and his master's in the field of museum curatorship at the State University of New York College at Oneonta/Cooperstown. He participated in graduate work at the Munson Institute of American Maritime History, where he studied under Dr. Robert Albion. Mr. Wegner began his government career in 1974 as a historical researcher for Admiral Rickover in the Navy's Division of Naval Reactors and was then an exhibits archivist at the U.S. National Archives. He has been curator of ship models for the Department of the Navy since 1980. He has published numerous scholarly historical articles presented at many symposia and has written *Fouled Anchors: The "Constellation" Question Answered* (1991). Mr. Wegner has contributed to *Rickover and the Nuclear Navy* (1990),

Naval History: Sixth Symposium (1987), *Dictionary of American Military Biography* (1980), *The American Image* (1979), *In Peace and War* (1978, reprinted 1984), and *How the Battleship* Maine *Was Destroyed* (1976).

Mr. Wegner has been a consultant to the federal government regarding the history and architecture of the warships *Monitor* and *Constitution*. He was the 1993 recipient of the Peterson Award honoring his work on the origin of the USS *Constellation* and is a member of the American Society of Naval Engineers, the North Atlantic Society of Oceanic Historians, the Nautical Research Guild, and the U.S. Naval Institute.

Ib Hansen was born, raised, and educated in Denmark, where he survived a stint in the Danish underground resistance during World War II. He graduated with honors from the Technical University of Denmark in 1946 with a master's degree in civil and structural engineering. After a two-year sojourn in subarctic northern Norway to support government efforts to restore towns destroyed in World War II, he settled in the United States, and he became a U.S. citizen in 1951. He took up the profession of structural engineering and worked on the design of bridges, including the Mackinac Straits Bridge, the Sault Ste. Marie International Bridge, and the James River Bridge in Richmond, Virginia.

In 1960 Mr. Hansen became a researcher at the Navy's David Taylor Model Basin (now the Carderock Division, Naval Surface Warfare Center), where he took up structural dynamics, weapons effects, and ship protection. In this work he has participated in and directed numerous tests of ship structures exposed to explosions, studied war damage caused by weapon hits on Navy ships, developed methods to predict explosion damage to ship structures, and developed methods for the design of ships to withstand explosions. He has written more than one hundred reports on these subjects, as well as lectured on them at the Massachusetts Institute of Technology, the Naval Postgraduate School, and other places. During his thirty-four years in this field he has received the Meritorious Civilian Service Award twice, the Navy Superior Civilian Service Award, and other performance awards. He is currently head of the Surface Ship Protection and the Submarine Protection Departments at the Carderock Division of the Naval Surface Warfare Center in Bethesda, Maryland.

Robert Price graduated from the Michigan College of Mining and Technology (now Michigan Technical University) in 1943 as a chemical engineer and did research on the photography of underwater explosions at Woods Hole Oceanographic Institution until 1947. He then joined a branch of the Naval Ordnance Laboratory at Indianhead, Maryland. Continuing his photographic work, he obtained high-speed pictures of explosions at ocean depths of up to two miles. In 1956 Mr. Price moved to the main naval ordnance laboratory at White Oak, Maryland, to better participate in several nuclear tests. His work on conventional high explosives involved systems for both firing and instrumenting full-scale tests at sea and small-scale tests in water tanks. He designed and supervised the construction of a high-gravity tank and centrifuge at White Oak.

After the USS *Scorpion* disaster in 1968 Mr. Price participated in the analysis of the accident and follow-up experiments. Subsequently, he advised on damage to the plating of the *Sansinena,* a tanker that exploded in San Pedro, California, and developed a rapid-analysis program for evaluating underwater explosive capability. Other programs of his were useful in locating explosions relative to the observer, to the ocean bottom, and to the ocean surface. Mr. Price's pioneering contributions to the scientific study of the effects and tracking of underwater explosions led to his being chosen in 1975 to aid in the writing of this book. Before his retirement in 1983 he had twice earned the Navy's Meritorious Civilian Service Award. He holds two patents.

The **Naval Institute Press** is the book-publishing arm of the U.S. Naval Institute, a private, nonprofit society for sea service professionals and others who share an interest in naval and maritime affairs. Established in 1873 at the U.S. Naval Academy in Annapolis, Maryland, where its offices remain, today the Naval Institute has more than 100,000 members worldwide.

Members of the Naval Institute receive the influential monthly magazine *Proceedings* and discounts on fine nautical prints and on ship and aircraft photos. They also have access to the transcripts of the Institute's Oral History Program and get discounted admission to any of the Institute-sponsored seminars offered around the country.

The Naval Institute also publishes *Naval History* magazine. This colorful bimonthly is filled with entertaining and thought-provoking articles, first-person reminiscences, and dramatic art and photography. Members receive a discount on *Naval History* subscriptions.

The Naval Institute's book-publishing program, begun in 1898 with basic guides to naval practices, has broadened its scope in recent years to include books of more general interest. Now the Naval Institute Press publishes more than seventy titles each year, ranging from how-to books on boating and navigation to battle histories, biographies, ship and aircraft guides, and novels. Institute members receive discounts on the Press's nearly 400 books in print.

For a free catalog describing Naval Institute Press books currently available, and for further information about subscribing to *Naval History* magazine or about joining the U.S. Naval Institute, please write to:

Membership & Communications Department
U.S. Naval Institute
118 Maryland Avenue
Annapolis, Maryland 21402-5035
Or call, toll-free, (800) 233-USNI.